Great Australian Fly-Fishing Stories

LES HAWKINS

ABC
Books

Published by ABC Books for the
AUSTRALIAN BROADCASTING CORPORATION
GPO Box 9994 Sydney NSW 2001

First published August 2006

National Library of Australia
Cataloguing-in-publication entry:
Hawkins, Les.
Great Australian fly-fishing stories.

ISBN 10: 0 7333 1895 9
ISBN 13: 978 0 7333 1895 5

1. Fly fishing – Australia – Anecdotes. 2. Fishers —
Australia – Anecdotes. I. Australian Broadcasting
Corporation. II. Title.

799.1240994

Internal and cover illustrations of the Blue Charm Fly by Chris Hole
Designed by Luke Causby, Blue Cork Design
Typeset in 10/13pt Baskerville by Asset Typesetting Pty Ltd, Moruya
Printed and bound by Griffin Press, Adelaide, South Australia

5 4 3 2 1

Dedicated to the memory of my fishing companions,
with whom I spent untold happy hours and who
now fish the ever-flowing Elysian streams.
Otium cum Dignitate

ABOUT THE AUTHOR

It was when he was transferred to Albury on the banks of the great River Murray in the early 1960s that Les was introduced by a friendly enthusiast to the delights and mysteries of fishing with the fly for the trout that abounded in the nearby lakes and streams. Like the quarry he still pursues over 40 years later, he became, in his own words, 'immediately hooked'.

As interest in the sport grew, he gathered a group of fellow enthusiasts together to form Greenwell's Fly-fishing Club, named after one of the world's best-known trout flies. He was granted life membership of the club in 1977.

Les was elected President of the Australian Fresh Water Fishermen's Assembly in 1991 and again in 2003, and was Secretary of the Australian Recreational and Sportfishing Industry Confederation for 9 years (known as Recfish, this is the body that deals with the Federal Government on all matters concerning recreational fishermen).

A true bibliophile since childhood, Les Hawkins began buying books on fishing many years ago. The authors were many and varied until he began to specialise in books by Australian writers. When away on a fishing trip, an anthology of fishing stories took his interest, leading him to believe that a book of this nature featuring Australian authors should be published to display our own home-grown talents.

With his usual enthusiasm, he began writing to publishers and authors seeking approval to publish a chapter or two from some of the best-known Australian books.

CONTENTS

PREFACE

During World War II most of our teachers at Fort Street Boys' High School were people who had retired but been called back into the education system because of the need for men in the armed forces. I was among the fortunate pupils who had the benefit of our English master, George Bowman. I can still picture him, tall, gaunt, bespectacled, with a military moustache, softly spoken but with a love of literature and the gift of passing it on to others.

So I learned to love books, a passion that is with me still. The result is the great number of fishing books I have read, allowing me to enjoy authors from around the world and, particularly, from Australia.

One of my favourite books is *The Armchair Angler* (1986), edited by Terry Brykczynski and David Reuther. It contains dozens of chapters, from such noted authors as Ray Bergman, Theodore Gordon, Zane Grey, Roderick Haig-Brown, Ernest Hemingway, G.E.M. Skues and Izaac Walton, to name a few.

Other books of similar kind are O*utdoor Life's Anthology of Fishing Adventures* (1945), *Great Fishing Stories* (1946), T*he Fireside Book of Fishing* (1959), *A Creelful of Fishing Stories* (1932) and *A Treasury of Fishing Stories* (1946). Although written some time ago, the magic of these books is timeless, and they manage to transport the reader into the realms of imagination.

A unique advantage of fly-fishing is the choices it offers: you may fish dry fly, wet fly, streamer or nymph, fish upstream or downstream, study entomology, tie flies, build rods or read about it in the various types of books written on these subjects (when a visit to a lake or stream is not planned).

As a collector of fly-fishing books by Australian authors, I have had the great pleasure of reading countless wonderful stories. Many of these warrant inclusion in digest form to display these authors' remarkable ability to create a mental picture that takes you with them as they fly fish Australia.

This book is the result of many hours of chatting, telephoning and writing to authors and publishers, but it would not be here without unstinting and gracious help from people such as Rick Keam, Andy Braithwaite, Mick Hall, Peter Gibson and Bill Classon, to mention just a few. Please forgive me if I have missed anyone; perhaps a 'senior moment' can be blamed.

Many stories deserving of inclusion have had to be omitted due to space limitations or copyright restrictions, but I have endeavoured to present a selection that is as rich and varied as possible.

This book is not mine; it belongs to the publishers and the gifted, imaginative writers who generously granted permission to use their work.

Sparse Grey Hackle once said, 'Some of the best fishing is to be found not in water, but in print.' Also Izaac Walton's well-known quotation, 'God never did make a more calm, quiet, innocent recreation, than angling', leads me to believe that man needs an escape from the daily problems of living. If he cannot go a-fishing, then at least it can be done vicariously, in the printed word.

Les Hawkins, 2006

PETER
LEUVER

PETER LEUVER started fishing as a boy, and in his early twenties tried skindiving mixed with saltwater fishing around Sydney. While reading books on fishing he became fascinated with pictures of trout flies. In the late 1960s he made a fly rod and caught his first trout on a nymph in the Queanbeyan River near Canberra.

Since then he has learned to tie flies and use them. He has also bred pheasants and ducks, which kept him supplied with beautiful feathers and capes.

In 1983 he started to write and illustrate a monthly column about trout flies for the magazine *Fishing World.* He is an artist/designer and lives in Sydney.

His book *Fur & Feather* was first published in 1991 by Kangaroo Press (now Simon & Schuster), and is still in print, which is some indication of its continuing popularity.

The following chapter, 'The Bredbo', revolves around what is alleged to be Australia's first trout fly and I am grateful to Simon & Schuster for their permission to reprint it.

CHAPTER 1

The Bredbo

As far as I've been able to ascertain, the first Australian-designed trout fly was the Bredbo. 'The Bredbo!' you say. 'I've got one of those in my fly box.' And well you may, because it is still a popular fly with those who use the traditional wet fly. The Bredbo is mentioned in Howard Joseland's fine little book *Angling in Australia and Elsewhere*, published in 1921:

> *One of the most killing flies is the Bredbo and this, I think, may lay claim to being the first artificial locally made fly. The original was tied at Jindabyne about 1896 by Mr C.R. Burnside and Dr A.J. Brady, who with myself may be said to be among the pioneers of fly-fishing for trout in New South Wales. It was, however, not generally recognised that our trout would take the artificial fly freely until about 5 years later. In those days the few anglers who visited or resided on the stream used little else but the natural grasshopper.*

Joseland also admits to using a natural grasshopper and an artificial as a dropper. That is a fascinating admission but not surprising, as trout were only introduced into New South Wales in the late 1880s.

Did most people fish with bait, lures or flies in those days? There are records of big trout being caught in the Great Lake of Tasmania with spinners covered in eel skins. Devon spinners were also a favourite. Another method was to impale an entire small baitfish on a series of treble hooks. There was a bib at the fish's head which made the whole thing spin or gyrate through the water. With all the trebles spinning around the baitfish like grappling hooks, any trout that came within a few centimetres of the bait would have found itself in dire trouble.

River fishermen also used devons, grasshoppers, worms, frogs, nets – anything, in fact, to catch the fish. The early settlers that we see in old photographs standing in front of their humble, rough-hewn log dwellings had large families and few comforts. They cleared the bush with an axe and killed their own food. Can you imagine those hefty sons of the soil tying their own trout flies when plenty of fresh bait was freely available? I suspect the fly fishermen were those with more time on their hands, the townspeople or the gentry or perhaps visiting Englishmen who wrote about their experiences and adventures in the Antipodes.

Trout were introduced into Tasmania in 1864–66. The eggs were imported from Britain, and it was the first time salmonid eggs had been transported to another continent.

Trout were released into Victoria in 1871–72 and into New South Wales in 1887. However, the Bredbo was not designed until 1896, 10 years after F.M. Halford, one of the originators of the dry fly in England, published *Floating Flies and How to Dress Them*. Thirty years had passed between the introduction of trout to Australia and the design of our first fly. Lots of fishing was being enjoyed, but obviously with English patterns.

Where were all our fly tiers? We have always been an innovative people, but we are a conservative bunch. England was still considered 'home', even to native-born Australians.

So English flies, rods and other tackle were widely used for trout fishing. After all, England was where our brown trout came from. Even so, I'm sure someone must have made flies out of possum fur, lyrebird herl or brush turkey wing slips. Although research by Bob Dunne, the antiquarian fishing bookseller and writer, has bought to light locally designed flies for fish such as perch (bass), native grayling and even mullet, there is not a mention of a locally designed trout fly from Tasmania, Victoria or New South Wales.

Enter Dr A.J. Brady and C.R. Burnside. The fly they designed was a grasshopper imitation and fished wet, in the tradition of the time.

But it's a beautiful fly. The English wet flies were a fairly sober lot. Their colours were brown or fawn with an occasional white wing or hackle. They were the Greenwell Glorys and the March Browns. Our little Bredbo was a brave departure and a good introduction to our infant fly-fishing scene. It never made the transition to a dry fly. If a dry grasshopper was used, it would have been a fly such as Howard Joseland's Hopper Hackle.

Who were Dr A.J. Brady and C.R. Burnside? Burnside seems to have disappeared into the mists of history, but Dr Brady was on the first committee of the NSW Rod Fishers' Society. It was started in 1904 by Howard Joseland, A.D. Hall and T.W. Carr. Its first president was Justice R.E. O'Connor of the High Courts, who held office from 1904 to 1907. Dr Brady then held office from 1907 till his death in 1927. After that Joseland was president till 1929.

Howard Joseland, author of the now famous and first ever book on fly-fishing in Australia, was an architect who lived in the Sydney suburb of Wahroonga. He has been likened to America's Theodore Gordon as his country's godfather of fly-fishing. Joseland came along a lot later than Gordon and was far more diversified. He taught us how to fly fish for perch (bass) and even how to catch fish in the surf with a fly. He even went as far as making a greenheart rod, and suggested Australian timbers for the making of a fly rod. He studied Halford and applied his techniques here. He was the first to study mayflies and other trout food. He fished extensively in the Snowy Mountains of New South Wales. In his book he illustrates nine flies he designed himself to cover the essential trout-feeding situations, from mayfly patterns to an ant pattern.

Jack Ritchie, author of *The Australian Trout, its introduction and acclimatisation into Victoria*, has been fly-fishing all his life, and his father fished before the turn of the century. I consulted Jack about the first Australian trout fly and he in turn consulted Tony Brothers, fly-tying master of the VFFA, and in reply said they both believed it to be the Bredbo. Jack's father noted in his diary for 1907, 'Call at Eastways in Sydney and get fly of which they have eyed samples. The "Bredbo" with grasshopper wings and gold body. Found very successful with it in the Snowy.' In 1909 the diary records that it was the most successful fly above Jindabyne.

The Bredbo was, of course, named after the little stream that starts its journey high up in the Great Dividing Range and then gurgles downhill in a westerly direction past the village of Bredbo, crosses the main Canberra–Cooma road, and ends the journey when its waters join the Murrumbidgee River nearby. It was certainly one of the most popular flies right up to the 1960s. The 'eyed hook' samples referred to by Jack Ritchie's father were hooks with the normal ringed eyes we are familiar with today. Traditionally, flies were tied with a gut leader tippet attached.

Now the interesting thing about the Bredbo is that it has the golden pheasant tippets tied in at the side to represent the grasshopper's legs, an innovative step in those days. Not even one fly sports legs in Mary Orvis Marberry's book of 1892, *Favourite Flies and Their Histories*. This book is a prodigious volume of flies collected late last century in the United States and includes flies for trout, salmon and bass.

That grand old lady of Australian fly-tying, the late Elsa Lowrie, was in her seventies when she died in January 1991, and she fished right up till the time of her death. She had tied flies from her early teens. When I asked her if she knew what Australia's first fly pattern was, she said in her letter that she believed it was the Bredbo. She also gave her version of the dressing:

Body	Lime green floss, Binding, dark green floss silk (twist)
Hackle	Grouse
Underwing	Two triangles of golden pheasant tippets
Overwing	Brown Turkey (speckled black)

So here we have probably the first version with the golden pheasant underwing. The body colouring and hackle must be an alternative, because it's obviously not the fly with the gold body that Jack Ritchie's father fished with at the turn of the century.

Some of our other popular wet flies also sported underwings: historic old flies from the 1920s such as the Joseland Favourite, Moonbah, Tarana; even Elsa's famous Glen Innes Hopper has a red slip hidden between two grizzle hackle points; these were beautiful, graceful old patterns, and it was sad to see their passing.

Both John Veniard's *Fly Dressers' Guide* and F.A.D. Griffith's *The Lure of Fly Tying* describe the Bredbo's modern dressing. M.E. McCausland's 1949 book, *Fly-fishing in Australia and New Zealand*, has a colour plate of the Bredbo, and if you look closely you'll see the legs sticking out at either side. He also describes a general grasshopper pattern that has 'legs', a lemon silk body, oak turkey wings and grey hackles. Seeing both forms have been popular for so long, they are both shown here.

The original tie:

Hook:	12
Body:	Yellow floss silk ribbed with gold wire
Wing	Hen pheasant wing feather
Legs	Three or four golden pheasant tippets tied in at the head along each side of the body
Hackle	Brown partridge back feathers tied in underneath

Later version:

Hook:	12
Body:	Yellow floss silk ribbed with gold tinsel
Wings:	Speckled hen wing feather; underwing, pheasant tippets
Hackle:	Brown partridge back feathers tied in underneath

JACK
RITCHIE
OBE

THE FOLLOWING article appeared in the 1991 edition of *Basic Flyfishing* (Kangaroo Press 1993). The research for the article was carried out by the late Jack Ritchie OBE, who generously gave his approval to reprint from his book *The Australian Trout, a history of the introduction of trout into Australia*.

John (Jack) Gowar Ritchie (1915–1992) was a metallurgical engineer. He served in a range of capacities in state and national angling organisations, including a term as President of the Australian Freshwater Fishermen's Assembly. He was an active member of the Royal Historical Society of Victoria.

CHAPTER 2

The Early Days in Australia

In the middle of the nineteenth century our forefathers, who were mostly of British descent, were acclimatising Australia with the introduction of many of the things they had left behind when immigrating, such as trees, plants, birds, animals – and fish.

Edward Wilson, born in London in 1811, came to Australia in 1841 and settled in Melbourne. After a short period in cattle grazing he turned to journalism and purchased the *Argus* newspaper in 1848. He remained a senior partner until his death.

A tall swarthy man with dark penetrating eyes, he was a radical in his writings and quickly established a reputation for the *Argus* in fighting the good fight on many issues of injustice and government maladministration. One of his first interests in retirement was to found the Acclimatisation Society of Victoria in 1861 and become its first president. The early annual meetings, in which the governor of Victoria, Sir Henry Barkly, took a keen interest, make fascinating reading. They deal with the importation of such diverse species as English thrush, blackbirds, sparrows, starlings; game birds such as pheasants and partridges; cashmere goats, angora goats, English hares, bees and fish such as roach and tench as well as salmonids. The Society received substantial government financial support, including permission to use an area of Royal Park – now the Melbourne Zoo. The first trout-rearing ponds were built there.

The *Argus* of 14th April 1864 wrote on the Society's activities: '[We are] seeking to stock this country with new, useful and beautiful things ... to provide for manly sports which will lead Australian youth to seek their recreation on the river's banks and mountain side ... rather than in the Cafe and Casino.'

By mid-1864 it was evident that Wilson was suffering from a serious eye complaint and this would necessitate his return to England for surgery. We meet Wilson again in England, when he becomes involved with the Australian Association.

Let us turn now to Tasmania, where, starting in 1841, there was growing interest in the possibility of introducing Atlantic salmon (*Salmo salar*). However, the problems seemed insurmountable: a cold-water fish to which high water temperatures are lethal needed to be transported either as fish or ova, in sailing ships through the tropics in voyages lasting 3 or 4 months.

The first attempt was made in 1852 in the *Columbus*, with salmon and trout ova in a 60 gallon tub of water and a bed of gravel. The ova all hatched but died as the temperature rose during the passage through the tropics.

Following this failure, the first suggestion of using ice was made.

The next attempt was made in 1860, and from this date the project became closely associated with James (later Sir James) Youl in London and Morton Allport in Tasmania. James Youl had been born in Sydney, Australia but his family moved to Tasmania (then called Van Dieman's Land) in 1819, where he enlarged the Symmons Plains property developed by his father.

In 1854 he returned to England and in 1861 the Tasmanian Government appointed him as their accredited agent in London – without salary!

There he became associated with Edward Wilson, then back in England, and others in the Australian Association. This association raised £600 by private subscription to finance the next trial in the *Sarah Curling*. The 30,000 salmon ova from the River Dovey in Wales were contained in a trough fed with water cooled by running through an ice house. The last ova died on the 59th day out, when all the ice had melted away.

The project had now attracted the support of the Tasmanian Government and they appointed salmon commissioners, one of whom was Morton Allport. Hatching boxes and rearing ponds were constructed on the Plenty, a tributary of the Derwent River, these being based on those at Stormontfield on the Tay in Scotland.

The next trial was directed by Youl with the help of William Ramsbottom, sent from Tasmania to accompany the shipment of 50,000 salmon ova, again from the River Dovey, in the *Beautiful Star*, a small steamer of 120 tons. The ova were carried in trays on beds of gravel mounted in a swinging frame over which iced water flowed, hopefully to counteract the movement of the ship. This swinging apparatus was a total failure, but, after the last ova died, Ramsbottom found that a number of ova which Youl had placed in a small box in the ice house were still alive, even though they died after hatching. This observation gave the clue to the technique which was successful in the next shipment.

Youl pressed on with financial support from both the Tasmanian and Victorian governments and the Acclimatisation Society of Victoria.

During 1863 Youl carried out experiments in the Wenham Ice Company's vaults in London. He found that running water was not essential, being cut off from air was not fatal and light was not required for survival of the ova. Furthermore, if the ova were packed in moss in small boxes and covered in ice their development could be delayed for various periods up to 120 days and then they could be successfully hatched. Youl wrote, 'It appears that the best way next year is to place the ova direct in an ice house.' He then located a suitable ship, the *Norfolk*, of 953 tons, a speedy three-masted full-rigged clipper, and the owners, Messrs Money Wigram and Sons, kindly donated 50 tons of space. The ship was to sail for Melbourne on 20th January 1864.

The ice house was built on the lowest deck amidships, the boxes were ready, the ice ordered, and then at the last moment Robert Ramsbottom (William's father), who had secured ova for Youl on previous occasions, found that the fish in the River Ribble had already spawned. In desperation Youl appealed, through *The Times*, to proprietors of salmon leases to help with ova so that he would not lose the chance 'to get this noble fish out to Australia'. This letter was dated 6th January 1864, only 14 days before the *Norfolk* was to sail.

Even so, no ova were forthcoming up to the 14th January; a week to go and Youl was in despair. However, within 2 days of sailing, salmon ova from the Severn and the Dovey were received. Youl and his helpers worked around the clock to pack the 90,000 ova for transportation and the owners delayed the sailing for a full day. The last block of ice was placed on board at 4 pm on Wednesday afternoon and the *Norfolk* sailed on Thursday morning, 21st January.

Included in the salmon shipment were 2,700 trout ova from the famous Itchen River, the Wey and the Buckinghamshire Wye, both tributaries of the Thames, donated by two noted English pisciculturalists, Frank Buckland and Francis Francis. Although Youl had not planned to include trout ova in the shipment, he took the diplomatic course and placed them in the ice house.

The *Norfolk* made a very fast voyage of 84 days and docked in Melbourne at Railway Pier on 15th April 1864. Picture the exhilaration when, on examination, most of the ice was intact and about 80 per cent of the ova were still healthy.

Her Majesty's Steam Sloop *Victoria*, mounting three 32-pounder guns, was selected to transport the ova to Tasmania, a noteworthy achievement, as *Victoria* was the colony's only ship of war. The sloop arrived in Hobart on the 20th April 1864 and the ova were transported to the prepared spawning beds on the Plenty.

On the 4th May 1864 the momentous event transpired: trout began to hatch, and salmon began on the following day.

Let us return to Melbourne, where eleven boxes of salmon ova had been left in the Victoria Company's ice works. They hatched on 7th May 1864 and were later released into Badger Creek, a tributary of the Yarra Yarra River.

Many years passed before rainbow trout were introduced, firstly by New South Wales Fisheries (1894), who consigned ova to Queensland in 1896, and then in 1898 by both the Ballarat Fish Acclimatisation Society and the Geelong and Western District Fish Acclimatisation Society in Victoria. The ova were secured from New Zealand, reared in specially constructed ponds, and then released from around 1894 to the turn of the century.

Thus, with remarkable co-operation between government, acclimatisation societies and dedicated men, the salmonid fishery was established. Further shipments of trout, sea trout and salmon followed and to date Australia can boast one of the best and mainly disease free fisheries in the world.

To prevent the introduction of diseases, the Australian Fisheries Council prohibited importation of salmonids and their ova in 1970.

Regrettably, this was overturned in 1999 when, due to the lowering of international trade barriers, Australia was forced to accept wild-caught salmon meat, initially due to Canada and the US challenging Australia in world courts. It is hoped that this decision does not bring about the introduction of many diseases, such as whirling disease, which are prevalent in other countries.

RON
McKENZIE
AOM

A COMPOSER, conductor, writer, poet, philosopher, fly fisherman and devoted family man, he practised as a public accountant in Wangaratta, Victoria.

Joining the RAAF in 1940, his Wellington aircraft was shot down over Holland. He wrote about his experiences as a prisoner of war in his book *An Ordinary War.*

Ron was noted for his subtle sense of humour, which pervades his book *The Ratbag Mind of Dinas Vawr.*

A tireless worker for many voluntary organisations, he is best known by anglers for his involvement in fly-fishing. He was awarded the Order of Australia Medal for his service to the sport of freshwater fishing in 1984 – he was the first in this field to receive such an honour.

In 1947 Ron joined Wangaratta Fly-fishing Club; he later became involved in the Victorian Fly-fishing Association, the NSW Institute of Anglers and many other state organisations. He was involved in the foundation of the Australian Freshwater Fishermen's Assembly, serving terms as secretary and president. He was awarded life membership of that organisation.

Ron will be remembered not so much for what he took out of our fisheries, but rather for what he put back into his most loved sport.

The following chapter, 'Who Wears the Waders', is from *The Ratbag Mind of Dinas Vawr.* The proceeds from this book were given to the Australian Freshwater Fishermen's Assembly to assist in the publication of papers dealing with freshwater fisheries and their environs.

I am indebted to Ron's wife Enid for giving her kind permission to include this particular chapter.

CHAPTER 3

Who Wears the Waders

The counsel of others may help make a fisherman, but (*pace* Izaac) it doesn't make him compleat. The distinction between fishwives and fishing wives is too rarely noted by the male in his youthful confidence that he knows it all, and that she wouldn't like it anyway.

It is true that there are men and women who don't enjoy fishing. Often this failing arises from beliefs that bait is messy and stinks, that fishing is cruel, that fish aren't good to eat, that places are full of flies and mosquitoes and snakes or sharks and stinging things.

Admittedly, bait can be messy and sometimes it stinks. For these reasons and from natural laziness, and because I find it more fun, I prefer fly-fishing for trout, though more often than not I use bait or spinners from rocks or beaches, or in estuaries. Fresh bait can be kept odourlessly in the refrigerator, though domestic strife may result if the angler cooks such baits as sun-cooked prawns in this way.

There is much assumption in a statement that fishing is cruel. It can be; few fishermen approve of others who suffocate fish by leaving them out of the water. That the hook hurts fish is open to considerable doubt, if not completely disproven by the fact that many fish will take a bait over and over again; I once hooked the only eel in a rock pool seven times running, and have on several occasions caught trout a little time before and identified them by a fly lost to them in the earlier encounter. That a fish is tired after a fight cannot be denied, but trout, in common with many other fish, always seem to me to be more angry than frightened while hooked. In years of fishing I have only once seen evidence of a fish hooked on a fly failing to recover quite quickly when returned to the water, if properly handled: on that occasion it wasn't observed that during release a gill had been damaged. The fish was eaten.

The subject of cruelty recalls that a beautifully spoken and elegant lady once troubled friend Michael and me by saying, in tender tones, 'Oh! The poor little thing', while we were becoming nervous wrecks with 7 and 8-pounders in the Eucumbene River. Taught to roll-cast, and using two flies, as was our custom at the time, she surprised herself and us by hooking a very big fish almost immediately. Obeying screamed instruction implicitly, she handled it well, but was tiring as quickly as the fish after about three-quarters of an hour. The fish surfaced and rolled; a 10-inch rainbow grabbed the dropper and the great brown escaped. Hauling in the little rainbow, our dear friend, whose language was always beyond reproach, dashed it on the rocks crying, 'You bloody rotten little pink bastard!' I couldn't resist a quiet, 'Oh Helen – the poor little thing!'

Places are full of flies and mosquitoes and snakes or sharks and stinging things. Fortunately, places are also free of them; places of exquisite beauty, places of geological or botanical or zoological or historical or other interest. If one requires heaven, probably the best thing is to be good and die young.

It is arguable whether my wife is a better fly fisher than I am or vice versa. Oddly enough, this is probably the only subject we don't argue about. There is no reason why a woman shouldn't fish more skilfully than a man except perhaps in those areas where great physical force is required. Very few fish require great physical force; it is probably true that more fish are lost through the application of considerable force than for any other reason.

These things are not arguable, though: that a wife who fishes understands her fishing husband better than one who doesn't, that a husband who fishes understands his fishing wife better than he will understand a non-fishing wife, and that the shared pleasures are considerable – places, people, things. And fish, of course.

Incidentally, the best way to interest your wife in fishing is to buy her a rod and reel that are themselves things of beauty. I know.

Having annoyed mine for several years by disappearing altogether or by leaving her with nothing to do for hours if she accompanied me (and returning to her some hours after the scheduled time) I tried it and it worked. After all, if it doesn't, you have a beautiful new rod and reel.

As only a fisherman could think like that, I suppose one could say that, in one sense, the making of a fisherman was then complete. But the beauty of fishing is this – every fisherman knows that upstream, past the next rapid, will be something he has never seen before.

PHILIP WEIGALL

PHILIP WAS born in Melbourne but spent his early years exploring the foothills of Mt Buller. A beautiful area surrounded by 'classic' trout streams such as the Jamieson, Howqua and King. This is where his love of trout fishing began, and it has been a guiding influence in his life ever since.

Despite returning to the city, attending university and starting work, Philip managed to put thousands of kilometres on his four-wheel drive in the quest to perfect his fly-fishing techniques.

He wrote his first articles on fly-fishing in 1989, and since then has been a regular contributor to *FlyLife, Freshwater Fishing, Victorian Lifestyle, Victorian Fishing Monthly* and *New Zealand Fly Fishers Annual.*

These days, he lives southeast of Ballarat in Victoria with his partner Jane, son Daniel, and their water-loving dog Badger.

Philip's books include *Trout'n About* (1994), *The River Behind the Hill* (1999), *Call of the River* (2002), *Victorian Fly Water* (2003) and *Trout Stories* (2004).

The following chapters are from *Trout'n About* (with permission from the Australian Fishing Network).

CHAPTER 4

The Hard Country

Down towards Antarctica, far to the south of Australia, a cold front begins to form. Out here there is nothing but ocean, cold, grey and lifeless. The wind shrieks and moans, whipping spray from the water that forms as droplets of ice on the feathers of a lost seabird. To the horizon and beyond in any direction there is nothing, But in the sky above, the invisible atmosphere is changing. The air pressure – weight of air on the sea – starts to drop. In the distance, the pressure rises. Like a ghostly canyon that cannot be seen by human eyes, the low pressure system deepens, and the high pressure mountains around grow taller. The wind becomes an aimless scavenger, tearing harder and harder at the ocean below. Air as frigid as death drifts into the canyon, slowly accumulating giant clouds. Then for no discernable reason, the whole mass starts moving. Not to the west as usual, but north towards a huge continent, benign and warm by comparison to these barren wastes. The migration of the icy mass goes unnoticed by man. Only the tiny electronic beeps of satellites on the edge of space, and a whirring computer in a skyscraper basement thousands of kilometres distant, mindlessly acknowledge its existence.

'Just one more bend,' shouted David Trounce, my companion on this trip, 'then we'll head back for a bite to eat.' I waved an acknowledgement from my snowgrass seat on the hillside, a couple of hundred metres away, and crunched another mouthful from a muesli bar. It had been a pleasant afternoon on the Bogong High Plains in mid-summer.

Earlier we had cast caddis patterns to eager trout on a small mountain lake, and for the last two hours we had followed the meandering feeder stream as it twisted and turned at random through the alpine meadows. The scene up the valley was soft and reassuring. We were above the tree line, but willy wagtails flitted for insects in the heath and currawongs glided effortlessly above. Here and there were colourful wildflowers, and even the granite boulders were wonderfully textured and warm to the touch. The light breeze was crisp, but not cold. It would have been easy to lie back on the soft tussocks for an hour or so and close the eyes.

Looking down the valley, though, a different face of the region was revealed about 2 kilometres downstream, where the little stream plunged into another world. At this point the yellow/green landscape of the high plains ended, replaced by dizzy precipices, towering crags and bare rock. Forested slopes beneath the escarpment seemed impossibly steep, and the hazy lowlands were a faraway planet. And high on the dark peaks, in places where the sun never shone, blatant drifts of snow filled the ravines and pockets on the mountain sides. This view was a reminder that the benevolence of the high mountains was transitory, and the scene of warmth and tranquillity up the valley was somehow deceptive.

I turned back to watch David, and it was good to see his smuggler rod bending to the weight of a trout. Dave has a love of stream fishing, and although he enjoyed our earlier session on the little lake, there was no denying he was happiest casting a dry at the gravely riffles and undercuts of a stream, especially alpine water like this one. Dave is like me in that he can quickly adjust his expectations to match particular water, so that while the half kilo trout were merely the norm, a trout of that size in the stream was less common, and catching one was cause for a little whoop of pleasure and maybe even a satisfied chuckle. I'm not saying we won't follow you through a hundred metres of blackberries if you can show us where the big one lives, it's just that we like to keep a perspective on these things.

Dave's success was obviously a spur to fish 'just one more pool', and I was more than content to sit back and watch from my natural grandstand. In fact, the general comfort and tranquillity were making me a little drowsy. I think I actually nodded off for a few minutes. When I opened my eyes again, I felt something was not quite right. Nothing obvious – but something was different. Then I noticed. Everything was quiet. The birds weren't calling out, and the chirping cicadas and buzzing flies had fallen silent. The breeze had picked up a little, and the sun was lightly veiled in high cloud – not much, but enough to suck a little heat out of its rays. Subconsciously I glanced in the direction of the car. Dave's white Subaru was just visible as a matchbox-sized object down the end of the valley near the lake. I looked to the west, and thin tendrils of cloud were appearing like smoke from behind the bulk of the largest mountain. I went to call out to Dave, but he was already coming up the hill toward me, stopping now and then to glance over to the west.

'Looking interesting over there,' puffed Dave as he reached me. I agreed. By now the sun was a hazy white glow in the strange cloud above, while the dark mass on the western horizon had already doubled in height. The speed of change in the elements around us was awesome to watch. We started walking briskly toward the car. The appearance of the country had changed from inviting to hostile in 15 minutes. Without the sun, the snowgrass hills looked bleak, the boulders cold and forbidding. The effect was accentuated by the increasing moan of the wind and the waving tussocks. Two hundred metres from the car, the first drops of sleet stung our cheeks. The approaching cloud caught us, and visibility was lost down to 10 metres – the car vanished. The wind was shrieking now, and flakes of snow were mixed in with the sleet. I fixed a bearing on the car moments before it disappeared, and we almost walked straight into it. Vests and rods were thrown carelessly into the boot, but we left our thigh waders on as we bolted into the front seats.

It was a great feeling to be out of the wind, which rocked the Subaru as Dave started the engine. We headed up the road, following the snow poles in the headlights although it was still mid-afternoon.

Mist, sleet and snow raced across the front of us. After a few kilometres, the road began to descend and we were soon surrounded by the moderate protection of a hardy snowgum forest. Shortly after, we were back at the chalet, which lay just below the lip of the high plains. A warm fire and dry clothes greeted us. At times like this it seems almost worth getting wet and cold so you can fully appreciate these little comforts. After hot showers we poured a drink and looked out the windows. The storm was in full force by now, and even here, below the tree line and in comparative shelter, the windows rattled to blasts of wind. Back towards the high plains, the sky was completely black, and the mountains had vanished. By now, snow would be settling up there. The massive cold front, spawned days ago in the far southern ocean, had arrived.

CHAPTER 5

'The Poker'

We continued up the river. By late afternoon the valley was completely in shadow, and right on cue the expected upstream barrier appeared. The stream had gouged a chasm in the sandstone, and from this it spilled down a staircase in a series of cascades and plunge pools. None of these were spectacularly high, but at least two exceeded 3 metres in vertical drop – too much for a trout to negotiate. And at the base of the cascade was the rare jewel we hoped to find – a huge, dark pool gouged out by aeons of water on rock. Of unknown depth, it was roughly circular – perhaps 30 metres wide and 40 long. Here and there the skeletons of long-dead trees protruded from the water – testimony to the violent floods that carried them from who knows how far upstream.

The lazy banter of the last few hours died away. Here was a pool that could hold a really big trout. We couldn't know that for sure, but all the signs were there, even at first glance. For the last few hours every decent bit of water had been disturbed by vigorous rising trout, usually several. Yet the surface of the water before us remained unbroken, save for where the cascade plunged straight in at the head.

In honour of the seriousness of the situation, the rules were changed. Five casts each, alternating until a fish – hopefully *the* fish – was caught. Mark went first. The red tag was changed for a Tom Jones. I sat back on the cool sandstone and attached a weighted brown nymph, lengthening my tippet at the same time.

The foaming head of the pool was the obvious temptation, but Mark knew better, and methodically covered the banks and snags nearer. Although outwardly competitive, I think Mark and I were not really concerned with who caught the big trout (still an assumption), but rather that it was caught. Nothing happened on any of Mark's casts, adding to the ominous atmosphere. No little 'pannies' snatched at the fly, no fingerlings splashed behind it. Then it was my turn, so I crept a little further up the pool, casting in a grid pattern and pausing to allow the nymph to sink deep before beginning a slow retrieve.

In one mossy corner of the pool, a raft of foam had formed. I had been watching this on and off for several minutes, when I thought I saw a streak of brown briefly disturb the white foam. Uncertain, I cast anyway. Slowly I drew the nymph toward me. A tiny muffled bump translated down the line – possibly a rock or log. I kept retrieving, then drew the fly up to recast. At that moment a white shape a metre below the surface caught my eye. In an instant I realised this was a gaping mouth; then the black shape it was attached to came into focus, darker than the pool itself. I slowed the nymph almost to a stop. But the trout seemed suddenly suspicious, and just hung there with fanning fins, eyeing the nymph from a distance of centimetres. I twitched the rod, and it moved as if to take the fly, then turned and slowly swam downward, disappearing forever in the gloom. 'Jeez,' Mark breathed, having crept unseen to behind my left shoulder. 'How big do you reckon?'

'Two feet at least,' I replied, 'but did you see the size of his head?'

'Yeah, an old cannibal,' Mark agreed, 'but what a trout all the same.'

Small streams are looked down on by some fly fishers. When you've spent good money on neoprene waders, a powerful graphite rod and a weight forward line which you can shoot 30 metres, a part of you wants to stand chest deep in some swirling river or vast lake and create beautiful patterns with your fly line, or hear the reel scream as a big rainbow powers over the horizon. Crawling through willow thickets or bow-casting 3 metres from a stooped position lacks the same degree of glamour. And when the biggest pool is only as big as a carport, the trout can hardly take you to the backing.

But there is more to small streams than meets the eye. The intimacy of having all the action unfold in close proximity more than compensates for the slightly claustrophobic sensation of not being able to throw a long line. And the babbling creeks teach you things that can only be learned when you are seeing trout and their little world from close quarters. To observe from a few metres distance several wild trout in a sunlit mountain pool is a revelation. Watching how they utilise the currents and patches of cover, how they hunt their food and the way they interact with one another is both fascinating and educational. For all the appeal of our big rivers and lakes, I'll always make time for the small streams. They keep you on your toes.

MICK
HALL

I HAD intended to reproduce a chapter from Wing Commander L.J. Wackett's book *Studies of an Angler*, but Mick Hall has written a précis which captures the spirit of Wackett's theories and his biography superbly. Anglers still discuss and argue these theories wherever they gather.

Mick Hall is a professional fishing writer, fly-fishing guide and instructor and a member of the Professional Fishing Instructors & Guides Association. Mick is well known for his regular fly tying articles in *Freshwater Fishing* and at the Blackridge Flyfishing School at Eildon in Victoria.

Heavily involved in fly-fishing from his early days in the Red Tag Fly-fishers Club, he was involved in the formation of Southern Fly Fishers Inc., and Yarra Valley Fly-fishers Inc., serving as foundation president of both clubs.

Today he can be heard on radio 3AW Melbourne and 3AK Melbourne fishing shows and is a regular panel member of 3SER's fishing program.

Over the years he has been involved, with varying degrees of participation, in the Council of Victorian Fly-fishing Clubs, the Australian Fly Tiers Guild, the Australian Trout Foundation, and Fly Fish Australia.

Mick has written articles for *The Flyfisher's Journal* (London) and the *Art of Angling Journal*, an American periodical.

The following article appeared in *The Flyfishers Annual* (2002), and is reproduced with the kind permission of Helen and Bill Classon, of *Freshwater Fishing* magazine.

CHAPTER 6

Lawrence Wackett:
A Study of an Angler

Once he got an idea, he was hard to stop. Long-serving Australian Prime Minister R.G. Menzies said that 'my only complaint ... was that he thought and spoke so fast it was sometimes difficult for me to keep in step with him'. Arnold Gingrich called him both a 'Little Jack Horner' and a 'worry wart', confessed to knowing nothing about him, but praised him for the single most original angling chapter in a quarter-century. Leonard Wright wrestled with its theories on trout behaviour to develop his own related ideas.

Who was the man? Lawrence Wackett was born in 1896 at Townsville in Australia's northern tropics. A year later his father suicided in despondency over business affairs, leaving a widow with three small children to raise in difficult circumstances.

His surroundings triggered the boy's interest in nature, exploration, hunting and fishing. Nearby was a large freshwater lagoon with a variety of fish and a tidal river with barramundi. He was able to holiday on the Murray River at Cardwell, and at 13 spent a month on then largely uninhabited Magnetic Island, where a Danish beachcomber with a sailing dinghy introduced him to reef fishing.

At 6, Wackett already understood the workings of a model steam engine his father had given him. He became passionately interested in machinery and engineering. Later, his scientific promise won him a scholarship to Duntroon Military College. However, he cut short his course to volunteer for the Australian Flying Corps.

Wackett served in Egypt and France, where he devised the first system for air-dropping ammunition to troops. After nursing his badly hit biplane home from 20 zigzagging miles of photography deep behind the Hindenburg Line, at a height below 500 feet, he was awarded an immediate DFC (Distinguished Flying Cross).

After the war, Wackett married Letty Wood. Enrolling at the University of Melbourne, he quickly completed his unfinished BSc, intent on a career in aeronautical engineering. Moving to Sydney, he built planes and flying-boats at the RAAF experimental station at Randwick. During this time he enjoyed fishing for luderick, particularly at Port Hacking.

In 1936 a consortium of Australian manufacturers formed the Commonwealth Aircraft Corporation to construct military aircraft. Wackett, who had left the RAAF as Wing-Commander, was appointed manager and chief designer. The Corporation was located in Melbourne.

The Trout Years

The Melbourne years fostered Wackett's love of trout fishing. Free weekends and the occasional holiday would see the family camped on the streams of Gippsland or in the Snowy Mountains. He became a member of the exclusive Waterfall Farm Fly Fishers Club, which was limited to 20 members. Its lodge was an old farmhouse at Khancoban on the Geehi River, which in those pre-Hydro days was Australia's finest rainbow trout stream. Perhaps Wackett's visits to America on aircraft business awoke his interest in such syndicates. In 1943, Eugene Wilson of the United Aircraft Corporation introduced him to private club water in the New England countryside, where he enjoyed himself greatly with the dry fly.

Wackett's son Wilbur became one of the first four fighter pilots posted to New Guinea. Shot down near Lae, swimming for 8 hours and surviving the close interest of several sharks, he eventually overcame malaria to walk 400 miles over the Owen Stanley Range to Port Moresby. His epic feat was celebrated in several publications, including George *My Brother Jack* Johnston's *New Guinea Diary* (1943). In September 1944, Squadron Leader Wilbur Wackett perished over home soil while returning from a night flight over the Timor Sea. The crash was attributed to bushfire smoke and failed radio communications. The following year, in the midst of victory celebrations, his infant daughter died.

Lawrence Wackett sought solace from his grief in activity. In 1946 he self-published a small book dedicated to Wilbur and limited to 500 copies: *My Hobby Ii Trout Fishing*. Encouraged by the reaction, he continued to approach his angling with the same scientific mind that drove all his activities. Over the following 3 years he immersed himself in English flyfishing literature and some from America, including the work of Ray Bergman, who impressed him as a practical fisherman. He read Halford, Dunne, Skues and Taverner, commenting that Taverner's *Trout Fishing from All Angles* presented a considerable amount of collected scientific knowledge not usually found in angling books. Among Australian writers he enjoyed R.L. Blackwood's *The Quest of the Trout* (1926), C.R. (Reg) Lyne's many articles, and R.H. Wigram's *Trout and Fly in Tasmania* (1938).

Wackett's second and major book, *Studies of an Angler*, was self-published in 1950. Today both works are considered collectors' items, and copies in good condition are quite valuable.

The new book was nothing if not original, bringing applied science and technology to bear on previously unexplored areas. Wackett clearly believed that there is always a better way to do or build something. Long before carbon fibre fly rods, he saw the future in a tubular form of the strong, lightweight materials then being developed for advanced military aircraft. He thought it certain that the cracking problems of the earliest plastic fly lines would be solved through applied science. But above all, he focused on trout behaviour and on his innovations with trout flies.

Barometric Pressure

The 60 pages that *Studies of an Angler* devotes to barometric pressure and trout are as controversial and intriguing now as they were then.

As his introduction makes clear, Wackett's intention was to present the evidence for his case, leaving it to others to consider, debate and perhaps disprove. The bare elements are as follows.

Trout spend most of their time near the lower limit of the available depth range. They tend to maintain themselves in a state of neutral buoyancy (hydrostatic equilibrium), which requires the least work. When leaving position to take food, they experience short pressure changes which they counter with muscular effort. However, Wackett argued, a sustained fall in barometric pressure creates a small but incessant excess of buoyancy in their swim bladder.

Wackett maintained that in trout this bladder is practically a sealed chamber, because the pneumatic duct from bladder to gullet is extremely narrow. Pressure readjustment has to take place mainly through the slow process of osmosis, during which time trout experience physical inconvenience. The relatively small side fins also have to work harder for the fish to remain in position, leading to muscle fatigue. At such times trout are not inclined to rise to natural or artificial flies.

The process is complicated by a range of other factors including altitude, water temperature and pH, the condition of the fish, and their size. However, Wackett's field data – extended barograph printouts matched with observations of feeding activity and fishing success – clearly showed that something important was happening, whatever the explanation.

First critic off the taxi rank was Victoria's Director of Fisheries and Game, Alfred Dunbavin Bultcher. An advance copy of *Studies of an Angler* had been sent for review to the *Australian Shooters and Anglers News*. In vol. 4, no.1 (October 1949), Butcher maintained that:

The so-called primitive fish – primitive because they are not so far removed from their ancestors as other fish – have an air bladder from which a tube opens to the gullet. These are called physostomous fish and belonging to this group are the salmon and trout ... briefly, the function of the air bladder in those fish which possess one is to keep the fish comfortable under a variety of conditions.

Butcher cited a range of examples, but ignored Wackett's argument that trout have 'neither the adequate usable duct of a primitive fish, nor the efficient absorption organs of a ductless fish'.

In the following issue, angling editor B. O'Loughlin defended Wackett in a long article detailing other aspects of his theory in greater depth. He quoted writers such as Eric Taverner, who had cited *The Cambridge Natural History* as stating that, 'Gaseous secretion and absorption are comparatively slow processes ... [taking] from a few hours to several days.'

As an ardent dry fly angler, Wackett's theories were heavily slanted towards his preference. He conceded that trout affected by a sustained falling barometer might under some circumstances take flies or baits sunk down to them in their resting locations. However, he associated the artificial nymph only with fishing to bulgers, even though he played with experimental dragonfly nymph (mudeye) imitations and when desperate would occasionally use these insects as bait.

Entomology

Wackett's perspectives on entomology were limited, giving the impression that Australian mayflies and their nymphs are important only in Tasmania. He claimed he had never seen a large hatch of duns in progress. Despite his barometric theories, trout can feed enthusiastically on the little blue Baetids that hatch on cold days with intermittent showers, and the flotillas of lambda duns and other 'March Browns' that emerge in squally or even snowy weather on the lakes.

In fairness, little was known of Australian mayflies at that time. Wackett was influenced by Dunbavin Bultcher's 1947 pamphlet *The Freshwater Fish of Victoria and Their Food*. Though based on field studies, it involved a limited range of waters where mayflies were less important than caddis larvae and other food sources. Even Dr R.J. Tillyard's *Insects of Australia and New Zealand* (1926) lists only 20 known species of Australian mayfly. Today around 100 are known to science, with an estimated further hundred as yet unclassified.

Wackett was more excited by terrestrials. He gave beetles, wasps, bees and ants considerable attention, emphasising exact imitation. One story is revealing. After noting a resemblance between the body and hackle of a Red Tag and the flying Malacodermid beetles in his garden, he later met the same beetle on the stream:

> The very next time I went fishing ... I looked for similar insects along the river and found them. Since then I have nearly always seen them during the summer months ... I continued to use the Red Tag fly, but cut the red appendage off, and found it equally acceptable to the trout. This was important, for it made the imitation more closely resemble the natural I had selected.

Sceptics might suggest that if a tail-docked red tag was no better than equally acceptable, the trout cannot have been deterred by the red appendage in the first place. But Wackett went one stage further. He developed a precisely moulded copy of a Malacodermid, with a downward-curved body and wing cases in the flight position.

Wackett's development of thermoplastic fly bodies and wings was revolutionary and preceded Lee Wulff's similar experiments by several years.

Tasmania's great flyfisher and tier R.H. (Dick) Wigram wrote, in his book *The Uncertain Trout* (1951):

> *It has been a long time since any radical change in artificial flies has been produced by the fly dresser. Halford's patterns, which first appeared about 1886, were hailed as the last word in artificial fly-dressing. Dunne produced a fly which when oiled was claimed to represent the correct body colour. Every conceivable variety of material has been tried by the fly tier in the hope that his reproduction would bear closer resemblance to the natural insect. It remained for an Australian angler, Wing-Commander L.J. Wackett, to invent the true copy of the natural fly. The full process is explained in his book* My Hobby is Trout Fishing *and the results are incredibly good. I have used these flies. If they were obtainable commercially there would be no need to use any others. Wing-Commander Wackett's duns and spinners all have detached bodies and the balance is perfect. As both the body and wings are made from plastic, it is, to all intents and purposes, indestructible.*

Wackett's body and wing units were press-forged from thermoplastic material between a pair of pantographs – engraved die blocks heated over a gas jet. The finely detailed moulds included mayflies, wasps, beetles and ants. He also developed a bee but encountered flotation problems, though finding it an extremely effective wet fly on the streams he fished.

The process allowed insect bodies to be made in any colour, including subtle combinations achieved in successive pressings. There are surviving specimens in orange, faded red, olive and black. Following the final pressing of the body and wing unit, a few barbs of cock hackle were glued in as tails and a hackle wound behind the wing. Other tiers experimented with a hackle in front of the wing and with removing the wing entirely. There were good practical reasons for both variations.

Wackett stated that 'the best policy is to omit wings wherever a hackle will suffice', except for spent spinners and terrestrials. His mayfly spinners did not imitate the spent insect – species like the red spinner *Atalophlebia australis* conduct their swarming flights over the water and are actively taken both on it and above it – so it is strange that he incorporated a single upright wing into his mayfly design. It featured a tapering front spar which was meant to flex down during casting and then rebound. This does not seem to have worked entirely as intended.

Bob Roles relates that in the early 1970s, he and Tom Edwards borrowed a set of the mayfly moulds that had been in Dick Wigram's possession. Together they made up a range of the flies and experimented with them. While the flies looked good and sat correctly, they were prone to spin during casting and to twist nylon tippets.

A parachute hackle wound around the wing base may have eliminated the problem: it is surprising that Wackett's accurate criticisms of conventional fly design did not lead him towards alternative hackling options. However, the gut leaders of that era were stiffer than nylon and twisting may not have been a major issue. It should also be noted that Wackett himself made several pressings of each fly to squeeze the wing to the thinnest possible membrane.

On the stream, the flies certainly had their moments. In Sir Hudson Fysh's angling memoirs *Round the Bend in the Stream* (1968), the Qantas founder recalled how several highly experienced anglers were frustrated by a difficult cruising brown trout on the Murrumbidgee at Bolero. Deciding to persevere, Fysh tried all options without success until remembering a 'magnificently made' Orange Wasp given to him by 'Wackett the craftsman, the orange body cast in a mould and the transparent wing lifelike when mounted with ginger hackle … It seemed irresistible to any trout, and indeed I regarded it as too precious to use except on special occasions.'

The fish must have recognised that this was one of those occasions. It promptly took the Wasp, first cast.

Wackett was convinced that all flies in the future would be made in this manner. As with Lee Wulff's similar experiments in America, it was not to be. The Wackett patterns do not appear to have ever been produced commercially, and the few that have survived were privately made. Today they are collectors' items fetching around $100 each.

Knighthood and Retirement

In 1954, Wackett was knighted for services to aviation. After acknowledging some 500 congratulatory letters, and in search of 'contemplative rest', he spent a week fishing at Waterfall Farm.

In retirement, Wackett worked on a bewildering number of inventions, ranging from an adjustable plumbing wrench to new roof tiling systems to entire prefabricated houses. To his frustration, none achieved commercial production. He did find a useful purpose for one prefabricated construction. Among the members of the Waterfall Farm syndicate was Archbishop Sir Frank Woods of Melbourne. To provide the Archbishop with a quiet private space for his morning devotions, and maybe the other members with undisturbed sleep after a hard night, 'Wack' donated a wooden aircraft crate as an annexe. It was promptly named Bishopswood.

When the drought of the late 1960s brought poor trout fishing, Wackett turned his attentions back to the sea, revisiting the reef waters off Queensland and fishing for yellowfin tuna off southern New South Wales.

In 1970, whilst handling a canoe stored in his garage rafters, he fell 3 metres and became an incomplete quadriplegic. With typical initiative, he then devoted much of his time to inventing aids for the disabled. He died in 1982, having left his mark in an amazing range of activities. The Sir Lawrence Wackett Centre for Aerospace Design Technology at Melbourne's RMIT University perpetuates his contributions to aeronautics. Fittingly, it is located at Fishermen's Bend.

The Legacy

In *The Fishing in Print* (1974), Arnold Gingrich states that *Studies of an Angler* contains a higher information quotient in one chapter than any angling book in the following 25 years. Like Dunne, Hardie, Mottram and Hewitt, Wackett was 'a true original of the Little Tommy Horner persuasion – always poking a thumb in, probing around to at least lift a corner of the curtain veiling the mysteries of our subject'. However, Gingrich cannot resist unleashing his wit on the same thinkers. He labels them 'worry-warts' and mischievously portrays Wackett as arguing that trout are 'literally [sic] blown out of the water by changes in temperature and pressure'.

Leonard M. Wright Jr's *The Ways of Trout* (1985) considers Wackett's work carefully. Wright is one of many anglers to note that trout in deep lakes can accelerate from a depth of 6 to 9 metres (20 or 30 feet) to swim near the surface with no obvious distress. He cannot accept that the barometric equivalent of a depth change of less than 1 metre will put trout off feeding for up to 3 days, as Wackett had argued. However, Wackett foresaw this objection. He argued that the critical factor was not the amount of excess buoyancy but its duration.

Wright believes that 'the Wingco' mistook the wood for the trees. In his own theory, the principal trigger for widespread and active feeding is a rapid trend of water temperature towards 17°C (63°F). Falling barometric pressure puts a lid on this trend because it is associated with heavy cloud layers.

The reader is left reflecting that both writers are on to something important, but that it has not yet been satisfactorily explained. Until then, it is enough to appreciate that Wackett was a dynamo of ideas. His chief legacy is the example set by his constantly inquiring mind.

HAROLD DOWN

HAROLD DOWN was head of Grimwade House, Melbourne Grammar's Primary School, in the 1950s, and a keener fly fisherman would have been hard to find.

One of eight children, all boys, he was born in Benalla, Victoria and spent all his available spare time in the rivers around central Victoria. He often remarked that trout fishing was his major love after family; disliking the seaside and saltwater fishing, he loved the sight and sound of running water as it cascaded over rocks and falls.

Melbourne Grammar Junior School had around 100 boarders during his term as headmaster, and as he was country born and bred himself, he related easily to those lads from the bush, teaching them the rudiments of fly-fishing, including how to tie trout flies, during his and their spare time.

Harold served in France and Egypt during World War II. His section was almost wiped out after running out of water in the desert. This may explain why he loved rivers and streams over other waters.

A hardy fly rod was produced for him and named 'The H.P. Down Rod'.

Down passed away in 1975, at 80 years of age.

My thanks to his daughter Elizabeth for her assistance, and her permission to reproduce this chapter from *Out Fishing*.

CHAPTER 7

A Fly Fisher's Tale

'Hoppers! Great Scott! He's catching hoppers!' we exclaimed with bated breath. But that's the end of the story.

You'll understand our surprise and concern only if you are prepared to be led quietly up to the climax. It may take several pages of print to get you to it, but a beginning there must be, and, like most beginnings, it will probably prove a little tedious.

Though our circle of intimate angling friends consisted of priest, pedagogue, retired naval officer and another we shall shortly meet, the occasions when we could all go fishing together were rare. The duties and obligations of our several callings nearly always reduced the party to three. It is not often that triangular associations are successful: domestically they are positively dangerous. But our fishing threesomes had stood the strain fairly well, until one of the party announced himself as a purist, a dry fly purist.

He was already known to a wide circle of friends as the best-dressed man on the stream. No one minded that very much, but when he boasted the additional vanity of absolute allegiance to the dry fly, and advertised the fact by constantly wearing one in his hat, we felt he was giving himself unwarranted, superior airs.

On dry fly and dry fly only he'd catch them, and catch them he did. I saw him hook and land a 3-pound brown from a stream that was running a banker and with water as red as the raddle crayon that farmers use on sheep. 'What about the dry fly now?' he said triumphantly to the Church, as he held up a thing that looked like an axe-handle, but was a brown trout. 'You're a lucky devil, and no mistake,' remarked His Reverence as he flopped his worms into the head of the pool. The event had definite repercussions on the social triangle. The Purist's efforts with the dry fly often produced more fish than any other two of us could catch by almost every legal variety of fishing, which included not only wet fly and spinner, but also the humble worm.

We became jealous of the dry-fly devotee's success, and said he had become conceited; at least we thought he had, for he even talked about getting a fishing suit camouflaged in tints of earth, water and sky, with a few bulrushes and blackberry bushes thrown in. The camouflage suit never got beyond the stage of being suggested, for our ridicule of stream-craft that needed such support was too hot for the Purist, who rounded things off by saying, 'I was only joking, anyway.'

'Surely, it's bad enough to sneak up on the poor trout with felt soles, without making yourself invisible besides,' the Church commented. The Purist was the only one of the three of us who could afford felt soles. Both socially and piscatorially, he was the best dressed man for miles around.

'I don't like fishing with fellows who come on to the stream in their worst clothes,' he would sometimes say. 'The trout is an aristocrat, and an angler should be suitably dressed when he goes in pursuit of such a sporting fish.' The Purist always was 'suitably dressed': he was the envy of all of us, and in aristocratic appearance a fit protagonist for the most elegant trout.

And so some sort of division occurred. The best-dressed man had created a sort of special class for himself by becoming a little too expert and exclusive. More or less against the wishes of His Reverence, the Purist tended to choose his own water, gave up the sort of chatty fishing which we all enjoyed so much, and flogged away with an intense earnestness that compelled us to recognize him as our superior. He definitely worked on his fishing, while we only played at it.

'It's not the fish one gets,' the Church remarked one day, 'but the joy of companionship on the stream, the mutual sharing of thoughts and opinions, that constitutes the pleasure of fishing for trout.'

'Yes,' I agreed, 'but you must admit that he catches the fish.'

'Well, let him have all the fish he can get,' the Church retorted. 'He's lost something I wouldn't lose for all the fish in the world. That's just you and me, me bhoy, a-wanderin' up and down and trying to solve the problems the Great Creator has set us.'

'We do get a fish now and again too,' I remarked.

'Shure,' replied the Church, 'but the trouble is there's too much jabberin' and walkin' about between the again and now. Anyhow,' he went on, 'the trout's a rovin' animal. Ye niver can tell where he'll be. If you expect him to be here, he's shure to be there, and he's more often there than here.'

'You're a tonic, Your Reverence,' I said. 'The stream wouldn't be the same without you.'

'Well, not quite the same, if you're speaking exactly, now, but almost the same. In all my fishin' I haven't altered it much, but one day I hope to get into something that will make the water drop a few inches and it won't be with a dry fly neither. I'll put on a wet as big as a young swallow and land a whopper, before the Purist's floater has had a chance to sail across his neb. God helpin' me so I will!'

'I wonder how he's doing?' I asked. 'We ought to go upstream to see how he's getting on.' The Church thought it might be a good idea, and added, 'We'll see him afar off as he'll be wadin' the water. He'll be floggin' the stream as my old grandfather used to flog his poor donkey to town, way back there in Cork on a market day.'

Then the devil entered into my soul, and I gave expression to a doubt that I had been harbouring for some considerable time.

'Listen,' I said quietly, and as though I was rather ashamed of introducing the subject, 'has it ever occurred to you that this getting away on his own upstream all day may not be connected with fishing the dry fly? Has it ever occurred to you that it might be connected with …?'

I paused for a moment before I could get it out, but the Church slapped me on the back and said, 'I'll say it for ye, me bhoy, connected with grasshoppers.'

'How did you know?' I almost whispered.

'How did I know? Ye don't think I've been coming with you all these years troutin' without knowin' what you're thinking? We Irish are loike that,' he said. 'We know what people are thinkin' before they speak, especially among friends – and enemies. My ould mother saved me from many a lie by just lookin' into my wicked heart and sayin', "Now, Denis, it's no good thinkin' ye can tell me a lie, tell me the truth" – and, believe me, when she talked to me so, I was thinkin' up a lie; but when she said that, I knew it was the truth, and nothin' but the truth I'd then have to tell. God rest her dear soul.'

We continued to plod our way upstream.

'Where you see red water like that,' said the Church as we were passing a puddle beside the track, 'there's iron in the ground. That's mineral water, shure.'

'Well, what about that one?' I asked, as I pointed to a green fluke-infested pool a little further on. 'That's mineral water, too,' he said with a roguish smile. 'They'd drink that in Oireland.'

'I'll leave it to you,' I said, but the Church vowed he was never thirsty when he was hunting for trout, and I knew he was up to his leg-pulling tricks again.

'Now about this grasshopper business,' I said, 'it would never do to let the Purist know what we suspect. It's a good job he's not gifted as you say are the Irish, who can often read what's in another's mind before it's put into words.'

'It would be the end of everything,' the Church said. 'If he's catching 'em on hoppers, may the Good Lord preserve me from ever seein' it.'

'I think I'd swear it was a dry fly even if I found him with a hopper kicking his legs in protest against being impaled on a hook,' I remarked. 'There'd be forgiveness in heaven for a lie like that, wouldn't there?'

'Now, me bhoy, we're fishin' and you're not treatin' me professional like, I hope, but I'd be gentle in such a case if you made a confession to me. Ye wouldn't be harming anyone, and the Purist might get such a froight he'd never be cruel to grasshoppers again.'

'He'd be a pure purist then,' I said, and the Church burst into a hearty laugh.

Thus, with occasional sallies of wit, we had already passed some considerable distance upstream from where we had confided our secret suspicion to each other.

We hadn't passed him on any of the bends where the track cut across narrow necks of land, had we?

'Let's have a look at the water,' said the Church, 'and see if he's done this stretch.'

Yes, the Purist had fished this part of the stream, for there were the flat pad marks of his felt-soled wading boots: they were unmistakably his footprints.

'He's got out here for fear of being drowned in that deep pool there,' I observed. 'See where the water has dripped from his waders.' Water drops had left little bullet-like depressions in the fine dust alongside the imprint of his wading boots.

'Ought to be here somewhere, unless he's having a sleep,' said the Church.

'He's a kangaroo for travelling fast,' I remarked. 'Covers a lot of ground even when he's not fishing intensively, but when an evening rise is on, two pools will do him then.'

'By the Holy Virgin!' the Church exclaimed, as he clasped my arm and prevented me from taking my next step. 'Talk of the Devil and he's shure to appear.' His eyes were fixed, staring ahead like one who had seen a vision that had sealed his lips. 'To the right of the bend,' he said in a whisper, and pointed with a finger as if he were taking aim with a revolver. And there to the right of the bend was the Purist – catching grasshoppers!

'Hoppers! Great Scott! Catching hoppers!' I gasped, as I watched the self-sworn dry-fly Purist lunging now here, now there in the grass.

'Wish we'd left yesterday,' said the Church. 'We'd never have known.'

'Let's approach without any noise and catch him in the act,' I suggested, for I had envy in my heart. 'Caught red-handed,' I whispered, as we proceeded cautiously, so as not to break even a twig.

The Purist continued with his grabbing, first here and then there amongst the long dry grass, as his winged quarry apparently either hopped or flew away from his reach.

'He must have a dozen by now,' murmured the Church. One hopper might have been excused for a specially difficult fish, but the Purist was obviously laying in a store.

At last we sneaked up to within a few yards, both shouting a mighty 'Good day' in a tone that almost implied 'Hands up! Surrender! Fall on your knees and beg forgiveness!'

But the Purist did none of the things we expected him to do. He went on groping among the grass, and scarcely lifted his head to justify his 'hoppering'.

'I put my line out to dry,' he explained, 'but the twig I attached the fly to broke, and I've lost the blasted thing in the long grass. I waited for you two so long I thought I'd have a little snooze, and I've forgotten exactly where I hitched up the confounded line. Every yard of ground seems the same here.'

Then we all went 'hoppering' to find the line that had been lost. It was the good fortune of the Church to discover it, but for a long time he spoke never a word. He was obviously doing a self-imposed penance of silence for having been guilty of unworthy thoughts about the Purist.

'Any fish?' I asked.

'Two: not bad fish, 16 inches and 18 inches.'

'What did you get 'em on?' I queried.

'Orange Quill dry fly,' the Purist replied casually, and continued winding the lost line on the reel.

At the end of the day we walked home three abreast with the Purist in the middle. Doubtful and suspicious though we had been, we felt we should act as a guard of honour to atone for our sins in thinking the Purist had been deceiving us. And so we trudged along together, one doubter on his right hand and the other on his left.

R.H.
(DICK)
WIGRAM
1901–1970

WIGRAM WAS educated at Winchester and emigrated to Australia in 1924. He settled in northern Tasmania, where he tied and sold trout flies – many of which he designed to represent Australian insects – wrote newspaper fishing reports and later ran a tackle business. He fished England and Tasmania for over 20 years before he published *The Shannon Rise* in 1938. The 'Shannon Rise' began happening when the Miena Dam, built between 1920 and 1922, increased the water flow into the Shannon River. The 'Rise' was a phenomenon: Snowflake Caddis moths hatched in such profusion that they almost smothered the air. Anglers from around the world would arrive, and jostle each other, side by side.

Regrettably, the Tasmanian Hydro Electric Commission diverted water away from the Shannon in the 1960s. The Snowflake Caddis hatched for the last time in 1963.

The next chapter, 'The War Years', is included so that readers can get some idea of the precautions taken to protect the Tasmanian Hydro scheme during World War II.

The Shannon Rise is much sought after by collectors, as are his other books *Trout and Fly in Tasmania* (1938) and *The Uncertain Trout* (1951).

CHAPTER 8

The Shannon Rise

The amazing hatch of moth that takes place each year on the Shannon River at Miena provides what is possibly the finest dry-fly fishing in the world.

The larva of this moth, the Snowflake Caddis, lives in a cocoon of minute pebbles or debris woven together with silk. These abodes are attached to logs and rocks in the fastest water available, as the larvae can live only in fast water and die very soon if removed from it. They are very active and feed on any small living organisms that come their way. When fully fed, the larva creeps into its cocoon and turns into a pupa. In this form it remains until the time is ripe and, when the weather is suitable, it rises from its home and shoots to the surface, immediately being transformed into the winged adult. Practically all the flies seen during a hatch are males. The female seldom escapes from the water, as immediately on emergence she is set upon by a horde of males under whose weight she is forced down into the stream, living only long enough to release her fertilized eggs before being eaten by the trout or drowned.

The female is larger than the male, and being full of eggs, is greatly relished by the trout; in fact, many of the fish pick out the females and allow the males to drift past unmolested.

The moth usually starts to hatch during the first week of December, the actual date depending to some extent on temperature and atmospheric conditions. During the last 8 years it has occurred four times in November, the earliest date being 12 November, and four times in December, the latest being 15 December.

The Shannon flows from the Great Lake down to what is known as the Shannon Lagoon, three-quarters of a mile below. The river is fairly wide and shallow for the greater part and has a stony bottom. The water is as clear as any chalk stream, full of ripples, strange currents and eddies, fast flowing, and with banks entirely free from bushes or tall vegetation.

As the moths hatch out and drift in droves down to the lagoon, fish crowd up the river eager to get near the source of supply and settle down to a month or two of heavy and easy feeding. The first few days of the hatch are by no means the best for fishing, but after a week or so, thousands of fish have moved up into the river, and sport begins in earnest. The hatch of fly when at its height is phenomenal. Countless millions of moths swirl and eddy over the water; the banks are alive with crawling flies. Viewed from a distance, a white mist appears to hang over the river, in which fish from two to five pounds in weight rise steadily throughout the day.

CHAPTER 9

The War Years

When the war came in 1939, the moth was not disturbed by the ravings of a paperhanger, and not having heard a gun fired in anger, hatched as usual on or about the last day of November. There were a few new faces at the Rise during the first war years. A few anglers came from the tea and rubber countries, planters and civil service men who were taking their leave in Australia, as passages to England were impossible, and enjoying a new experience in fishing, as excited as children at seeing so many trout in one place and all feeding at the same time.

When Japan made her treacherous attack on Pearl Harbor, we were already on the Shannon. The news took all rods to the wireless set, and we had no heart for fishing. Some of the familiar faces were already missing. It was a sad year and an anxious time for everyone. Most of us packed up and returned to the city. There was little pleasure in sport at this troubled time.

During the following year the military took over the only hotel. It was believed by the High Command that Japanese planes or saboteurs might strike at the dam in an effort to cripple the Hydro-

Electric scheme and flood the Derwent Valley. Some humorist worked out that if it was high tide in Hobart when the dam was blown up, the water would be over the post office clock.

Sentries patrolled by day and night and machine-guns were placed behind piles of sandbags at each side of the river. No planes came over and no cloak and dagger men were seen near the dam. No mines came floating down the lake in a northerly wind. The bored soldiers froze in their sentry boxes as howling gales hurled spray far above their heads and the wind shook and buffeted their wooden shelters.

The Shannon still flowed swiftly between its bare open banks and the moth, unheedful of the fact that men all over the world were killing one another with frightful weapons, hatched, bred and were eaten as before.

During those years the anglers were fewer. I think one felt an uneasiness, as of stolen time. I had many letters from old friends in the fighting services who were anxious to know what sort of a Rise we had. Were the fish up to standard? They hoped the war would soon be over and they could return to their beloved Shannon.

I believe it was in 1943 that a cricket match was played on the west bank of the river – Anglers versus the Army. The wicket was not all that might have been desired, as many of the boulders with which the earth was strewn had roots weighing several tons hidden away underneath the grass and these had to be left intact (shades of Trent Bridge). Undeterred by balls that never actually arrived at the crease or shot off at an angle of forty-five degrees, the visitors batted first, and if my memory serves me, were all out for the magnificent total of 29. (It was only possible to hit balls on the full toss.)

The Army innings was held up for some time while the angler's wicketkeeper was retrieved from the river bank whence he had rushed as soon as his wicket had fallen. Needless to say, the Army won with several wickets in hand. As no boundaries had been fixed before the match started, one of the sergeants ran fourteen off a ball that went in the river. A case of beer was then presented by the Anglers, and victors and vanquished joined in a drink at the nineteenth hole – well, it was as much like golf as cricket.

It was then that the soldiers, who took a keen interest in the angler's sport (many a fat trout was sent up to the mess), decided to build a foot bridge just below the dam, and thus save that weary walk back to the bridge and up the eastern bank should the fishermen decide to cast from the other side of the river. The little bridge was a wonderful help and it was with thoughts of gratitude to our Army friends that we used it for many years, until quite recently: it was washed away and has not since been renewed.

War on such a gigantic scale must end, and by 1946 the American uniform which we had occasionally welcomed at the Shannon Rise was no longer to be seen. Lend-Lease returned to the States with, we hope, pleasant memories of the fishing on our crack river. They were fine chaps and I hope someday they will come back and try again. This time they may catch some fish. As one young Colonel said to me, 'They are certainly lunkers, but, boy, do they know their stuff.' He took six big ones back to Melbourne. I know, because I gave them to him. A few days later he wrote, 'When I showed them to the Chief he said I was a goldarned liar.'

The war was over and there was great joy. The men would come home, and the world, it was hoped, would settle down to an age of peace in which people could live their lives secure in the thought that the four freedoms promised would be theirs at last. There would be time to work and time to play, and there would be the countryside free from the scars and reminders of madness. There would be the old Shannon Rise without the shadow of anti-aircraft defences, and the men who loved the Shannon would cast their flies again, surrounded by the old familiar figures in their waders and raincoats. Not all of them would be there. Three of my dearest friends would not lay a line across the water again. They are with me each time I fish the Shannon. I see them in my mind and I hope that they may know that they are not forgotten.

HARVEY J. TAYLOR

HARVEY TAYLOR has been involved in most forms of angling since his early childhood, from fishing the small inlets and bays of Victoria to game fishing offshore along the east coast of Australia. He has been an active writer for the major Australian fishing magazines for many years.

Since moving to Tasmania in the late 1980s, he has concentrated on trout angling: he has written three books about Tasmanian angling and its identities to date. He is very involved in angling clubs and member associations, is on the executive of the major angling bodies in Tasmania, and gives much of his time voluntarily to the sport.

This extract is by courtesy of Blubberhead Press and the author.

CHAPTER 10

Shannon Rise Revisited

Tasmania has attracted the trout angler for over 100 years – the wily brown trout, and the fighting rainbow trout in selected areas have made the lakes and streams of the island state a Mecca for local, interstate and even overseas fishermen. The natural beauty of the Tasmanian wilderness areas provides an added appeal to the angler.

Situated roughly in the middle of Tasmania is the Great Lake, a large and natural expanse of fresh water at an altitude of over 1000 metres. It is the source of attraction for a high percentage of anglers, locals and visitors alike, and over the years some remarkable catches have been recorded there. The lake was originally stocked with trout in 1870, when a party of pioneers carried a billycan of fingerlings from the Plenty Hatchery, in the Derwent Valley north of Hobart, for release into the lake. In those days it was a long and tiring journey on horseback, so different from the simple drive in a car that is possible today.

At the turn of the [twentieth] century the offspring of these original fish were being caught from the lake, with weights averaging 5 to 10lbs and reaching over 20lbs. The area was attracting those anglers who were prepared to rough it in order to get to this wonderful and developing fishing region.

At the southern end of the lake the Shannon River ran out, a small and rocky stream in normal times, not too wide nor too deep. The river of course rose and fell due to the fluctuating levels of the Great Lake, so around 1900 the pioneer anglers who had fished this area since the late nineteenth century erected a rock wall across the Shannon in order to back up the water and so improve the fishing conditions.

The following entries from the Miena guest house logbook illustrate just what the anglers of the day could enjoy as a normal bag.

2nd January 1900	1 fish: 3lbs
6th January 1900	4 fish: 6, 11½, 11 and 15½lbs
27th December 1901	3 fish: 8, 6 and 6lbs
15th January 1904	9 fish: 9, 5, 10, 8, 4½, 14½, 8½, 8½ and 8½lbs
11th November 1906	11 fish: 2½, 6½, 7, 4, 4, 12, 4½, 5, 7, 2½ and 7lbs

In 1911 the Hydro-Electric Power and Metallurgical Co. completed a small dam at the head of the Shannon, in order to regulate the flow of water to a power station then under construction at Waddamana. In 1916 the government took over this scheme and its new Hydro-Electric Department built a more substantial dam across the river to raise the level of the lake. This replaced the early rock dam built by the anglers. Before the erection of this dam, two to four fish per rod per day was the average. Once it was completed, this number increased dramatically to around 15 to 20 fish, with an average size of 6lbs and little or nothing below 3½lbs.

A greatly improved multiple-arch structure, the Miena Dam, was erected at the outfall of the Shannon in 1922 to ensure a constant flow of water down the river to the Waddamana power station. This increased the depth of the lake by another 6 metres. (A third rockfill earth dam was built downstream of the arch dam in 1967, increasing the water level a further 3 metres, and in 1982 this dam was raised by another 6 metres.) A large volume of water passed out of the lake through the Miena Dam's sluices, keeping a short stretch of river below it continuously in spate. After passing under a road bridge, the river widened out into the artificial Shannon Lagoon, a large body of rather shallow water formed by the backing up of the river by a second dam some 5 or 6 kilometres downstream. The course of the river itself through the lagoon was marked for a considerable distance by levees, which were the raised banks of the original river channel standing just clear of the water level.

The advent of the early dams created a fast, constant flow of water down the Shannon, and in these conditions the Snowflake Caddis [moth] thrived. Their love for fast, clear, cold water enabled them to breed in countless numbers over the short distance between the dam and the lagoon. During the hatching season large quantities of dead moths washed up onto the shore, and their masses in flight were like clouds, so dense were they. If ever an environment offered an ideal breeding situation for the Snowflake Caddis, it was this stretch of the Shannon River.

The river, from the lake to the lagoon, ran through low tufted grass banks, for a distance of no more than a kilometre. Its width was between 20 and 50 metres, a lot narrower in places, with an average depth of about a metre. It was probably the most fished short length of water anywhere.

The trout would cruise the lagoon waiting for the magic moment when the Snowflake Caddis would hatch. This seemed to take place at almost the same time each year, usually at the end of November or in the first week of December. For the hatch to commence, the water temperature needed to reach around 10–11°C (50–52°F). The warmth of the sun at this time of year enabled this to be achieved, although sometimes it did not occur until Christmas, and one year it did not happen at all. The onset of the moth was the signal for anglers, from near and far, to converge on the Shannon River. Telegrams were sent from the nearby guest houses to a regular clientele – 'The hatch is on', or just 'It's on' – which was all that was needed to start the procession of anglers to the river.

Once the hatching began, the moths were at first few, but gradually the numbers built up, until such time as they were everywhere, in ears and noses, up shirt sleeves, in waders – clouds of white were blotting out the sun, and falling onto the water surface, where they were gobbled up by the eager waiting trout. At the height of the hatch, any angler, because of the numbers of fish in the river, could be selective and pick from perhaps twenty fish in his area. Selecting a fish was easy, presenting the fly not too hard, but having the selected fish take your particular fly was the challenge: with the hundreds, if not thousands, of natural flies, yours had the odds stacked against it. A lot of anglers used to take a slightly larger fly than the natural ones in order to achieve a take.

Most of the larger fish tended to congregate in the middle of the river. It required a good cast to reach them, but once there a take was usually the order of the day, as these fish did not seem as timid as the smaller ones feeding near the banks on both sides of the river. The majority of the fishing was done with the dry fly, although when the quantity of moth had reduced somewhat, a small wet fly accounted for some nice fish.

To give an idea of how many fish were in a section of the river when the hatch was on would be extremely difficult, for they would congregate in such numbers, and [were] of such a size that would be hard to believe. As an indication, the 1937 regulations required any fish taken under 15 inches (38cm) to be returned as undersized!

Finale

It was in the middle of the 1950s that the Hydro Electric Commission decided to divert the waters of the Great Lake northward to service a new power station to be built at Poatina. The development of HEC storages had already been adversely affecting the Shannon River. The water was cut off for longer periods of time from about 1938 onwards (the Tarraleah scheme), and the fishing continued to fall away until the total redirection of the Great Lake outfall in 1964.

As the flow of the Shannon became irregular, a swell of opinion arose among anglers, tourist bodies and others who wished to retain the magnificent angling that the river had provided. Little success was achieved. The Southern Tasmanian Licensed Anglers Association's report of 1964 sums up the general picture:

> *The opening of the Poatina power station resulted in the diversion of waters northwards from Great Lake by closing the gate at Miena and shutting water off the Shannon River between Miena and the Shannon Lagoon. The effect has been to reduce the Shannon River into a series of pools and the level of the Shannon Lagoon will be lower than it has been for many years. However, this may yet provide good fishing. The loss of the Shannon Rise has been well discussed by the HEC and anglers and the Government in 1956 and again in 1963.*

LES
HAWKINS

THIS ARTICLE is from *Trouting Tales*, by Les Hawkins (Kangaroo Press, 1996).

CHAPTER 11

Trouting Tales – Kiandra

Jauntily perched on a knoll alongside Pollock's Creek and only a short distance off the Snowy Mountains Highway, for many years stood a weekend hideaway for members of the Poachers' Club.

Poachers they were not; precisely the opposite. It was a loosely knit body of enthusiastic fly fishers with the motto 'There are no rules, and don't you dare break them.'

The hospitality of its members was known to the hundreds of anglers who frequented the upper reaches of the Eucumbene River and who, inextricably drawn by the brotherhood of the rod, would call in for coffee or an ale when Poachers were in residence.

The shack's history warrants chronicling here, for sadly in 1970 it disappeared forever and there are few of us left to re-tell its story.

Prior to World War II, two brothers, James and Ken Parkes, purchased a small area of land at Kiandra, near Pollock's Creek, and moved a weekender cottage from the south coast of New South Wales to their selection. Jim, being the elder of the two, had the deeds registered in his name.

A typical outside 'dunny' was built on the thunderbox principle, and in later years it became a noted landmark when it, like the leaning tower of Pisa, took a drunken lean to one side. A length of three by two was used to prop it up and make sure that an occupant did not suffer an indignity whilst the dunny was engaged.

At the outbreak of war, Jim Parkes enlisted in the Royal Australian Air Force and was trained in the Empire Training Scheme in Canada. He served with distinction as a fighter pilot during the Battle of Britain, and, sadly, lost his life when shot down during a dogfight over London. Regrettably, he died intestate and his estate passed to his mother.

In 1944, the Kosciuszko State Park was reserved for the purpose of conserving and preserving one of Australia's most important catchment areas and the wonderful natural phenomena found in it.

Later the privately owned land at Kiandra was purchased by the Kosciuszko National Park Trust, with the property owners given permissive occupancy until their death.

Following the re-purchase of these lands, what many have referred to as an act of bureaucratic vandalism followed. The historic buildings whose owners had passed on were burned to the ground: such lovely old buildings as the home of Bob Hughes, known as the skiing postman for many years, and one of the great characters of Kiandra. (His name is preserved forever in several books, particularly *Historic Kiandra* and Klaus Hueneke's superlative books on the Snowy Mountains area.) The old post office, where for many years Bill Paterick tended the mail and read the rain gauge, was also destroyed, together with many fine buildings whose owners I do not know.

Early one Sunday morning in 1970, Barney Banbrook and I were polishing off the remains of a hearty breakfast when a park ranger (known by the uncomplimentary nickname of Yogi Bear) called to request the name of a person to whom they could write officially and request the Poachers to remove their belongings. The building was marked for destruction.

Mrs Parkes had passed away, and thus the National Park Trust wished to resume possession. I volunteered my name and address, as I knew I could contact Ken Parkes at work on the next day and mount a campaign to preserve our tenure.

Whilst waiting for the expected letter, we carried out an intense campaign to members of parliament and the Kosciuszko National Park Trust, apparently to no avail, as notification was received by me one Tuesday some weeks later. The letter had been signed by the Park Superintendent, advising that the shack was to be destroyed on the following Sunday. This short time frame did not allow for the troops to be mustered for evacuating our goods, so I telephoned the superintendent and pleaded for more time. At least until the weekend after the deadline; in view of the circumstances, we were verbally granted that time.

On the Saturday morning of the agreed weekend, three of us arrived in a VW Kombi Van ready to load and remove our goods, only to find a blackened square and some foundations where the shack had stood. We were stunned and amazed at this treachery, for if one could not believe the promises of the chief administrator, then one may start to doubt the veracity of the Queen of England.

We learned that the contents of the shack had been taken to storage at Yarangobilly Caves, from whence we recovered most but not all of our goods.

Some of the Poachers characters are well remembered: old Barney, who had the wonderful habit of preparing his gear for the day, walking out the door, studying the sky, wetting his finger and holding it in the air to determine wind direction, saying, day after day regardless of the weather, 'Good day for a Wickham's Fancy.' Barney was an excellent and proficient fisherman who had a heart of gold and never hesitated to pass on his knowledge. One of his favourite sayings was, 'There is no knot or tangle that with an infinite amount of patience a fly fisherman cannot make ten times worse.' His face was so craggy that he was sometimes described as 'a goat looking through a barbed wire fence' or [as having] a face that resembled a photo of the Snowy Mountains taken from two miles high.

Another character was Charles Kinsella, who had a pathological fear of snakes and carried a .38 pistol in a holster whenever he went fishing. Shades of John Wayne!

One favourite of mine was Bob Roles, who spent an entire season in the shack; I have never yet known another fly fisher who could consistently lay out his fly line on the water as straight as an iron bar.

Ken Parkes was a marvellous raconteur and frequently entertained us with jokes and stories. One of his tales went like this, delivered in a perfect Oxford English accent complete with all the appropriate gesticulations.

A subaltern, young Cholmondley Fotheringham-Smythe, was posted to the British regiment at Peshawar that guarded the Khyber Pass. Reporting to his commanding officer on arrival, he presented his papers.

'Good to have you with us, Fotheringham-Smythe,' said the Colonel, with his moustaches waving from side to side as he spoke. 'As a matter of fact, I'm off to Blighty for a spot of leave in a few days, but before I go there are a few things I must warn you about. Firstly there are the Thugs, dreadful fellows. Keep a close eye on them; they'll have a wire around your throat and your money in their pocket quick as a wink. Then there are the Indian women of loose virtue. Keep away from them, Fotheringham-Smythe – disease, you know. But the most dangerous of all is the "snake of the plains". Absolutely deadly, kills you in seconds if it gets you.

'There you are riding your charger along the bridle path and lying across the track you'll see it: brown band, yellow band. Avoid it like the plague, old chap.'

Some time later, whilst reclining in his armchair at the services club in London, enjoying a sherry and his long overdue leave, the Colonel looked up and saw an apparition appear in the entrance to the members' lounge, completely swathed in bandages from head to toe. 'By the living Harry, that looks as if it's young Fotheringham-Smythe!' he exclaimed. Arising from his chair, he walked over and said, 'Good Lord, young fellow, what happened? I know – don't tell me – got mixed up with the Thuggees.'

'No sir,' mumbled Fotheringham-Smythe.

'Ah, then you must have been caught out fooling with those Indian women.'

'No sir, not the Indian women.'

'Don't tell me it was the snake of the plains?' said the Colonel, recoiling in horror.

'Yes sir, it was just as you said. There I was riding my charger along the bridle path when I saw it lying there, brown band, yellow band, just as you said, sir. My charger reared in fear and I was thrown to the ground on top of that horrible apparition. Thinking quickly, I ran my hand along its length attempting to squeeze it behind its head and immobilize it. But sir, have you ever caught a tiger by the testicles?'

The old Kiandra pub was a great place to have a drink and relax after fishing; you could always find a local or one of the road workers who could regale you with stories and the history of Kiandra.

Tourist buses stopped there frequently, and one un-named publican would walk along the other side of the bar where the tourists were perched on stools and gently pat the rounded bottoms of the young ladies. He got quite a few slaps, but his bed was rarely lonely! Later, Alan and Robina took over the licence. I became very friendly with them, often working behind the bar to give their one permanent bartender a rest.

When 'streaking' was all the rage, a large group of tourists and locals were having a noisy night, alcohol was flowing freely, the bar was full of cigarette smoke and a mate of mine said, 'I am going to be the highest streaker in Australia.' He then proceeded to disrobe in a small nearby room and ran into the bar clad only in his goose-pimples!

Following a visit to the pub by a team of reporters, this episode made the Melbourne *Truth* newspaper. A long and humorous article with a photo of Robina playing pool topless must have raised a few eyebrows in the liquor licensing board, for the hotel lost its licence soon after.

One Easter night my streaker mate and I were unable to fish at all due to heavy rainfall that had caused the Eucumbene River to burst its banks. So we were carrying out bartending duties to pass the time and allow the bartender time off. During the evening three huge German men entered the bar, torn and bleeding. 'What happened to you blokes?' we inquired. 'We rolled der volksvagen down der hill', was the reply. It transpired that they were travelling from Tumut to Cooma and missed a turn on the wet road; the VW rolled end over end and finished in a gully right side up. These guys calmly got out and walked about 10 kilometres to Kiandra!

'Ve vill haff a large scotch and a schooner chaser pliz.' We duly dispensed their drinks, and after a number of rounds, the pain must have disappeared, for they decided to play pool. Now these guys were big, all over six foot (183cm) and weighing about 18 stone (114kg). The alcohol was taking effect and they were becoming very boisterous towards the end of the night. One of them said, 'I show you what a good German man can do.' and proceeded to crawl under the pool table and lift it completely off the floor using his back.

This was greeted with thunderous applause by the remaining drinkers, who were by now approaching that wonderful state of nirvana that is reached after spending a great deal of money on booze. If they were not tipsy by then they were wasting their money, as my dear old granny would say.

Sensing that these giants may be encouraged to perform more feats of strength and possibly create some uncertainty as to the ultimate well-being of the hotel, Alan asked them to quieten down. He produced his 'people tamer' from under the bar. This 'people tamer' was the large end of a shortened pool cue, and although a bookie wouldn't give odds if a stoush eventuated, the Germans, as good gentlemen should, decided to retire, much to everyone's relief.

The fishing in those days was splendid; rarely did you see another fly fisher on the stream, and if you did you went out of your way to say 'g'day'. (You probably knew him anyway.) I am talking of the days when you would take the silk flyline from your reel and coil it around a specially constructed line winder or hang it out to dry overnight. In the morning it would be strung between the fence and the shack and special preparations [would be] used to dress and polish it. Then [it would be] wound back on to your reel. A far cry from the low-maintenance fly lines of today.

The upper reaches of the Eucumbene are unusual, insofar as there is no vegetation on the edges of the stream, only snowgrass. This results in extremely few hatches where the whole surface of the stream is swarming with countless rings. Fishing is usually a matter of knowing the likely lies and casting to tempt the fish to your fly.

Ten o'clock in the morning was our usual starting time. The sun usually warmed the air sufficiently for the sparse insect life to become active by then. It is one of the few streams where fishing can be satisfying all day, except of course for those rare hot, brassy and windless days.

One very special day for me dawned with low cloud, on the verge of a fog, calm with a drizzle of rain, enough to sit on your clothing like a myriad tiny silver pin-pricks. At home one would think it was a horrible day, but it was ideal for fishing, so Barney and I selected our favourite stretches of water and set off with instinctive optimism.

(In the early days of my fishing career, in a similar manner to most novices, I was keen to prove to my peers that I was worthy of inclusion in their select band of 'expert' fly fishers. My intention was to catch and kill as many fish as I could. Therefore in the tale that follows I ask for my readers' understanding.)

My first choice of fly was a Murrumbidgee Wonder, size 16 dry; this fly usually proved a good pattern on dull and overcast days, with its bright red hackle, peacock herl body and tiny red-dyed grizzle hackle tip tail. Today was no exception. The fish were in a co-operative mood and evidently inclined to feed. Within a short time a stout 2-pounder (1kg) took my fly with a deliberate and confident rise, and it went into my creel, a hessian sugarbag, kept wet to keep the contents cool. I moved a little upstream with unquenchable confidence, champing at the bit to get at the next fish.

On the next bend of the stream I came across one of my favourite pools, a right-angled bend in the river creating a deep undercut bank on the current side and a large quiet backwater on my casting side. The water was gin-clear and flowing at classic level. 'Poseidon, protector of all waters, grant me a special day,' I pleaded as I cast into the bubbling run at the head of the pool. An immense black shape rose and followed the fly but then, much to my chagrin, turned away. Further casts of my little fly failed to entice that black shape to rise again, so I sat and let the pool settle down while I pondered the alternatives.

I could hear the derisive laughter of Poseidon as he thundered, 'Mere mortal, you will work hard for your fish this day.'

'OK, venerable one, I received your message. Impatience and impetuosity will be subdued. After all, I have all day to fish.'

Would a wet fly or nymph, or a change of pattern, bring about the desired effect? My lofty brow wrinkled with concentration as I wrestled with this mind-boggling problem. Poring over an open fly box, my eyes inescapably drawn to the dry fly section, I spotted my favourite Eucumbene fly, a Geehi Beetle. Tying on a number 12, I crept back to the head of the pool and cast again into the current tongue. The fly bobbed and danced in the current only a few metres before it disappeared in a swirl that caused an involuntary lift of my rod tip.

Thank goodness I didn't react too violently and break the tippet, which had happened many times before as a result of a sudden and savage rise.

The rod tip pulsated and bounced and I could feel a weighty and muscular fish trying to escape the pull of my line. As it leaped from the water, the buttery yellow of its flanks told me it was a brown trout. My teachers had taught me to follow a leap by raising the rod tip and then dropping the tip in order to prevent the weight of the fish breaking the leader or tearing the hook from its mouth as it plunged deeply back into the water.

In typical brown trout fashion the fish went to the bottom and sulked; it shook its head frequently in an attempt to dislodge the hook, but I had been taught this trick too, and let the fish have some slack until it tired of this tactic. Eventually it wearied and I was able to guide it to the slack water at the edge of the pool and into the net. It weighed 3½lbs (1.6kg).

The day continued in the same manner, and I finished fishing at 2.30 pm with my bag limit of 10 fish, which totalled 26lbs (12kg). Easily my best day, before or since.

By the time I had finished fishing I was some 2 miles upstream, and 26lbs of fish is a heavy load to carry back to the shack, so I hid them in the snowgrass and carefully noted the spot, then trudged homewards to collect the car and drive back to collect my fish.

Writing about big fish reminds me of one weekend spent in the company of Don Haberecht of Nariel Fish Farm fame. We had decided to try the Murrumbidgee River at a spot 20 km north of Kiandra known as the Skeleton Hut. The Skeleton Hut was just that, the framework or skeleton of a shelter hut built by those hardy stockmen who tended cattle on the long plain during summer. Unfortunately time has wreaked its havoc, and now the hut has completely collapsed.

By scaling along and over a steep ridge an angler can reach some water that is rarely fished due to its inaccessibility. Don and I had decided to fish together on this occasion, each fishing for 100 metres whilst the other kept him company and spotted fish. At one point a rock ledge protruded into the river. Don walked onto this ledge and cast into the centre of the stream, which was about 20 metres wide and quite deep.

The fly drifted for a few seconds, then disappeared in a huge sucking rise. Don set the hook and the fly line knifed upstream like the periscope of a nuclear submarine. When three-quarters of his fly line had been stripped from the reel, I yelled for him to turn the fish or it would finish up in Canberra. 'Turn the bloody thing – how?' he moaned. 'I can't do a damned thing with it.'

By now the whole fly line was in the water and Don was on his backing; it did not matter what he did, he could not control that fish. It can now be chronicled as a matter of historical fact that the leader, fly line and backing all reached the end of their travel and the fish disdainfully snapped the leader like a length of rotten string and proceeded on its way totally unconcerned at the entire episode.

Don turned to me and said, 'I might as well have stood near a railway line and hooked the Melbourne Express, for all the control I had of that fish.'

PETER
JULIAN

PETER JULIAN is a schoolteacher by profession; he is married, with two children. As well as taking regular excursions to Tasmania and the Snowy Mountains, he has fished in Britain, Europe, North America and New Zealand.

He loves to head for the hills with his fly rod, and it is when he is casting Red Tags and Royal Wulffs up the runs and glides of Victoria's northeast streams that he feels most satisfied and at home. Being a teacher does give him some time to pursue his favourite recreation.

Peter was an early columnist for *FlyLife*, and his articles and photographs have appeared in *Freshwater Fishing, Northeast Angler, On the Road* and online at bluemanna.com.au.

The following article is from *Fly-fishing for Trout Down Under* (Kangaroo Press [now Simon & Schuster], 2001).

CHAPTER 12

20/20 Vision

As the shadows lengthened, and the light beamed in horizontal shards of yellow, there was a sense of anticipation. As always, the Snowflake Caddis moths were the first to appear, dancing up a storm. But the young angler waited.

Soon the clouds of spinners could be seen above the tea tree, and he knew that sport was about to begin. A feeling of anxiety surfaced as he wondered, momentarily, whether he was in the prime spot. Upstream, the water barrelled through a set of rapids, ran silently and efficiently through a glide, spilled into a pool 50 metres upstream of his position, made its way to the tail, and then began its descent through another untamed rapid.

The little fish started first, but the young angler resisted the temptation to cast. Then he noticed another subtle sip over on the far bank, near the protruding roots of an overhanging red gum. Realising that his current fly was too gaudy for a potential whopper, he snipped off the Royal Wulff and tied on a smaller Grey Wulff, clipping the hackles on the underside to reduce its apparent size, and to make it easier to sip through the thick surface film.

A moment later, and he had the line airborne. The first cast landed just short of the desired location, but this was just what had been planned: better to cast the first one short in case the fish has drifted back, rather than risk landing the thick fly line on the fish's nose and scaring it into its tangle of snags.

The second cast straightened out perfectly, the grey fly sinking onto the surface with barely a ripple. It drifted a half metre and then disappeared into a barely distinguishable sip, the tippet disappearing into the faint spreading rings.

With breath held, a few heartbeats later the young fisher raised the rod tip.

Instantly, the silence over the river was shattered. The fish launched itself three times, and then, changing tack, bore downstream. The leader did not stand a chance when the fish found the first roots and popped the tippet, before the boy even had time to take stock of his chances.

Breathing again, he sat down on a tangle of driftwood and surveyed the scene as the light faded. There were other, smaller, fish rising now, but none with the characteristic sip of his former adversary, which, no doubt, was skulking among the thickest knot of roots it could find.

As the boy's pulse returned to normal, he reflected on the fish that he had caught, and reflected also on the others, like this one, that had got away. He remembered having watched a platypus eyeball him as he, in turn, had stood motionless eyeballing the platypus. He recalled the excitement of fishing all day until exhaustion, knowing that he was worn out but always wanting just one more cast, wanting to find out what was around just one more bend in the river. He recollected the crowded solitude of the past week, when his family was camped beside the stream and he was out on the water. He remembered the smell of eucalyptus smoke mixed with bacon and eggs in the morning and sausages in the evenings.

As the light faded completely, he realised that there was much for which he could be grateful. With these thoughts, he hitched up his waders, fondly cradled the battered fly rod his grandfather had given him, and headed for camp. Tomorrow would be another day of wilderness, of anticipation, of discovery.

SIR
HUDSON
FYSH

HUDSON FYSH was born in Tasmania, and served as a pilot in World War I, but he is best known as one of the founders of Qantas and managing director of that airline for many years. He was also an ardent trout fisherman: *Round the Bend in the Stream* is his book of fishing reminiscences.

During a conversation with Sir Hudson's son, John, I was interested to learn that John had suggested the title of the book as *A Bend in the Stream* ... but it was eventually changed.

His favourite rivers were those of the Snowy Mountains area in New South Wales, but he also fished for trout and salmon in New Zealand and Scotland, and for mahseer in India; he put a fly over famous rivers in England, far rivers in New Guinea and Austria, and waters in North America and Japan.

His book recaptures happy days in lovely places in the company of birds, animals, wildflowers, fish and fishermen.

My appreciation and gratitude to his family for allowing the reader to share in Sir Hudson's reminiscences.

CHAPTER 13

Fishing the River Test

The essential Test remains to us. She is still the greatest trout stream in the world.

J.W. Hills, *A Summer on the Test*

Hills, who in 1934 wrote that charming book *A Summer on the Test*, not only felt that the river was the greatest trout stream in the world, but also that it was the most charming in its atmosphere and surroundings, and, together with the other Hampshire chalk streams – the ltchen, Kennet, and Driffiel – the most difficult to successfully fish. This latter attribute was, of course, essential in the fly fisher's code. Indeed, an attempt to write something about the Test after only a comparatively few visits seemed presumptuous, except that I was fortified by Hills, who wrote, 'Anyone who has fished for a generation or more ought to have something to say, however inefficient he may be.'

Well, I had fished for over two generations, and after sampling the Test and savouring its surroundings and atmosphere, felt that no dedicated dry fly fisherman's experiences were complete without having matched his wits against the wily Test trout.

A short river of some thirty or forty miles, the Test has its source in perpetual springs and meanders down its whitish chalk bed through the villages of Long parish and Stockbridge and the town of Romsey till it reaches the sea at Southampton. The river, with its picturesque bridges, is flanked in many parts by wide valley water-meadows interspersed with carries, or by-pass streams, which all hold fish. Cows graze on lush green pastures, snipe drum, and cuckoos call from the woods along the river. The spring-fed chalk stream does not flood, rains being absorbed into the heavily grassed meadows, and this enables house building right up to the low river banks, which are studded with venerable homes, their red brick or mellow stone blending into the countryside, and the old barns and cottages with their thatched roofs. Nothing seems to have changed much for centuries, and the buildings lend charm and atmosphere to the river and evoke its history. As far down as Romsey, the Test is a trout stream, and then in its few miles to the tideway it holds salmon and sea trout.

The history of the Test goes back for many centuries and the Doomsday Book refers to the Abbess of Wherwell, who owned a fishery at Long parish 'for the use of the Hall'. Then in 1396 the great Convent of Romsey had an abbess who granted one William Berill permission to build a fulling mill on the river, but it provided he was not to fish without a licence. It was about this time, in 1420, that a fisherman named Piers Fulham wrote a pamphlet which is claimed to be the first book in the English language on angling, perhaps an extravagant claim. It was entitled *Treatyse of Fysshynge wyth an Angle* – which seems to connect with the origin of my own name.

It was at Romsey that I had my first introduction to fishing the Test. This was in July 1945, during wartime, when I was invited down for the weekend by Geoffrey Akroyd to stay at Timsbury Manor. Though the Manor grounds were in a dilapidated state owing to shortage of staff, I am not likely to forget the old Victorian house, and the time when we went out through the walled kitchen garden, with the scent and colour of the ripening English wall-grown peaches, to the much older chapel with its chained bible.

This dates back to the reign of Henry VIII, when he issued a proclamation that a bible prepared by Coverdale and of the largest size, called 'the great bible', should be read in the churches, and these volumes, sometimes more than one, were chained to stands in each church so that the people could read them, or have someone to read the sacred words to them. The process of hand printing was, of course, very laborious in those days, and the churches did not wish to see the books stolen. As I turned the leaves of this old bible it took me far back into history.

I was familiar with gun rooms, but it was at the Manor I had my first introduction to a rod room, where a dozen or more rods were laid out on horizontal racks. Reels, lines, and other gear were also there in neat array, while the casts of some large fish caught on the beat adorned the walls. All was presided over by the river keeper, who also acted as gillie to the master and to visitors.

I was taken for a tour of the water by the river keeper, and in the nearby carry, flowing through the usual Test lush green water-meadow with its grazing cows and bird life, in the shelter of an overhanging beech-tree, after a cautious approach, I was shown a large trout, 'hooked and lost by his Lordship last Wednesday. He will still be dour.'

Nothing was moving on the main river. Though it was a beautiful morning, there was no hatch, but the gillie decided that I should fish, which I did for an hour without success, and with my instructor insisting on choosing and tying on every fly and showing me exactly where to cast. I became fed up with this procedure and, after lunch, when I was to fish again, gave my tormentor the slip and got off on my own. The result was one small brown trout, returned to the water, and a grayling of about three-quarters of a pound which I did not know what to do with, so brought it back with me, and it was disgustedly thrown to the cats. At least I had achieved a long-felt ambition and had caught a trout on the Test. However in those war days the Test was not at its best, and Geoffrey Akroyd bewailed the uncut weed-beds, and the lack of proper restocking.

Grayling, I find, are regarded in different ways in different places. On the Test, which must be kept pure for its trout, they are treated as vermin and are not considered a good sporting fish, or good for eating. In some other parts of Britain they are more accepted, and on the Continent, in Austria, I found them a much prized fish, considered excellent for the table. Actually the grayling which are to be caught in the Test, up to three pounds or more, can be seen rising to the fly in much the same way as the trout. The fish accepts in the same way, and is a fair fighter when hooked. A beautiful silvery coloured fish with a large reddish dorsal fin, it definitely ranks amongst the sporting freshwater fish of England and the Continent.

Akroyd and I were, however, to fish the evening rise, which would be good, and my expectations were great as we sat down to dinner at about 8.30 p.m. During the long meal I got more and more restive as time passed, and the first signs of dusk set in. By the time we got to the peaches it was 9.30 p.m. and slowly getting dark. I could see my chance for a fish vanishing. On the river there were one or two good fish feeding, rising with their almost imperceptible dimple close into the bank. A few casts, darkness descended, undue haste produced a line tangle, and gone were my hopes of hooking one of the big fellows.

Not long after my visit to Timsbury Manor, it was all arranged for me to fish the famous Broadlands water for salmon at Romsey, but this plan fell through. Broadlands, of course, is the palatial home of Lord Louis Mountbatten, which is separated from the Test, broad-flowing here, by an immense area of carefully cut greensward. The view of the Manor from the old Romsey Bridge is breathtaking; then when one turns the other way the little gardens of reed-roofed cottages flank the river, half a cast away, with a backdrop of the town and the old abbey and pointed church spires.

On another occasion, down near the tideway at an inviting pool, I unsuccessfully fished the Rolls-Royce water; moving salmon thumbed their noses at us the day long. The Hampshire Avon was another unsuccessful venture; we tried for salmon, then higher up for trout – I am afraid that in the bigger water coarse fish and eels had about taken over. Then came a gap of some 10 years before, a much improved fisherman, I fished the Test again, higher up the river in the rightly famous Long parish and Stockbridge areas.

Close to Stockbridge is situated the Houghton Club, where fishing records have been preserved since the year 1822; it is no doubt the premier and most exclusive Trout Fishing Club in the world. It is exclusive so as not to overcrowd the few miles of water, and there are only twenty members. I had a standing invitation from the late Lord Beaulieu, a member, to visit the club and fish there but could never exercise this as visitors were not allowed till after 16th June. The practice is to put in large fish, both brown and rainbow, of two pounds or more, and as the river is very good, river care being phenomenal, good catches are taken. The daily limit is ten fish, and all fish under a pound and a half must be returned.

Early in June 1965, when attending an executive committee meeting of the International Air Transport Association, I had the opportunity to fish the Test at Gavelacre, on the upper river between Long parish and Stockbridge. I was the guest of the late Lord Knollys. His lovely old red brick home was in a magnificent Test valley setting, with tall beeches and flowering chestnuts surrounding it, and a thirty-yard strip of lawn separating it from the river. We sat in front of the house and had our tea amidst a profusion of red roses which climbed the walls, and looked at the trout nymphing in the stream and grubbing amongst the weeds, their dorsal fins and tails coming out of the water.

The little 50-yard run of water on which we gazed came from a cascade under an old rustic bridge, then rippled down on its hurrying way till it emptied over the tail of the run into quieter water overhung with leafy boughs from a stately grove of beeches. A mother duck and her little chicks breasted the stream, the little fellows darting here and there. At the back of the house a little by-pass had been run through the rose garden, and here a number of tame trout, hand-fed, were on the fin under the shelter of some overhanging elms. In its whole setting, I thought I had never seen anything so beautiful, so peaceful, and so alluring to a fisherman. During tea I was also told the story of how, as an experiment, one of the by-pass trout had been netted and taken down the river, where it was released. Sure enough, in a day or two that trout had found its way back up the river, passing its brethren, travelling through devious and difficult channels to take up its old position. It was there again, waiting for its daily ration.

Next morning, with lunch in my fishing bag and armed with Lady Knollys's rod, I was dropped at the bottom of the main river beat, the Test here for some miles running as two distinct rivers. Dry fly only was the rule, a limit of four fish, and no wading, since the river banks were cleared for casting. I fished a 3X cast with a small dry fly of local reputation. The river itself ran clear and hurrying with a ripple here and a run there between low grassy and tussocky banks. The depth was a mere 2 or 3 feet, and the chalk bottom could be seen patch-worked or streaked here and there with weeds, the fronds trailing and swaying in the current. The weed growth in the chalk streams is, of course, great, and careful cutting is necessary each year.

The morning was clear and windless. It was a bright day with little fly on the water, the mayfly hatch being over, and through the clear water 20 yards upstream I could clearly see a nice trout rising. Its cavernous mouth opened wide as it engulfed the odd spinner or dun as it drifted down. Casting carefully, I put my Iron Blue over him, and that trout was off like a shot, having, I think, seen not only myself but my rod as it flipped forward, and also my line and gut as it hit the water. I felt I would have to stand further back or get down on my knees, casting a longer line, and I would have to look for some ripple-helping broken water.

As I worked my way up the stream, fishing the odd rise here and there, I found myself scaring those fish every time I cast. My longest cast – I am not a long caster – was a good 6 feet short of what I felt it ought to be. On several occasions I cast with a dozen good trout in view, only to see every fish dash off like a maniac as soon as my line hit the water. I realized the truth of all that had been said about the Test being a difficult river, and only one for the experts.

I crossed a narrow rustic footbridge and stood watching the clear water flowing below, with an odd fly or so on the surface, together with the bits of grass, weeds, and green leaves, which so often float on this stream. Someone cutting weed upstream. It was lunch time, and I opened my tin of beer and ate my sandwiches, sitting on one of the little benches set here and there along the river in strategic positions, where the angler can sit and watch for movement on some favourite pool or run up ahead. As I sat there, a picture of the river which was quite unforgettable formed in my mind. On this lovely summer day from the thick woods cuckoos constantly called, and blackbirds just sang their hearts out. Thrushes sang, too. Snipe made twisting flight over the marsh and swifts hawked insects, swooping low.

With the afternoon the light had changed. I sensed some balance had tipped in favour of the fisherman, and when from my seat I saw a trout rise with confidence beyond a leafy hawthorn bush in the riverside, I dropped my lunch, grabbed my rod and using that bush as a shield cast around it, dropping my fly onto that typical brown trout lair close in to the bank, where I had seen the last rise. A strike! I had him this time. I tightened on what felt like a good fish as he tore off upstream. Not a bad fighter, which, when I had him out, scaled just under two pounds.

I came to 'the stew', a small stream bypass of the river netted at both ends, and also over the top to keep predator birds out. This little stream held fish for release in the river as required; some of them looked two pounds in weight, and I learned later from the river keeper that he had recently netted twenty of these fish up to two pounds and put them in the main stream. The fish had been fed on raw liver and, of course, when released tended to congregate nearby and try to get back to such a God-given food supply.

I caught three easy fish up from the stew, all just under two pounds, and ended the day with another nice brownie further up, and a grayling of a pound and three-quarters which was considered a good fish for the river. Emptying my bag, with the four beautiful, well-conditioned fish before me, I noticed that three of them had the typical brown trout features of red and dark spots and brown to russet general markings, with yellowish bellies – earlier in the day I thought I had never seen anything more beautiful than one of these fellows jumping, animating the river scenery and flopping back with a splash. The fourth fish was dark and steely blue, with never a spot on him, and akin to our Australian Lake Eucumbene brown trout, and rather like the deep trout of Lake Taupo.

I was mystified, and in a chat with the river keeper, with the trout laid out before us, I was told that the dark silvery chap, an ounce under two pounds, was a 'stew fish' which had been feeding on chopped liver before release in the stream, while my other three were fish which had been in the river for a long time, existing on their natural food of shrimps, nymphs, and fly of various kinds.

On another visit to the Test I fished with Sir Charles Dunphie on his stretch a few miles up towards Long parish from Gavelacre – a delightful beat with the rather broader Test flowing in a single channel between beeches, oaks, and a variety of undergrowth thickly clothing the river banks. For this reason wading was in order, and interesting fishing it was, trying to flick the fly in under some particularly low branch hanging over the water. No mayfly appear on this stretch, and it was thought better without them, a theory with which I hardly agreed. It was rather an unproductive day, with one $^3/_4$-pound fish, and my main memories are of the delightful river, the company of Sir Charles, and our attempt to negotiate past two very belligerent white swans which were nesting on a little island.

My most recent visit to the Test, and perhaps, unhappily, my last, was to Gavelacre in the first week of June 1966. This was not long before the death of my kindly host, Lord Knollys. Lady Knollys was greatly incapacitated, and to still enjoy a little of her beloved fishing she used to sit in a wheelchair out on the lawn on the river bank, and landed a trout or so in that way. The ever-changing movement of the river with its fish, bird, animal, and insect life which she loved, could also be watched.

At early morning-tea time I looked out of my rose-entwined casement window at the river and the finches twittering on the bird table under the large pine trees. A lovely balmy morning, and I noticed a large greyish moth fly in through my window – a female mayfly which I still have in my pocketbook. I thought this a good augury for the day, and that a hatch of this fly, delectable to the trout, would be on, and so it proved. It was a wonderful day. Out on the river where the lovely chestnuts were in bloom in their red masses, a mayfly or so was floating down and the fish were taking them.

Much has been written about the mayfly which some Hampshire streams have and some haven't, and which varies in the intensity of the hatch, if there is a hatch at all, from year to year. About the last week in May they appear, and last perhaps for 14 days. In a heavy hatch the fly just whitens the water, and to expect a trout to take your artificial is out of the question. However, trout just gorge on these insects and, most importantly, big fellows come up from their lurking depths. The time to fish the mayfly is when a few insects are coming down here and there, or shortly after the rise is over and the fish are moving and looking for more. The imitation used is a big sparsely hackled fly such as I cannot imagine trout mistaking for the real thing; but, mysteriously, they do.

In the morning on the river I had caught two fish around the 2-pound mark and was feeling pleased with myself. I had seen a very good fish rise, which I could not attract with a variety of flies. In the afternoon I went back for him, and was fortunate to see the fellow gulping the odd mayfly as it floated over. A long cast; no drag; my fly steadily came back with the current and, wallop! I tightened, and was playing a larger fish than I had before hooked on the Test. When it was safely netted and on the bank I was surprised to see I had a rainbow trout which, on the scales, went just a shade under three pounds. Back at Gavelacre great surprise was expressed at the catching of a rainbow, which it was thought must have come up from the Houghton Club water lower down the river. I believe this was the largest Gavelacre fish recorded in 1966. That day with the mayfly-fishing was comparatively easy, and I understood how, on some hotel waters, permits to fish cost extra during the mayfly season.

I shall always have the most satisfying memories of the Test: of fishing it, of its incomparably lovely surroundings, and of the firm friends with whom I fished.

DICK
EUSSEN

THE FOLLOWING chapter is from *Barramundi and Tropical Freshwater Sportfishes* (Kangaroo Press, 1994), and is reproduced with permission from the author.

Eussen has been writing for outdoor magazines since 1957, and was one of the pioneers of four-wheel driving into the then often trackless areas of the tropics from the late 1950s onwards.

He has been very active in practical conservation issues, in particular in the Northern Territory's Barramundi Management Plan. As a member of the Amateur Fishermen's Association of the Northern Territory, he was one of the principal figures behind the push for a better deal for the barramundi – and amateur anglers in general.

CHAPTER 14

Fly-fishing

Fly-fishing for tropical fish, and in particular barra, is an attractive change from other methods of fishing. Its attraction drew me to the sport years ago and has kept me on the go when I feel like trying something more skilful. Make no doubt about it, fly-fishing with heavy 10 weight rod requires quite a lot of skill and fitness.

Years ago there was an arrogant attitude that fly-fishing was only suitable for trout and salmon. You had to be of the upper class, the old school tie and all that. Happily, different values apply today. Fly-fishing is a method of great versatility and can be used for catching anything from pan-fish to marlin. It's just a matter of matching fly rod, reel, line and flies to the target fish.

There is quite an increase in the number of anglers using fly-fishing gear in the north, working from tidal flats and deep estuaries to billabongs and upper river pools in the quest for barramundi. There are many exotic places in the world which have top challenges and reputations as fishing paradises, but in reality Australians don't have to travel out of this country to find that what remains here is perhaps the finest fishing in the world today. This is especially true of our northern coastline.

The Right Gear

No matter what you fish for with a fly, the right equipment is needed to produce the target fish. If you are after jungle perch or sooty grunter, fly gear in the 6 weight class will be fine. However, that is inadequate when you are chasing barras. For them you need what is known as saltwater fly fish gear.

One of the most versatile outfits you can use is a 2.7 metre rod designed for a 9 weight line. It can handle the best that freshwater barra are capable of and do a very good job on 90 per cent of saltwater barra also.

However, when fishing saltwater inlets and tidal shores, the best rod is one designed for a 10 weight line. Fishing in this sort of an environment is always risky, in that a monster queenfish, trevally, cod, shark or something even bigger will take that fly and take off into the deep blue. Anyone who has ever hooked 15+ kilo barracuda or Spanish mackerel will know exactly what I am talking about. Under such conditions, the heavier, more powerful rods and lines provide better control and generally make casting with big flies a lot easier, and they provide a better degree of control in turning a fish. Even small fish in tight rocky foreshores running with the tidal flood can be trying with a rod that lacks backbone.

Conditions are the major factors which will decide the choice of fly-fishing outfit you will use. You must consider the rod components. Graphite rods are lighter, more powerful and also give better casting performance than fibreglass ones. They cost more, but are well worth the extra money. A good saltwater rod should have ample numbers of large, stainless steel, snake guides, at least one aluminium-oxide stripping guide – two is better – and a large tip guide to prevent leader connections from getting snagged during a cast.

Good saltwater reels can be more expensive than rods, and this is true when we come to the choice saltwater corrosion-free reels. These have several features which freshwater reels don't have – or need. One of these is an adjustable drag system. Unlike freshwater fish, which are normally played from the line, the barramundi is often played from the reel.

That is why the adjustable drag is so important. This drag must be strong, dependable, saltwater resistant and capable of releasing line smoothly, without hang-ups. The reel must also balance the rod, otherwise casting can become very tiring. The drag adjustment button should be easy to locate, and should allow the drag to be tightened with a few turns, as opposed to only one turn or less on cheaper brands. Saltwater water reels should accommodate at least 200 metres of 15kg backing, plus the fly line. Micron or Dacron is the best backing for flyfishing reels. A reel that is to be used as a freshwater reel should have at least 50 metres of 10kg backing.

Reels should be capable of taking interchangeable spools: for example, one spool may be loaded with a sinking line and the other with a floater. Make sure that spools are easy to change under field conditions.

Fly reels come in different designs: direct drive, reverse and multiplying reels. The strongest and most reliable are the direct drive reels, as they have fewer moving parts. They take in line with each turn of the handle without slipping. They are also the least expensive.

While drag is important in fly-fishing for large fish, it is often over-emphasized, and can result in too much drag being used. For the majority of fish, no more than 1 to 2kg of pressure is needed to hold and turn fish. If you are breaking off too many fish, the chances are that the drag is too tight or the reel is not letting line flow smoothly.

Fly Lines

Fly lines are available in many tapers and densities and it is very confusing for beginners to select the right one. Much of the available information comes from expert casters who can lay a 30-metre cast out before breakfast. Shooting heads, 'saltwater tapers' and other specialty lines do increase casting distances, but not noticeably so if you are just starting in the game. Novice casters nearly always have trouble with these lines till they become more skilful. The whole truth of the matter is that you don't need to be able to cast 30 or more metres. Most fish take the fly in close, with 5 to 10 metres being the most common strike distance.

Under such conditions the standard weight-forward taper is more than adequate when used in 8 to 11 weight designations. As casting skills increase with practice, distance will grow also, and it is then that some of the 'expert' lines may be used to gain that 30-metre cast. I use both sinking and floating lines when fishing for tropical fish. The floater is easier to cast across shallow tidal flats and other shallow bodies of water. As large streamers and poppers are the norm in such conditions, the floater is the best choice.

There are many sinking lines. The intermediate full-sinking line is the best to cast with, and it sinks to desired depths quite well. As you gain experience you may feel the need to purchase extra spools for the reel and invest in sink-tips, lead core and other lines. It's all a matter of experience and the time of the day to find out where the fish really are. But as beginners' lines, the intermediate sinking and floating lines in weight-forward are the only ones needed.

Leaders

The leader's role is to put some distance between the fly line and the fly. In trout fishing the leader's role is to deaden the impact of the fly in the water. But in the tropics a noisy splashing leader is normally an advantage. The fish are attracted to the splash, which can, with some practice, be made to sound like a school of bait being hounded into the shallows. It always brings the wolves in. The long tapered leaders used in trout fishing are almost impossible to cast with when using large flies or poppers.

Many anglers in the tropics use a single length of 6, 8, or 10kg breaking-strain monofilament tied directly to the fly line as a leader. My own method is to tie a 15kg butt section, 1 metre in length, directly to the fly line, using a 'nail-less' nail knot. A metre length of 8kg monofilament is attached to the butt section with a blood or barrel knot as a tippet. For barra, another 30cm length of heavy shock tippet, 15kg or more, may be tied directly to the butt section or the tippet. While shock tippets are very much a nuisance, they are a must on fish that have cutting edges and abrasive skin. Barra are well known for their razor-sharp gill rakers.

Wire may also be used for the shock tippet, and the connection can be made with a small swivel. The fly can be tied directly to the shock tippet with an improved clinch knot, and in the case of braided wire, with a half loop. In no event should the total length of the leader exceed 2.7 metres, and in most practical uses the leader for barramundi need not exceed 2 metres. Of course if you are fishing under IGFA rules you must stick with the leader as laid out in the rules of the Association. As a matter of fact the chances of catching a barramundi for the record charts are very good on fly gear.

Flies

Selecting flies for barramundi is quite simple. As long as the fly resembles a baitfish, the barra will show interest. To get started, you should have a few Deceivers in white, green, blue–black and purple colours. I think that the Deceiver is the one great fly that will catch anything in the tropics. It casts well and imitates a vast variety of foods tropical fish feed on. Some needle or eel-like patterns are worth their weight in gold, and again this colour is one which works well on barra, as do pure blacks in gin-clear waters. Other flies for the north include Pink Things, Bentbacks, Clauser Minnows, Dahlburg Divers and many of the fish patterns tied by several makers who live in places like Townsville, Cairns and Darwin, where they peddle their creations through the local tackle shops.

Fly hook sizes should be matched to the fly line in use, and flies tied onto 1 to 6/0 hooks are commonly used on lines from 8 to 12 weight. My own preference is hooks in 4/0 size on 9 to 10 weight lines. Try to obtain some flies which have weed guards fitted to them, as they are extremely handy in weedy billabongs and pools. Remember, it's not all barra in such locations, as saratoga, catfish and tarpon also find these weedy places attractive.

I think that almost half the considerable amount of barra I have caught on the fly rod have taken poppers in the late hours of the day and early evening over shallow tidal flats, and on the end of billabongs and deep permanent pools. Poppers are deadly on barra, and they will chase them inshore if they have to. So get a few in the tackle box. They may be the savers which will make the tropical north fishing trip a success to be talked about. Keep the leaders short, and use at least a 10 weight outfit to keep poppers fitted with 3 to 4/0 hooks in the air in order to gain some distance during casting. When retrieving flies and poppers, do it with short, slow, jerky movements, recovering no more than 15cm of line any one time. This is especially important when working poppers during dull light conditions.

Barra are basically lazy fish and do not waste a great deal of energy chasing lures. If you have a fish chopping at your fly or popper but miss it each time, slow down the retrieve. A trick with poppers is to let them settle on the surface and wait for the circles caused by the splash to decrease before slowly moving the lure. Just a bit at a time: let it settle down, count to three and do it again. The strike will startle you in its intensity as the barra hits. It also works on other fish.

Using flies and poppers in association with the fly rod and line is a whole new ball game if you have not done it before. It is fun, and can open up a new world of fishing pleasure. The key to success is to recognize what food the fish are eating and then pick a lure which resembles the bait and work it till you strike the right medium. You must be able to recognize the different conditions – weather, winds, tides and phases of the moon and, of course, temperature, which affects all fish. That has already been explained in other sections of this book; what is more important is the right fly outfit. Know the area where you are going to fish, or hire a guide, or let a mate take you into the wilds where the fish are. The learning process of fly-fishing takes time but is good fun as long as you don't allow your frustrations to get the best of you in the early stages. They hit all of us, but we survive to discover and enjoy a whole new world of fishing.

JOHN SAUTELLE

JOHN SAUTELLE was one of those born fishermen who spent most of his life within reach of trout water.

Although born at Bombala, in country New South Wales, he was educated at the Sydney Church of England Grammar School. He played an active role in both rural activities and research into his hobby, trout fishing.

He was a foundation member and life member of the Monaro Acclimatisation Society, and its president for 7 years. As well, he was president of the Australian Freshwater Fishermen's Assembly, a foundation member of the NSW Institute of Freshwater Fishermen, and its president for 5 years. He was also deputy chairman of the Amateur Fishermen's Advisory Council.

John was one of the people who was instrumental in forming the NSW Rural Advisory Service, was advisory councillor to the Minister of Primary Produce, and a State councillor on the Agricultural Bureau.

During World War II John served with the 6th Divisional Cavalry. After the war he had at least two major achievements: he got his golf handicap down to single figures, and he was, with Mr N Douglas, able to persuade the then Commonwealth Treasurer, Sir Arthur Fadden, to establish the Commonwealth Development Bank.

Fishing for the Educated Trout is not a book of instruction, but in the course of a series of humorous yarns he manages to get in an amazing amount of trout lore from many countries, which he absorbed over more than 50 years of enjoying his sport.

I am indebted to his family, and particularly to his son John, for their permission to include the following chapter.

CHAPTER 15

Monaro in the Early Days

I count myself one of the lucky ones, in that I can say, 'You should have seen the trout fishing on Monaro in "the good old days".' There is very little risk of being contradicted when one talks of the fabulous fishing to be had there during the late 1920s and early '30s, because very few of my contemporaries were keen trout fishermen. Even so, there are some still fishing who can go back to the early 1900s, and I have been assured by a few of them that the fishing was even better then than when I first became really interested in trout fishing, about 1927.

Carl Massy and I used to open the season on the McLaughlin River, or 'Mac', as it is affectionately known to many trout men. We were sometimes accompanied by Allen Caldwell, and it was a red letter day when we met another angler on the stream – that pleasant state of affairs continued almost up to the early 1950s, when we gradually found more and more cars parked by our favorite pools, until today it is like Pitt Street on Friday afternoon during the opening weekend.

The only fish, apart from eels, in the Mac in those days were rainbow trout, and with practically the whole river to ourselves it was rare not to take one's bag each day. We generally returned anything under 0.9kg (2lb), and I remember one day when two of us kept nine fish that weighed 20kg (44lb) during five hours fishing. I fished with either worms, small spoons, devons, or Indian spinners then, not really becoming a keen fly man until about 1934, when my youngest brother Peter converted me one well-remembered day on the Campbalong Creek.

Peter was friendly with the well-known Sil Rohu at the time, who had persuaded him to try fly-fishing. Peter and I were fishing together, he with dry flies and me with a small devon. I had a couple of nice fish of about 1.8kg (4lb) each by the time I caught up with him, and felt rather pleased with myself. Just as I arrived at the pool he was fishing I saw a trout rise about 27 m (30 yd) below him and called out, 'There's one below you.'

He moved back and walked down, keeping low to gain cover behind some tussocks until he was opposite the spot where I had seen the rise. Just then the trout rose again a few feet further down; Peter cast his fly, a Red Tag, dry, about 2 feet below the still visible rings, and next moment I saw the fly disappear. The fish, a very good brown trout of 2.3kg (5½lb) was duly hooked and landed.

It was the first time I had seen a dry fly used and I was most impressed. It looked pretty easy, so I asked Peter if he would lend me a fly. He first of all greased my line, a silk Kingfisher, so it would float, tied on a fine leader and showed me how to tie on the Red Tag fly which he handed me. He then greased the fly with some of the line grease so it would not become waterlogged, and gave me instructions to count to three before lifting my rod tip if perchance a fish should take the fly. I could cast reasonably well for a short distance, so I went off downstream full of confidence.

Approaching a large pool, I saw what I took to be a small fish rise very close to my bank, almost directly in front of me. I cast the fly a couple of feet to one side and luckily everything was in my favour, and the fly landed gently with only a couple of feet of leader on the water. I saw a very delicate sup, my fly disappeared and, remembering Peter's advice, I counted religiously to three, lifted the rod tip and thought I must have snagged a log or something.

Walking up to the bank, winding in line as I went, I couldn't believe my eyes – there, a few feet away, was an enormous fish, barely moving, and with my fly plainly visible in one corner of her mouth. As soon as she saw me she raced out to the middle of the pool, jumped high in the air twice and then went straight to the bottom. I couldn't move her until I remembered reading somewhere that if one tapped the reel, keeping the line taut, a fish would sometimes become annoyed and swim out from whatever cover it had taken. In any case, it certainly worked for me then.

I had made such an almighty row in my excitement that Peter came down to see what it was all about. He also became quite excited, for it was a very large fish. When I had her pretty tired he tried to get the net under her but we could see she just wouldn't fit in the thing crossways, so I suggested he wait until I had her completely exhausted. I then held her head straight up, suspending her vertically in the water, and instructed Peter to place the net under the tail and scoop her out.

He did it perfectly, throwing her about 1.2 m (4ft) away from the water. She gave an almighty kick towards the river, getting rid of the fly as she did so. I literally dived on top and held her down until I was able to get a finger in the gills and remove her from danger. She was a magnificent female brown trout of 3.7kg (8lb 2oz) – by far the biggest trout I had ever caught, my first fish on a dry fly, and what's more, with my very first cast!

Naturally, I thought that meant the downfall of practically every large trout on Monaro – how little did I know, and how much I still had to learn! It was many weeks before I caught my next decent fish on a fly, but I was really hooked on that method of fishing for trout from then on.

I often wonder whether the fishing really was so much better then than it is today. Sure, for the few who fished the streams then, results, both in quantity and quality of fish, were better, but it is questionable whether the total yield of a stream was any greater than it is today. Certainly the challenge presented by today's fish population is far greater, and to my mind a day's fishing now is far more satisfying, though the number caught may be far fewer. There is no doubt, in my mind, that that trend will continue, especially in streams dominated by brown trout, which on Monaro would be at least 98 per cent of them, even though all stocking over the last 10 to 14 years has been with rainbow and brook trout only. The more brown trout are subjected to heavy fishing pressure, the harder they become to catch.

However, even today it is possible to occasionally take a bag limit on some streams on Monaro. On one occasion in 1976 I had nine fish, all brownies, before lunch from one of our basalt streams. They weighed a total of 13kg (28lb), which would have been considered pretty good, even in 'the good old days'! I guess better equipment, finer leader material, better-tied flies, the use of polaroids for spotting, and maybe increased expertise as a result of many years of angling, all help balance the odds.

The late Messrs Jim Gaden, Ben Payten, Billy Napthali and Frank King helped keep the stock of rainbows high in such streams as the Mac, Campbalong and Delegate rivers. They were all keen fly fishermen – very occasionally I had the pleasure of fishing with one or other of them, and what great company they were, going out of their way to help, especially for beginners like me.

The first freshwater fish I ever caught was a redfin, or English perch, in the Bombala River in 1917, on a handline with a worm. I can still see the line moving out slowly over the grass as the fish swam away with the bait, and savour the intense excitement when that fish lay kicking beside me! Those fish are looked upon as a menace in a trout fishery, as indeed they have proved in some areas, for example Lake Canobolas at Orange, in New South Wales. However, it isn't always so, because although they are still in the Bombala River in large numbers, I had one of the best season's trout fishing in that stream in 1976–77 I have had for many years.

The late Dr Geoff Maitland, son of Sir Herbert Maitland, sent me a photo of Dr Spiller Brandon holding a large rainbow trout which he caught in the Big Badga in the early 1920s. The caption says, 'Caught in the Badga. A trout caught by Dr Spiller Brandon, of Woollahra, in the Big Badga River, near Cooma, where the "Rainbows" are very large. It was 2 feet long and weighed 7lb 12oz.' It has been said that Dr Spiller Brandon was responsible for liberating brown trout fry in this stream, to the eminent satisfaction of most fly men, and the distress of many other anglers.

There is no doubt that species has done extremely well there. Although only rainbow and brook trout have been released there over the last 10 or 12 years, the majority of fish present are brown trout. Growth rate is exceptionally good, a number of fish over 4kg (9lb) having been taken there during the last few years. I myself took a magnificent brown trout on my first visit there, a couple of years ago, which took me 55 minutes to land. It weighed 3.7kg (8lb 2oz) and now graces a wall in my office, thanks to John Kirkpatrick, who was with me at the time, and who kindly made an excellent cast for me.

A school teacher from Cooma took another brown of 3.4kg (7lb 14oz) from the same pool later the same day, and my son John took a 2.9kg (6½lb) brownie from that pool last year.

Access to some of the streams in the early days was often a problem, at times calling for the use of pack horses. On one occasion Carl Massy organised Bill Patrick, postmaster at Kiandra at the time, to pack him and me in to the upper Tumut River. That was well before the Snowy Mountains Hydro-Electric Scheme got under way, and meant a four-hour ride from Kiandra. Bill had the horses ready when we arrived and we got away about noon, with a tent and sufficient provisions for a week.

It was customary for some of us Monaro men to have a rum at the first running stream we crossed when embarking on a trip in the mountains; a kind of offering to the gods of good fortune. On this occasion we crossed a small creek about half an hour after leaving Kiandra. I asked Bill if he would care to join us in our traditional toast to the trip, to which he agreed and I poured him a fairly good one. He thought this was a hell of a good idea and suggested we have 'one on him' at the next creek we came to – by the time we had crossed the fourth stream Bill was in great order.

Carl and I had the feeling Bill was bushed, in the true sense of the word, so we got out a map and compass and took bearings on a couple of peaks which we could identify. Resection showed us to be on a ridge we shouldn't be on – we had gone too far. We finally convinced Bill we were right, returned to the correct ridge and made our way down to the river at our chosen camp site on Geordies Spur. Bill had never seen a compass and map used before, and although he knew the country really well and was normally a very good bushman, he had to admit our 'new-fangled' ideas had some merit!

The following extract from a small booklet shown to me by Did Gadsby, written in 1904, and titled *Trout Fishing on the Goodradigbee*, highlights the difficulties encountered when organising a trip in that period. It is a description of a trip by three fly fishermen, apparently arriving at Queanbeyan by train from Sydney, and I quote:

To give an idea of how difficult of access the valley of the Goodradigbee is, it was well into the night before the river was reached, although the anglers started straight away from the Queanbeyan railway station in a well-horsed buggy upon the arrival of the train at 5.15 a.m.; the distance being only 38 miles, but the last 18 of these (from Urajana to the river) is over the roughest of mountain tracks, reaching an altitude of 5000ft above sea level, and where it is impossible to make anything but the slowest headway, though for that stage of the journey fresh horses were engaged. It was 9 p.m. when we arrived at the homestead of the Franklins, to whose hospitality we were indebted for that night's accommodation; for as it was raining hard and we had left all our own comforts far behind, we had no hope that these could overtake us that night.

Apparently the cart with all their camping gear had overturned at the foot of Brindabella Mountain, in the heavy rain and pitch darkness. However, over four days the party caught 141 trout, of which 46 were returned, and another '49 big fish were lost after being hooked and played for a shorter or longer time'.

Law enforcement, even just before World War II, was practically non-existent – even more so than it is today. Thus it was a great surprise to my brother Pack and me when we were asked to show our licences when fishing the upper reaches of the Bombala River one day in 1937. Luckily we both had ours with us, but Pack, being an honorary inspector then, and somewhat suspicious of the character who professed to be a Fisheries Inspector, asked to see his licence. He was carrying a rod and had a large bunch of worms impaled on a hook, as well as being accompanied by one of the greatest 'Ned Kelly' boys in the district. The poor fellow had to admit he didn't possess one, though we later established the fact that he was indeed a NSW Fisheries Inspector!

We had ridden about 10 miles to fish the river that day, and when we first arrived we felt our time wasted – the river was high and fairly dirty because of a heavy storm which had fallen further upstream the day before. We were about to leave when I saw a rise in midstream, cast a dry fly out and was immediately connected to a trout. From then on, for two hours, the water fairly boiled with rising trout and we caught 16 between us. That was an example of one of those 'days of a lifetime'; the reason for the intense activity was quite inexplicable.

From the point of view of the number of fish caught per angler, and the average weight of those retained, the quality of fishing must be considered to have been exceptionally good in the old days. However, I expect the definition of 'quality', as related to trout fishing, is something which has varying interpretations for different anglers. No doubt for beginners it really is important to catch fish, thereby retaining their interest and enthusiasm until they become more expert. For the 'pot hunters' or 'belly fishermen', quality fishing will be regarded as the ability to take their bag every time they go fishing.

For what I term the true trout fisherman, the challenge of fishing for educated fish, in difficult conditions, will constitute the hallmark of quality. That challenge will sometimes be presented to a trout fisherman early in his career, probably more so if he is a fly fisherman.

Mr David P. Borgeson, Michigan Department of Natural Resources, Lansing, Michigan, concluded a paper which he presented to a Wild Trout Management Symposium at Yellowstone National Park, US in September 1974, by saying that many anglers soon deliberately handicap themselves, if fishing is too easy, by self-imposed gear restrictions. He said:

> *To gain further perspective into the manner of angling quality I like to imagine how a man from Mars would record his observations on our fishing. His notes might read something like this:*
>
> *Earth, September 25, 1974: For many desirable fish species, in addition to commercial harvest and personal food gathering, earth men practise what they call quality angling. When fish abundance is high the quality anglers depress their own catch artificially, either by using relatively ineffective gear, which they call sporting tackle, or by setting severe limits on the number and size of fish to be taken. Apparently well-fed, he seems less interested in the catch than in honing and testing his angling ability against the most interesting and desirable of fishes. These fishes he calls trout.*

Although the relatively ineffective gear referred to above is self-imposed today, maybe the inferior tackle available in the old days, especially leader material, helped create a balance of equality as compared with today's 'pressure fishing'. Maybe, in view of that, there was little difference in the quality of fishing in the old days!

LEWIS RUSSELL

RUSSELL was a Scottish-born Melbourne journalist. Little is known of him as an author of fishing tales. This story, from *Let's Go Fishing* (Georgian House, 1950), was kindly sent to me by Rick Keam.

CHAPTER 16

A Day on the Delatite

Mount Buller looked down benignly over the valley, the Delatite River crooned happily and sparkled in the warm sunshine, an upstream breeze promised assistance for the use of a fly, and so I pieced together my rod at the pool above the Mansfield–Jamieson road and promised myself a good forenoon's sport. There was no need to hurry; it was just 9.30, and if I knew my Delatite, I didn't expect to see any feeding fish much before 10 o'clock.

I think often that those minutes before you actually start are the happiest of all: you are on the river again, there is a wide prospect to appeal as you lift up your eyes to the hills, recalling as you do so the words of the psalmist. Sometimes I even entertain the suspicion that my angling is just an excuse for me to get to the river, revelling in its ever-changing beauty, rejoicing in the life which goes on so unobtrusively and with such absorbed concentration of purpose in the waters and in the banks.

With the rod assembled and the line in its place, there is the business of selecting a fly likely to appeal to the trout. There is nothing on the water to serve as a guide, I pick a coch-y-bondhu with a suggestion of a palmered hackle – an addition made on the advice of a friend, Mr G.S. Catlow, SM, an ardent and skilful angler. The 'cocky' is a very good representation of the tiny wattle beetle, and when it is about, especially if there is a wind, the trout take it greedily.

But on this occasion it is not on the menu, for I fish up to the throat of the pool without even the semblance of a rise. Changing to a wet Red Tag I start again from the centre of the pool, trying to work my fly under the water to as near a sunken log as I can go with safety – a spot which usually yields a fish or at least an offer.

Apparently nobody is at home, but when I cast into the throat and bring my fly round to the top of the log there is a flash of golden brown, and as the fish dives I tense my wrist – tense, not strike – and the reel sings as the trout comes up from his dive and dashes upstream.

The flash of colour had told me he was a brown, and his tactics as he fought against the strain confirmed the idea. A rainbow would by this time have been all over the pool and up in the air several times; but true to his breed this fellow bored down to the bottom and across, obviously trying to get beneath the log – a log which had often in the past given a fish sanctuary and me a broken cast. With as much strain as the fine cast permitted, he was induced to come away, foot by foot, and then for the first time he showed himself, a beautifully proportioned fish, as I judged, of over 1lb. He dived desperately as he sighted the waiting net, and I let him run a good 30ft before again applying pressure. Really that dash against the heavy stream, plus the pressure of the line, had finished him, and as I reeled in he came quietly, if stubbornly, to the net: 1lb 4oz, said the scales, and there was quiet satisfaction in my heart as I proceeded to fish the next stretch, a fine stream, shallow on the left but deepening to 4ft on the other side below a high bank. It yielded nothing except interest. Two good fish followed the fly with curiosity but made no effort to take it; a third lunged wildly and hit the fly in passing; a fourth took it, jumped as he felt the hook, shook his head and was free – and that was all.

The pool above is one which always repays concentration. From flowing to the west, the stream at the throat is divided by a tiny island and then runs north. The pool is deep, with a sandy bottom, and is the home of grand trout who, as all trout do, take on the colour of their surroundings, in this case a light gold.

My fly disappeared into the rough water, and as it was swept round by the current it was seized by a rainbow, who stormed up in fine frenzy and leaped high into the air. A fish of 2lb or so, he was quite uncontrollable, and after some mad rushes, dives and leaps he managed to dislodge the fly.

And this incident illustrates clearly the chance – or mischance, if you prefer it – of wet fly-fishing. He took the fly unseen, and probably as he dived with it, hooking himself in the process, he realised he had been deceived, with the result that the fly had but an insecure hold.

Had I seen him as he dived and tightened my wrist, it is more than probable that the hook would just have grazed his lips. A small hook, a fine cast and rapid water is a combination that loads the dice heavily in favour of such a bundle of energy as a 2-pound rainbow. That the trout discovered his mistake in time was just my bad luck – or his good fortune. In any case, I had had my sport, so there was no call for lamentation.

After such a display of aquatic acrobatics, it was idle to devote further time to the pool, and so I walked on, passing a long, flat, featureless pool with water no more than 18 in deep. There are plenty of trout in it, but they are unapproachable. Many a time I have promised myself a visit when the evening shadows lengthen and the big fellows come out from their day hide-outs and cast off lethargy and roam about seeking what they may devour, but somehow or other I have never got round to it – probably because the pools below have been giving me all the sport I could manage.

This day, however, I learned that a big trout is as partial to duckling as I am myself. Walking through the reeds, a dozen little balls of fluff erupted from cover and plunged into the stream, flapping and paddling madly for the security offered by the opposite bank while the parent duck made wild spirals overhead. Halfway across there was a sudden flurry, the big nose of a brown trout of between 3 and 4lb shot up, a duckling was engulfed and the fish dived with a flick of a broad tail. That was a trout of quite an astonishing size to be lying in the open on such a day of sun. I once caught a trout with a partially digested blue tit in his stomach, but this was the first evidence I had that a big trout is partial to duckling.

A quarter of a mile further on there is a long, grand pool, the water increasing in depth to as much as 5ft, while the bottom in places has shelves of rock running across the stream, between which the trout love to lie. Never yet have I fished this pool without taking at least two fish from it, and this day was to be no exception.

My first client supped with fortune; I slipped on a boulder as I stepped forward with my net, and the metal ring struck his nose and knocked him off the hook.

Number two was a 10 in brown which had to be returned, but the third was a rainbow of 1½lb who fought with reckless abandon for a couple of minutes before, as is the way of a rainbow, caving in meekly.

Then another brown obligingly hooked himself, well downstream, and from the way he pulled I thought I had established contact with at least a 6-pounder. But the heavy water, plus the length of line I had out, had deceived me, as it has so often done before and will again, I hope, for when I had managed to get him out of the current into the slack water I saw he was not the third of that. Still, he went to 1lb 9oz – good enough for anybody's breakfast.

After that I felt I deserved the reward of a cigarette, and was enjoying it when a rider on a horse remarkably like that idol of race-goers 25 years ago, Heroic, splashed through the shallows and gave me good day. I commented on the resemblance, to be told that the horse was indeed a descendant of that brilliant, if wilful, thoroughbred, and then we had much good conversation, as Pepys would have recorded had he been there, in the course of which I learned something about sheep and shorthorns and their ways, of the pests and troubles which have to be faced, and the rewards which follow good seasons.

We parted with a word of advice: 'Try the pool up there below those trees; there is a 5-pounder there who has broken everybody who has had him on.' I did try; but all I got was a couple of browns just on the legal minimum, which I returned for, I trust, another day. Subsequently I learned I had been talking to the owner of the Delatite Station, Bob Ritchie, a gentleman known favourably for his quiet, unobtrusive and unheralded generosity, particularly to former members of the Forces.

Noon! I had had good fun; I had three nice trout in my bag; there was time to walk back to the car and get to Jamieson for lunch, that quiet hamlet which drowses happily in Nirvanic calm in its lovely valley dreaming of the gold days that have gone.

DAVID
CHURCHES

DAVID JAMES Churches was born in 1942 in Adelaide, South Australia, and until he was 4 years of age, lived on a property at Coomandook (SA). For the next 4 to 5 years he lived in Adelaide, before moving to Keith (SA), where he lived with his parents (apart from 3 years at boarding school – Prince Alfred College) until joining the Royal Australian Navy in 1961. David was a keen angler from an early age.

It was in 1964, when the navy posted David to HMAS *Barman*, outside Canberra, that he became interested first in trout fishing, then in fly-fishing. He has remained a keen fly angler ever since.

David has been a member and office-holder of the Canberra Casting and Sportfishing Club, the Cooma Trout Acclimatisation Society, and the Australian Freshwater Fisherman's Assembly, and is a Life Member of the NSW Institute of Freshwater Fishermen.

He is now retired. He lives in Canberra during the warmer months, and travels extensively away from Canberra during the winter months.

He has had a number of articles and stories published over the years.

CHAPTER 17

The Hang-on-the-Wall Fish

You must remember, I had been in the MacKenzie country, South Island New Zealand, for a week. On the first day I landed a 5.5lb rainbow trout that nearly spooled me in three magnificent runs, a 4lb brown trout in the confines of a small, snag-infested pool that tested the #5 Loomis pack rod sorely and 7 or 8 lesser fish in the 2lb range. On other days I had landed and released fish up to 6lb. The 6-pounder took me in a mad chase down the Tekapo River through three pools, before choosing to fight it out in a deep pool just above a dead willow snag.

I had seen the 12lb fish in Norm's office in the caravan park and been told of a 13lb fish coming in the week before. There was an 18lb fish mounted in the pub, and a bigger fish up the road at Twizel. I had seen two or three 'hang-on-the-wall' fish in the local rivers, and local anglers were advising that more fish were starting their spawning run up the Ahuriri.

The Ahuriri is a powerful river. You wade across with care. You cannot strip line fast enough to keep up with a dry or nymph coming downstream. This day I was fishing the upper Ahuriri, well above

Birchwood Station. Local advice was, 'Not many fish, but all were trophy sized.'

The day was bright, with a soft sky. A gentle northwest wind blew down the valley, nothing I couldn't handle. Snow glistened on the surrounding mountains. Skeins of Canada geese were winging down the valley. Paradise ducks were calling on a gravel bar nearby and a hawk was patrolling the base of the mountain. I had been casting to a 'double digit' fish that totally ignored my offerings before drifting back under the bank. Walking slowly upstream, I peered over a clay bank into the head of the next pool.

There, just below the lip of the pool, out of the heavy current, a long, dark shape flickered and weaved in the flow. The Ahuriri is a fast flowing free-stone river free from weed. It had to be a trout. A VERY BIG TROUT.

What fly? I had on a #12 Hare's ear Wulff that had proved successful on other fish. Carefully I worked out a cast and dropped the fly about 2ft above the shadow. The fly bounced down the chute into the pool. The shape flickered to the left and back again. A second cast a bit further up. Again the shape weaved to one side.

Retrieving my fly, I watched as the shadow weaved back and forth. 'Feeding on nymphs,' I mused. 'OK, what's in my hat?' Off came the dry and on went a halfback nymph.

Two more casts with similar results. Obviously my nymph was not getting down in the heavy current. OK, what next? I opened my nymph box and without hesitation I chose a brand new Sloan's nymph. Sloan's nymph? The one Rob's dad describes in *The Truth About Trout Flies*. Possum-tail fur and a mixture of green and brown seal's fur. These had enough lead to put a .22 bullet to shame!

I snipped off the tippet section of my leader and tied on an arm's length of 7lb Umpqua tippet. On the end went the Sloan's nymph. Another check of the pool. The shadow is still there, flickering and weaving in the current under the heavy flow of water dumping into the pool.

Setting my hat down round my ears, I worked out enough line. The weighty nymph was strange to cast, and took a bit to get the timing right. When I felt I had it right, I set the cast above the fish, shooting some line, but checking it at the last minute to cause the nymph to bounce back a little and sink on slack line.

Down came the line, then a check of the leader! I struck – hard. The shadow shuddered, then rolled into the current and was away downstream. Clearing the loose line, I had it on the reel, and in no time at all it was into the next pool, with the backing knot rattling in the runners. Through that pool, down a deep, fast riffle – more backing – and by the time it had reached the next pool, it was 70–80 yards away.

Unstable free-stone streams are not designed for sprinting. The Ahuriri rocks are likened to greased cannonballs. Keeping on the pressure, I set off in pursuit. Slowly I gained line, but my catch also slowly edged towards the tail of the pool. Momentarily, I relaxed the pressure when a rock rolled under my foot, and it was away again. Through the chute into the next run and down into a large deep pool with a slow back eddy.

If it left that pool there was no way I could keep up with it. A flood gate lay across the next run and the river dropped into a narrow fast deep cleft for about 400 yards. Wishing I had chosen to use something heavier, I had the Sage #4 bent further than ever before. The 7lb tippet was strained to the limit. The line slowly entered the back eddy, still 40–50 yards away.

Recovering line as I carefully picked my way downstream, my spirits lifted as I felt the backing knot come back down the runners. Then more line. Finally, I could see the butt in the water and deep, deep down was the dark shadow, slowly edging towards the main current.

No way! Not again. On went the strain with a vengeance, this time with the left hand assisting with the lift. Slowly the shape came back against the current, lifting in the water. I was winning. When the leader knot was at the rod tip, I could clearly see my catch.

I was stunned! It had run me 150 yards downstream, the line strumming in the water. Grinning, I kept the pressure on, and with the rod horizontal to keep side strain on, I ran it into the shallows and onto the gravel bar. Booting it clear of the water, I bent down and twisted my fly free of the hardest-fighting, 3 feet brown 3 inch manilla rope I have ever caught!

CHAPTER 18

Monaro Trout

Monaro waters contain wild populations of both Brown trout (*Salmo trutta*) and Rainbow trout (*Oncorhynchus mykiss*). Atlantic Salmon (*S. salar*) have been stocked in both Burrinjuck Dam and Jindabyne Dam; however, they do not appear to have become a self-sustaining population to this date. Although I have caught them, they are not the same class of fish, nor in the same condition as those caught in their home waters. Brook trout (*Salvenius fontinalis*) have also been stocked extensively in headwaters of most Monaro rivers. These have not acclimatised either, although I hear stories of isolated pockets of large brookies in some of the more remote headwaters.

In 1861, a Mr Alexander Black travelled by boat to Merimbula, then on to Bibbenluke, from where he traversed the Snowy from Paupong to Buckley's Crossing (now Dalgety). He also inspected the MacLaughlin, Moonbah and Eucumbene rivers and reported 'these streams were not excelled in appearance by the most celebrated salmon rivers of Ireland and Scotland'. Mr Black made this trip as a result of attempts to introduce Salmon into Australia, which had been carried out since 1849.

Early efforts in Monaro acclimatisation began in 1883, when Mr W. Beaty brought Crucian carp from waters near Goulburn and liberated them in Bullembalong Lake. Two years later, Bullembalong Lake was nearly dry, and Mr W. Hepburn of Coolamatong, together with Messrs Reuben and Alfred Rose, A. Crisp and H. Merrett, netted the lake. The captured fish were liberated again, some in the Snowy at Jindabyne, some in the Moonbah and others in the Snowy at Coolamatong crossing. Mr Amos Crisp put a few in a pond at 'Jimenbeuan', where they increased, and many hundreds were put in various lakes in the district.

Tasmania was the first of the colonies to successfully introduce trout. This first shipment arrived from England packed in moss-lined wooden boxes and surrounded by 30 tons of Lake Welham ice, in an ice house constructed deep in the hold of the steamer *Norfolk*. In 1864 the first ova were placed in specially constructed hatching troughs alongside the Plenty River, near Hobart. All the Brown trout in Australia and New Zealand have descended from this and one other subsequent shipment. Once the Plenty River hatchery was operating, Brown trout ova were supplied to hatcheries in Geelong and Ballarat in Victoria, and other hatcheries in Australia and New Zealand.

Messrs Campbell and Gale of Queanbeyan liberated the first trout in New South Wales in 1887. They purchased 300 Brown trout fingerlings from Ballarat, together with some Redfin perch fingerlings. These fish were placed into milk churns, two-thirds filled with water and 25 fingerlings to a churn so they would not suffocate, and transported by rail to Queanbeyan. There they were loaded onto pack-horses for the final leg of their journey. One can imagine the two men on horseback followed by pack-horses, the sound of creaking leather and the chink of milk churns breaking the silence of the dry Australian bush as they travelled from Queanbeyan to release the trout in the Cotter, Molonglo, Queanbeyan, Yass and Naas rivers. A small consignment was sent to Mr H.T. Edwards and liberated in the Bombala River at Bibbenluke. In the same year the Fisheries Commission of New South Wales also released 2,000 fingerlings in the Shoalhaven and its tributaries.

The first semi-official attempt at acclimatisation was when Mr Lindsay Thompson, Chief of NSW Fisheries, endeavoured to have a trout hatchery constructed on a site he selected at Berrima. When this did not eventuate, he constructed a makeshift hatchery in a disused kitchen at the rear of the Commission's Phillip Street headquarters.

During 1889, George Glading went to Ballarat, Victoria, and returned with 6,000 Brown trout ova, which were laid down in wooden troughs in the makeshift hatchery. Local water, filtered through charcoal to remove impurities and cooled by an ice screw to a temperature ranging between 55 and 62°F, was used. Seventy per cent of those eggs hatched and the fingerlings were released in a large number of streams throughout New South Wales. A magnificent effort under such rudimentary conditions.

In 1890 a consignment of 5,000 trout ova was received from New Zealand. Among this consignment were some Brook trout ova that were also hatched out in the Phillip Street offices; however, there is no record of the Brook trout being caught.

The first official release in the Snowy Mountains was by Mr Reuben Rose of 'Boloco', near Dalgety. In 1889, he obtained a consignment of thirty fingerlings from NSW Fisheries, which he placed in the Snowy River. The dry impersonal reporting style of the time does not record the means of transporting the fingerlings or the difficulties that were overcome.

A grazier, naturalist and Latin scholar, Mr Rose can rightly be regarded as 'the father of acclimatisation' on the Monaro; and Mr Amos Crisp of 'Jimenbeuan' was closely associated with him. One notable exploit of these two gentlemen occurred in 1889, with the introduction of Blackfish (*Gadopsis mamosa*) into the Snowy near Dalgety. Seven lightly hooked Blackfish were caught in the lower Delegate River. These were transported in billy-cans held in forked sticks resting on pommels of their saddles over rough country to a place on the Snowy 80 miles above the falls.

A further consignment of 50,000 trout eggs were received by the Fisheries Commission from New Zealand in 1894, among which were 3,000 Rainbow trout ova. New Zealand hatcheries had stripped ova from fish trapped in the Russian River in California, for acclimatisation in their lakes and streams. These were the first Rainbow trout in New South Wales and probably the first in Australia. They were hatched in the blacksmith's shop of an old stable at Prospect, where the officer in charge had to sleep in oilskins as the roof leaked so badly.

On 16 December 1894, Mr Amos Crisp netted Curlewis Lake, in which he had liberated Brown trout fry on 11 October 1891. Among the catch was a Brown trout, 25 inches in length, 15 inches in girth, that weighed 7 pounds. Mr Crisp took the fish to Mr Rose at 'Boloco', who forwarded it to Mr Farnell, President of the Royal Commission of Fisheries. Mr Farnell sent it to the Australian Museum where it was mounted. This received considerable publicity in the press of the day. (This skin and the letter from Mr Amos Crisp are still available at the Australian Museum in Sydney.)

On 18 October 1895, members of the Royal Commission on Fisheries arrived at Buckley's Crossing on the Snowy (now Dalgety) on a visit to the District to take evidence. The party was met by Messrs Reuben Rose, W. Morrice, the Crisp Bros, H. Merrett, F. Litchfield, H. Rose and J. Rutherford. Mr Miller, Member for the District, introduced the visitors. After Mr F. Farnell MLA and President of the Commission thanked Mr Rose for his hearty welcome, the Commissioner proceeded to take evidence. Reuben Rose, Henry Dawson and Henry Merrett were examined, and at the conclusion of the examination Mr Rose read the Commission his now historic report, 'The Progress of Pisciculture in the District'.

In 1896 a new hatchery was completed at Prospect. This hatchery was constructed of weather-boards with a corrugated iron roof on brick foundations. The dimensions were 40 feet x 20 feet, and it had a design capacity for 100,000 ova. Three rearing ponds of brick and cement were also constructed. One was 40 feet long by 12 feet wide and 5 feet deep; the other two were 30 feet x 10 feet by 5 feet deep. The hatchery commenced operations with 60,000 Brown trout ova and 50,000 Rainbow and Loch Leven ova from New Zealand. A return showing the number of trout (86,826) liberated and the waters stocked during the years 1889 to 1898 by NSW State Fisheries was tabled in the Legislative Assembly and subsequently published in the *Sydney Morning Herald* of 17 July 1899. The Prospect hatchery continued to supply trout to the state, and a new larger hatchery was later built there, complete with brood ponds.

The Monaro District Acclimatisation Society was formed on 5 July 1937 with Mr Alf Rose, a son of Mr Reuben Rose, as its first President, and Mr Jack Arthur was the first Secretary. Mr Alf Rose unfortunately had to resign for health reasons during the first year, and Mr H.H. Solomon, Vice-Chairman, deputised for the remainder of the year. At the Annual Meeting in 1938, Mr Jim Gaden, grazier of 'Woburn', Bungarby, was elected President as Mr H. Solomon had declined nomination in favour of a younger man. Mr Gaden served as President of the Society from 1938 to 1952.

Acclimatisation Societies were recognised by New South Wales

Parliament in 1938, and under the Fisheries and Oyster Farms Act were empowered to manage the stocking of streams in their own particular district and establish and operate their own hatcheries. A number of small hatcheries were operated on the Monaro over the years, but these were finally consolidated in the Caldwell Hatchery. Except for a paid hatchery Superintendent, all work was carried out in an honorary and voluntary capacity.

The Caldwell Hatchery was officially opened on 12 August 1939 by Mrs Alexander Caldwell in the presence of the Hon. G.C. Gollen, Chief Secretary, Mr W.W. Hedges MLA, Mr S.L. Anderson, Under Secretary, Officers of NSW Fisheries, members of Rod Fishers Society of NSW, Members of Monaro Acclimatisation Society, and local trout fishermen. Mrs Alexander Caldwell of 'Brooklyn', near Ando, donated ten acres of land on Bungee Peak Creek for the hatchery and in appreciation of her generous gift, the hatchery was appropriately named 'The Caldwell Hatchery' at the opening ceremony.

The Society's Annual Report for 1940 records the first year's operation at the hatchery:

> *The trapping of wild fish from district streams over a period of five months by Inspectors McBride and Foster did not result in a large number of brood fish being obtained. These brood fish were held in netting enclosures erected in the Bungee Peak Creek at the hatchery site. One female Brown trout taken from the MacLaughlin River weighing 8 pounds stripped 7446 ova. From ova collected in this manner, 29,000 fry were liberated. As well as the local fry, 82,000 Rainbow fry from NZ ova and 61,000 Brown trout fry from NZ ova were also liberated.*
>
> *Additionally, a further 50,000 fry from Tasmanian ova were hatched in hatching boxes maintained by Society members. One member, Mr Lionel Freebody, obtained over a 90% hatch.*

The NSW Government arranged for Mr A. Kean, Curator of Fish and Game, Department of Internal Affairs, New Zealand, to visit the state in an advisory capacity in 1940. Accompanied by Mr Maurice Brown, President of the NSW Rod Fishers Society, he travelled some 3000 miles and saw practically all our main streams and fishing localities. His remarks and observations were full of interest to both the conservation authorities and trout anglers in general. Two recommendations worthy of note and consideration were: centralise the hatcheries – a large, well-equipped hatchery is preferable to a number of smaller ones; and introduce food organisms into lakes (specifically referring to Burrinjuck and Wyangala).

Concerning the policing of streams, he said that no stream will stand illegal fishing for an indefinite period. He pointed out that in New Zealand they have rangers on duty continuously for 24 hours throughout the year and in spite of this they cannot keep up with the prosecutions. 'Therefore,' said Mr Kean, 'what must it be like in your country where there is no supervision.'

With the exception of 2 years (1942–43), the Caldwell hatchery was operated successfully by the Society until 1951. By that time it was realised that to meet the large increase in trout fishermen, the hatchery and equipment would have to be expanded. This was not only the opinion of the Monaro Acclimatisation Society, but also of the Central and New England Societies as well. Representations along these lines were made to the appropriate Minister by the three Societies and the Government made a grant of money available to achieve this objective. As plans and specifications proceeded for the provision of fingerling and brood ponds at the Caldwell hatchery, the water supply from Bungee Peak creek was measured and was below the amount required for a modern trout unit. It was realised, with much regret, that the Caldwell hatchery site would have to be abandoned as a sufficient head of water was not available to operate the equipment.

A number of sites were investigated, including Mawson's Mill, and 'The Peak' on the Murrumbidgee near Wambrook and Bridle Creeks. Finally a site at Paddy's Corner on the Thredbo River, 4 miles from Jindabyne, was selected. This site was on a property 'Forrest View', then owned by Mr W. Napthali, who had no objection to 12 acres being resumed for the hatchery. It was unanimously decided to call this the Gaden hatchery, in appreciation for the long and dedicated work carried out by Mr Jim Gaden as President of the Monaro Acclimatisation Society. In 1948, Mr Reuben Payten, who had worked the Caldwell hatchery part-time, was appointed hatchery supervisor, and along with his duties in continuing the operations of the Caldwell hatchery, he supervised the construction of the new hatchery on the Thredbo River.

The last year of operation of the Caldwell hatchery was 1950. The Society had secured 340,000 Rainbow trout ova from New Zealand, of which 240,000 were set down in the Caldwell hatchery. Mr Payten, while supervising the construction work at the new hatchery, operated the Caldwell hatchery as well by working alternate days on each project.

On 18 October 1950, while working at the Caldwell hatchery, Mr

Payten noticed that the barometer was rapidly falling to an extremely low reading. At the time, lots 1 and 2 had hatched, but lot 3, the last consignment of 90,000 ova, had not begun to hatch. Instead of returning to Jindabyne that night, Mr Payten went to 'Woburn' and discussed the matter with Mr Gaden, President of the Monaro Acclimatisation Society, and remained the night. That night a storm swept over the Monaro causing widespread flooding. The following day, Mr Payten prepared to set out for the Caldwell hatchery at daybreak, but was prevailed upon to call Mr Allen Caldwell at 'Brooklyn' first. Allen advised him that the MacLaughlin was '4 feet over the bridge' and it would not be possible to reach the hatchery. Allen Caldwell then telephoned his brother, who, on reaching the hatchery reported that the flow of water had stopped, the pipe being blocked by debris and many feet under water. Mr Payten was able to reach the hatchery the following day and a brief inspection showed that all the fry in lots 1 and 2 were dead, smothered by mud. On washing the mud from a tray of eggs from lot 3, most were still alive. Mr Payten then made several unsuccessful attempts to see if the water supply could be restored. Returning to the hatchery, he carried buckets of water from the creek and washed the mud from all the remaining eggs. By carrying water from the creek in trout cans he managed to keep the eggs alive until water was restored on the 4th day, and 60,000 fry were liberated that year.

On 31 October 1953, the Gaden hatchery was officially opened by Hon. J.F. McGrath, acting Chief Secretary. At the official opening, the acting Chief Secretary paid tribute to the unselfish pioneer work of local residents, led by Mr Jim Gaden, in the development of trout fishing in the Monaro, and in the establishment of the fine Gaden hatchery. The Minister also paid sincere tribute to the Society's Supervisor, Mr Reuben F. Payten, who, due to an unfortunate illness, was in hospital.

From these early beginnings and dedicated men, the Monaro trout grew and prospered.

During my research, I found the following letter:

To Whom it May Concern
Sir,
Allow me a small space in your paper to say a few words in regard to fish and fishing. Now that the fishing season will soon be open (I mean to the dinkum sportsmen who wait for it to open) let us hope they will do their

best to help keep our streams stocked. Some, no doubt, will say, 'How?'
The answer is this: Don't fish to see how many you can get. Is it not
better to get enough for a meal, or might we say two meals, than get
enough for half a dozen meals? Fish are not good keepers in hot weather,
thus many are thrown out and wasted. Next, the fish that are kept
undersize. Many persons may say, 'I have hurt that fish with the hook',
etc. You have not hurt that fish with the hook as much as you do by
dumping him on to a dry bank and picking him up with dry hands. If
fish are undersize, never take them on to the dry bank to release them, but
bring them to a shallow edge, and always wet your hands before handling
them. Any damage to the scales will cause a fungus to cling to the fish.
This fungus is picked up out of the water, and if the fish are not in good
condition, often die.

Robert L Ingram

This letter appeared in the *Bombala Times*, 9 September 1938. It is still
relevant today.

CHRIS
HOLE

CHRIS HOLE had three careers. His first was in the Royal Australian Navy, from 1952 to 1984. His second began when he retired and became a farmer in the Brindabella Valley (near Canberra), with a mile and a half of the Goodradigbee River running beside his land. The drought in the early 1990s came at a time when he was considering his third career. He was to become a writer and illustrator of articles and books about fly-fishing for any species of fish that would take his flies.

He sold his property to travel the world with his rods, watercolours and camera, resulting in three beautifully illustrated books about his travels.

His fish stories are unforgettable, particularly his ironic handling of the fish that got away. Chris's paintings and drawings are now included in collections throughout the world.

Sadly, Chris Hole passed away in 1999, only weeks before the World Fly-fishing Championships were staged in the Snowy Mountains – he, with others, had put enormous effort into this. His wife Gini was proud to represent him at the celebrity fishing day in his honour.

My thanks to Gini Hole, who graciously granted permission to use the following chapters from *Heaven on a Stick* and *Fly-fishing Across Russia, East Europe & Finland*.

CHAPTER 19

Iceland

Included in the niceties of New Cottage at Cliveden was a miniature landing stage in front of the house, complete with two-man fibreglass dinghy. The boat was padlocked to its landing for security, and the keys to the padlock, and the shed where the oars were kept, were hung on labelled pegs in a cupboard inside the cottage. My family and I occasionally paddled about the Thames in front of the cottage in the evenings, taking photographs of the ducks, casting the odd fly at rises and drinking gin and tonic. A pleasant interlude.

But the dinghy had a much more important task to perform, or so I thought.

I had ascertained that to land private fishing tackle in Iceland, it was first necessary to have all the bits and pieces which could possibly be contaminated in other countries – waders, rods, reels, boots, lines, knives and the like – fully disinfected, and a certificate to that effect signed by a veterinary officer within seven days prior to departure for Iceland. A most sensible safeguard that can only be applauded. Further investigation revealed that decontamination could be achieved by immersing the tackle in a 2 per cent formaldehyde solution for 10 minutes.

Therefore, while at New Cottage I rang the local vet concerning this matter. He immediately suggested that he should bring the formaldehyde to the cottage to carry out the operation because, he said, the clinic was far too small. On the face of it, an apparently simple solution involving only the bathroom at the cottage. But, on further consideration, I pondered: (a) that the vet wanted a peek at Cliveden and possibly the arena of Christine Keeler's affairs? Unlikely, because he could do that at any time without having to clean fishing tackle in formaldehyde. (b) he wanted a cup of tea or a gin and tonic after his task? The tea he could get at the clinic, and it was highly unlikely that a vet would drink gin and tonic at noon. Or (c) formaldehyde was extremely toxic and had such a revolting smell that he would rather remove it from his clinic? Almost a dead certainty.

So I pulled the dinghy up from the landing stage onto the front lawn, provided a bucket to carry and mix the water, put my waders, reels, boots, knives and other tackle on board, and stood by to receive the vet.

It should have worked like well-oiled clockwork. But when the vet arrived and we reviewed the situation, we concluded that it would take us ages to fill the dinghy with fresh water; moreover, we had no immediate source of rinsing water after decontamination, and no easy access to sewerage disposal for the 'leftovers' – we certainly were not going to put them on the garden or into the Thames. So, up to the bathroom we went, and completed the task reasonably efficiently with little residue odour and – very probably – a resultant super-clean sewerage system. Gini spent that night in London with friends.

During my planning of the Icelandic episode, it soon became apparent that I was to visit a salmonid fishery at the very top of world class in terms of fishing, management, water purity, scenery, exclusiveness and many other factors, including, unfortunately, price. For these very reasons I included Iceland in my travels, limiting the actual fishing days because of the cost. Reykjavik also provided a logical geographic stepping-stone to the Northwest Territories of Canada and to Baffin Island. I was excited about the visit; what's more, Gini was coming with me and we were both eagerly looking forward to it.

To avoid excess luggage charges on this, the first in a series of out-of-the-way flights in small aeroplanes crossing 65°N latitude, I reduced my kit as much as possible. Spare fishing tackle (we always carry too much), maps, outdated papers and files, unwanted clothing and an increasing pile of newspaper and magazine articles were boxed up and sent home by sea mail.

With considerable regret we left New Cottage after breakfast on 10 July, drove to Heathrow, returned the rental car which had served us so well and boarded the Icelandic flight to Reykjavik. An entirely new experience awaited us 70 miles south of the Arctic Circle. The trip to Keflavik Airport and on to Reykjavik was not entirely uneventful. I had mistakenly put my two fishing knives in my hand luggage and these were seized at the departure immigration point with polite efficiency and a promise of delivery (with all other personal luggage) on arrival in Iceland. I would never have had the courage to hijack an international airliner, least of all with an Everlast filleting knife, but sadly it was the last I ever saw of my fishing knives!

Then, at Keflavik Airport, having completed a number of forms in triplicate about the missing knives, as we passed through arrival procedures, I joined a substantial queue of ruddy-faced individuals holding rods and other fishing tackle – in itself, encouraging. Happy in the knowledge that I already held a vet's clearance, and in the belief that my processing would therefore be a formality, I was dismayed to find I had to pay the same fee (per rod) as those who had not had their tackle precleaned, and who were quite happy to wait 10 minutes while the Icelandic officials did it for them, without having to pay the vet's additional fee in the first place. To add insult to injury, the local decontaminant was an iodine solution and not smelly old formaldehyde. We live and learn, but I'm sure I could have been better advised about the regulations.

The day did not improve; we picked up another rental car and somehow became lost in Reykjavik looking for the hotel – the map proved to be outdated. We eventually found the place, settled in comfortably, and went downtown for one of the best seafood dinners I have ever eaten, the price – being roughly four times that to which I had become accustomed (even by then) – matching the quality.

After another daylit night like Norway, we left Reykjavik the next morning driving generally north towards Borgarnes, meandering along the banks of the fiords as we went. It was our first proper look at Iceland: I don't take in a great deal when my knives go missing – I get lost, and I pay too much for a wonderfully satisfied stomach. More relaxed that morning, we found a majestically stark country, a little like New Zealand but more darkly dramatic, whose pronounced volcanic origins provide the dominant colour which, in summer, is tempered by the greens of grasslands mantled by snow-capped blue–greys. Other than a further colour contrast etched by white concrete and iron dwellings with brightly coloured roofs, there was little else on the immediate canvas. There were no trees, and the resulting moonscape was somehow both beautiful and sinister. Nordurá Lodge, where we were to stay, was 30 minutes' drive from Borgarnes, on the banks of the Nordurá River, right in the middle of some of the most imposing of this Icelandic scenery. We arrived there in time for lunch and were greeted by Jon Borgthorsson, the executive director of the Angling Club of Reykjavik, with whom I had been planning our visit during the previous 18 months.

Set on top of high basalt cliffs looking down to the beautiful Nordurá, this oiled timber and weatherboard lodge of the Angling Club of Reykjavik is one of the best remote fishing lodges I have ever encountered. The club, which was established in the 1930s, and which has negotiated leases for fishing on the Nordurá and leaseback arrangements for the lodges they have constructed and extended over the years, is particularly well administered and runs the pick of the fishing in a country which could well be called the pick of fishing countries in the world. The lodge contains 13 double bedrooms with all facilities, and four more which share a bathroom. Thus a total of 34 guests can be accommodated, which is more than double the 12-rod allocation on three major beats covering over 25 kilometres on both banks of the Nordurá. Thus, when the house is roughly half full or more, actual fishermen come to share rods or bring non-fishing partners for whom walking or riding through the splendid scenery is a joy in itself.

As well as very adequate staff quarters, the lodge provides a large sitting room overlooking the river, a sauna, rod and drying rooms, a cleaning room for fish, and a large cold room. The dining room can support the maximum guest capacity at one long table which is probably the start point of the fishing day when breakfast is served at 6 a.m. The first fishing session is from 7 a.m. to 1 p.m., lunch is served around the long table from 2 to 3 p.m., the second session, when beats are changed, runs from 4 to 10 p.m. and dinner starts at 11 p.m. or later. The beats change again next morning and after each six-hour session; so, after three sessions, if the angler takes a second full day and a half (and most take a total of three days' fishing), he has seen some of each beat before he repeats himself. This makes it ideal for the newcomer (on a three-day visit), who can take a guide for the first three sessions before going solo for another three, covering the beats he has already fished and been advised about. Conversely, those familiar with the area have two goes at each beat in a three-day session, seeking out their favourite spots.

As we arrived on a Saturday, and I was not due to start fishing until 4 p.m. the next day, I had a full 24 hours to examine the area quite thoroughly, talk to other fishermen, take photographs and get settled. I wish I could make myself do this at every new place; it obviously pays big dividends, but it is very hard when only self-discipline (and not regulation) is there to enforce it, and the river is full of jumping fish.

When, at last, I came to fish the Nordurá, starting that Sunday afternoon at 4 o'clock, in warm, clear weather, I was unaware at the time that I had before me three days of something very close to Paradise.

Before describing those days, however, I shall endeavour to sketch briefly some of the background to Icelandic sport fishing for salmon, because it is so closely linked to the success of the industry as I saw it.

Until 1991, commercial harvesting of salmon was a moderately large and important business. In particular it involved mainly landowning farmers who either netted salmon in the main estuaries (primarily early in the season, when the bigger fish run to spawn and when the price of salmon is highest), or sold the rights to do so. In the case of the Nordurá, netting in the fiord area near Borgarnes effectively choked the early salmon spawning run of big fish, not only for that river, but for three other important rivers running the same fiord.

In Iceland there are several angling clubs, largest and most important being the Angling of Reykjavik (SVFR) with 2,200 members. There is also an Association of Angling Clubs, loosely aimed at consensus in the preservation of the salmon, and a further Association of Angling Rights Owners. In addition, there are several articles of legislation governing fishing policy. In 1991, initially for a year's trial period, the clubs and associations negotiated a deal with the netting rights owners to buy out those rights in order to stop netting to preserve and then enhance sport fishing (which, in any case, was producing a price per kilo for salmon which far outweighed that which could be achieved commercially). Subsequently, similar buy-outs were negotiated for 1992, 1993 and 1994. The value of purchase was negotiated around the average commercial price per kilo of wholesale salmon, allowance for indexation over the years, and the cost spread throughout the users in proportion to their expected usage. It was a brilliant scheme, resulting in great preservation of and an increase in the sport (and therefore revenue), while the old commercial netters – the farmers and landowners – gained a no-risk source of income, without effort or maintenance, while pursuing their other prime farming interests. A small commercial salmon industry remains and is maintained by limited specialised fish farming sufficient to fulfil the commercial need.

There being no such thing as a free lunch, however, the cost of the buy-out eventually had to be passed down to the user, the sport fisherman, who was already paying for his share of land and rights (his purchase of 'a rod' on a beat) and for his accommodation and meals, and for a small (lodge or owner) profit margin. The biggest factor, undoubtedly, is the cost of leasing land and rights. The associations and clubs negotiate leases from landowners, normally at the close of each season, in September. Leases are often negotiated for several years in addition to the next season. Costs are then passed on to the fisherman for his rod, and subsequently, accurate records of catches in specific areas are kept, which form the basis for the next lease negotiation, the more productive areas bringing the higher lease prices.

Additionally, salmon fishing in Iceland is regulated by legislation and by club and association rules. The season lasts from 20 May to 20 September, but only three months may be used in this period (normally 1 June to 31 August) and by law, fishing may only be undertaken between the hours of 7 a.m. and 10 p.m. and then only for a maximum of 12 hours during that period. Moreover, the clubs and associations work out and allocate the maximum number of rods that are allowed to operate on any stretch of the various rivers.

Clubs and owners, armed with all this information and accounting, lease their holdings, make their estimates and add the costs of netting buy-back, food, accommodation and profit margin, then sell rods to club members and outsiders in order to meet costs and leave a small profit margin.

The entire organisation is tight, super-efficient, totally pure and extremely environmentally friendly, but very expensive. Moreover, it is run entirely privately and is greatly admired by locals and overseas visitors alike. But that represents the very top end of sport fishing in Iceland.

At the other end of the scale, the average local or visiting angler may indulge in excellent fishing (particularly for trout) using farm holiday accommodation or camping areas, all at very reasonable prices, while having the advantage of those all important (and partly paid for) factors of purity, good management, conservation and wonderful scenery, and with no problems of pollution or overcrowding. In essence, I believe Iceland provides arguably the best fly-fishing in the world; it is only a pity that, for most, it is so remote – a factor which undoubtedly adds to its attractiveness.

Ingo was my guide for the first three of my six sessions of six hours each. For the first session we were given the furthest downstream beat together with one rod, shared by two fascinating Germans from Munich, and two rods fished by Frenchmen, part of a large and regular group who spent a great deal of their time and effort ensuring they had the best spots. Positions on each beat were meant to be exchanged at the three-hour mark but, over the ensuing days, this system became somewhat subsumed by Gallic confusion, resulting in the sub-allocation of river banks on given beats for the entire six hours, changing banks on the next occasion of fishing the same beat. This didn't worry me much. I thought all of the water was magnificent, but it would have been unfair to the angler who had only one 18-hour visit on three beats, when he would fish only one bank of each and not both.

Ingo and I crossed the river by flying fox and I started casting my big Hardy in what he described as the most difficult part of the Nordurá. Big, slippery rocks, fast-flowing water of unbelievable clarity and jumping salmon were my memories of that first session, when I caught no fish but twice went 'swimming' involuntarily in the icy waters. The beats were all different. The downstream one ran through a steep-sided volcanic canyon culminating, downstream, in a horseshoe bend with white water over most of its length save one or two mirrored pools. The next, upstream, cleared the canyon at a deep, sharp, white-water bend to broaden and slow in front of the lodge; the immediate rock faces remained quite steep and colourful but more vegetation was evident, and stark volcanic strata cliffs rose in the background to the east. That central beat stopped, upstream, at Laxfoss (the Salmon Falls), probably the most famous falls in the area and a scene (shared from our bedroom window) of breathtaking beauty. For me it was also the most productive beat. The final beat, upstream again, ran from Laxfoss to the next falls, Glannifoss, and above, through continuing steep country at first, then flattening into a wide valley where the river became more like a gravel-bottom trout stream, meandering slowly north to disappear finally into the mountains again. All of it simply wonderful fly-fishing country.

Ingo was a good guide, an excellent fisherman and a very pleasant companion on the river, even if he tended to cover the ground over the rocks on the first occasion like an express mountain goat – a little too fast for me. His (most successful) advice was to use a very small tube fly (about half an inch long) and a size 14 treble hook.

After only a few hours' sleep, bleary-eyed fishermen were awakened the next morning at six to be greeted by a really super day. The warmth was already apparent at that early hour (even taking account of the lack of night); there was not a breath of wind nor a cloud in the washed blue sky which hung, as though drying, from the surrounding mountain peaks. I had the uppermost beat that morning and Ingo took me way up the valley to the 'trout water', where I fished non-stop in that hot light, seeing not another soul all morning. My guide was a little worried about things being too bright and clear, but I made it evident that this was 'trout stuff' to me and said: 'Let's go fine and small.' He wouldn't agree to go lower than 10-pound Maxima (although I would have preferred 7), but the size 14 Blue Charm tube fly looked perfect. The first run was a glassy glide over pebbles, with a bank on the left facing downstream, and with me on a gently sloping gravel bank on the right. Centrally there was a rocky outcrop around which the water swirled and over which it glided into a deep green run, continuing some 200 paces downstream.

I started above the outcrop, casting across, letting the fly swing down as I slowly retrieved with a short, slow stripping motion, remembering to keep a low profile. After the fourth or fifth cast, when I was wondering if I shouldn't be fishing upstream with a dry fly, a beautiful silver shape jumped clear and splashed back into the water only yards from me. Instantly I became a believer! And two casts later, was connected to an extraordinary weight which just kept shaking the line: jolt … jolt … jolt! About 10 minutes later, after a very satisfying battle, I landed my very first wild Atlantic salmon of six and a half pounds. I hasten to add that, because of the old netting policy, the majority of fish in the Nordurá were then grilse, but the number of older and bigger fish returning to the river was expected to increase.

After fishing the length of that pool I tried one other, without success. On returning to the starting point on the first pool, however, I hooked a second, smaller fish on the third cast as the fly was drawn over the rocky outcrop into the deep swirl. At 8.30 a.m. I was all fired up, super-confident and ready to fish until I dropped in the total certainty that it was going to be a great day.

We left that pool and drove in Ingo's 4WD Niva downstream along the higher left bank of the river, slowly polaroiding as we went. Salmon are quite visible under such conditions, obviously so when they jump, but also when they hold in a lie in the water. In such clarity their broad backs and swaying fins can be seen for some distance from above when their colour appears to be a pale shade of earth green against the contrasting gravel, rocks and moss.

Five minutes along the track, Ingo stopped above some rocks where a stormwater overflow pipe ran into the river. Through polaroids we counted four or five fish and knew that others would be around. Backtracking upstream then crossing a shallow bank in the 4WD, we drove along the gravel to a position some 150 paces upstream from the fish. In I went and started casting across, close to the other bank. Cast, swing, step ... cast, swing, step ... cast, swing, step. I eventually approached the target area and could see the wash around the submerged rocks at the outlet. I don't believe I've ever been more certain that there were fish there and that I would catch some.

Such an attitude is very healthy. And the first time my fly swung over the wash there was a big swirl; I was connected to a small henfish (about four pounds) which fought like the very Devil. Three in the bag and it was only 10 a.m. I backtracked upstream in order to cover the rest of the wash. About halfway down into it this time there was a big swirl but no weight; I let the fly continue to swing, slowly stripping in line. When it was almost directly downstream from me, there was a bow wave from the direction of the wash and then an almighty slash at my fly, and line whizzed out under considerable strain. Backing up to the pebbles I settled down to slug it out; I was quite obviously connected to a good fish. Although he broke the surface with a lot of spray a couple of times, I did not see him fully during the first 10 minutes. But when, with him complaining physically, I brought my charge to within 15 paces of the bank, I suddenly saw that the fish (about an 8-pounder) had a mate keeping close station – a phenomenon I had witnessed previously with trout. Together they put on a battle in the shallow water that had me thinking for a while that the leader had caught around the second fish and I was trying to land a double-header! But it was not to be; suddenly the mate broke formation and headed for the deep water. My hooked friend followed with such suddenness and ferocity that there was a quick PING as the hook pulled out and I was left wondering if this was a well-rehearsed battle tactic.

As we returned for lunch, Ingo inquired whether my first fish that morning was, indeed, my first landed, live Atlantic salmon? After considering the landlocked fish I had caught in Australia and New Zealand, the wild Pacific salmon from New Zealand's South Island, and remembering I had not actually caught a salmon in Scotland in the 1950s, nor in Norway some weeks before my visit to Iceland, I had to admit it was. Doubling up with mirth, Ingo announced that there was an ancient ritual in Iceland that had to be performed by the angler on landing his first Atlantic salmon. Thinking dark thoughts about pagan Viking rituals (did I have to chew out its liver while it was still kicking?), I hesitatingly asked what this ritual required of me. Between shrieks of laughter Ingo indicated that, back at the lodge, in front of my fishing companions, I had to grasp the fish and ceremoniously bite off its adipose fin.

YUK! My black thoughts weren't that far from the truth!

Some will recall just how firmly an adipose fin is attached to the upper backbone structure of a salmonid, particularly if they have had to strip a fish after smoking it. I certainly wasn't looking forward to it all when they placed me with my fish in front of the lodge sign and lined up the cameras. As the condemned man, I made one last request: did I have to swallow the revolting piece of gristle or could I spit it out?

'Of course you spit it out,' they said. 'Who would be so stupid as to eat it?'

Mumbling something about 'anyone stupid enough to bite it off', I grasped the fish in both hands like a piece of watermelon and sank my teeth into the fin just above the line of the back. Thirty seconds later the revolting morsel was lying at my feet, congratulations and laughter enveloped me, and the bubbly flowed like the water in the river!

Strangely enough I did eat lunch – the morning had been so invigorating – and was eagerly back in the river, this time in the home beat in front of the lodge, at 4.10 p.m. I fished a flat, quickly gliding rocky pool, close in by the bank and not far from the lodge. For the first hour and a half, although salmon were jumping all around me, I couldn't seem to hook one. Then I remembered to 'think trout' again, switched to a 7-pound tippet and a size 14 fly, and promptly landed a 5-pounder. Ingo was asleep on the bank in the sun but joined me after I had landed the fish and we walked up to Laxfoss to fish the white water for the remainder of the session. When we arrived I noticed the Frenchmen on the other bank (chosen by them) giving the water a fair pounding, but apparently with little to show for it. Ingo led me to a good white-water run almost under the falls and changed my tippet to a 10-pound Maxima, keeping the small Blue Charm in place. On the third cast I was well connected to a 5-pounder and understood, by the time I landed him, the need for a stronger tippet in that particularly strong run. Before Ingo had reached the bank to bag that salmon I was hooked to a second one of much the same size. I only wished at the time that I'd had my camera with me to record the Gallic expressions on the other bank (although we became good friends later).

A short while later, and a little further downstream, I hooked another fish and, despite the hook pulling out, I knew I could do little wrong and was in the very grip of one of those truly red-letter days the like of which even regular fishermen experience only once in every 2 or 3 years. As we walked back to the falls to fish the white water again, I indicated to Ingo that, as I now had six salmon in the cool room (potentially 20 pounds of Graflax for Gini to take back to London for our friends), it would be greedy to take any more and that, unless I took a particularly evil looking jack fish or a trophy-sized monster, we should practise catch-and-release for the final hour. Fifteen minutes later a good henfish took my fly and gave me an excellent 10-minute fight before we gently beached her. If the expressions on the fishless Gallic faces on the other bank had been worth photographing earlier that evening, then the looks of total disbelief as the crazy Australian actually put his fish back in the water could have written a million words. Then, through the mosquito netting, polaroids and hats, I actually saw a couple of faces go chalk white when I made it obvious to Ingo, with 15 (expensive) minutes of the session still remaining, that I'd had enough for one day and started to head back to the lodge.

I was acclaimed 'top rod' that day, a matter of little importance in true fishing terms to me. It was all wonderfully enjoyable, and I had to admit to the highs and lows we fishermen endure as I compared Iceland and Norway, happy in the thought that I could change nothing anyway. Red-letter days must be accepted happily for what they are, as must the many blank days because of the expectations which always follow. Fly-fishing needs both – roughly in the proportions that they naturally occur – if it is to maintain its incurable mystique.

For once I could say: 'You should have been there on Monday' … and I was!

The next morning I arose out of the mushy trance of insufficient sleep, too much celebration, aching muscles, and with a horribly sore throat, to greet a cold and bleak morning. I had graduated from my three sessions covering each of the beats with Ingo and was on my own for the next three. Ingo had returned to Reykjavik, where he also worked as a flying instructor, and was arranging an evening flight for Gini and me to look over Gullfoss and other famous wonders when we returned to Reykjavik three days later. Meanwhile, he had loosely teamed me up with the two Germans and their guide, Kristian, in case I needed further advice or help. It was a kind gesture and I thoroughly enjoyed their company. The older German, Bernhard, had fished the Nordurá for 16 years; indeed, he had also fished Norway and a great deal of Europe, Alaska, Canada and South America ('Argentina and Chile were best in the 1970s'), and he had personally fished with Charles Ritz and other famous fishing identities. Yet he was an unassuming and quietly spoken man; he said he had a philosophy about the three stages in a fly fisherman's life. 'The most, the biggest and the most difficult?' I proffered. 'No,' he said. 'Catch fish, help others to catch fish, watch others catching fish.' I silently bowed to a superior, wise and humane philosophy.

His companion was a first-timer to the Nordurá who spoke little English (he had an equal right to say that I spoke little German), but who had a wicked and engaging sense of humour. Their guide, Kristian, was a multilingual Icelander, an excellent fisherman of long standing, a member of the SVFR and a great help to me with his knowledge of the area.

That morning we returned to the downstream beat to fish the horseshoe bend. After a fruitless hour together fishing two rods on one bank, Kristian suggested that I cross to the other side, saying that the Germans were keen to stay put and that he would help me to cross the river. I thus found out how sensible the Germans were. With arms locked together and Kristian sporting a staff, somehow we crossed that maelstrom and, what's more, Kristian returned on his own – finding a somewhat less perilous track than our outward route which we used together for my eventual return.

I climbed the hill, around which the river curved in its horseshoe formation, to fish the distant side while Kristian, who had returned to the opposite bank by then, directed me into my starting point with whistles and pointed arms. It was so cold that I was wearing long thermal underwear, my normal fishing attire, plus a thick jumper, my black oiled fishing coat and silk balaclava and gloves. My throat hurt like hell and I couldn't seem to find my deadly Blue Charm tube from the day before. How the mighty had fallen.

At least my position was sheltered compared with the Germans fishing on the other bank around the corner. So I sat on a rock and 'manufactured' a small Blue Charm by cutting off the first half-inch of a huge Norwegian tube fly of similar colouring, and giving it a substantial haircut. My spirits rose with the results and I started casting from the sloped rocky shore into the tight, fast white water in the first running pool. Below it was a short waterfall, after which the fast water broadened into a very long, deep pool surrounded by cliffs on the far side but with a good rocky beach on mine.

Cast, swing, step … cast, swing, step … It looked to be good fishy water and, even through the cold, I began to rekindle sparks from yesterday. Some 50 paces downstream from my starting point, and a similar distance to the waterfall, my fly swung over a submerged boulder into the deep green water beyond, to become snagged on the bottom. At least I thought it was snagged on the bottom until the 'bottom' began to shake its head!

But let us return for a moment to the evening before; around midnight, flush with success (and red wine) at dinner, a Norwegian chum and I were agreeing that we ought to 'go smaller' in this river. We reckoned we should 'raise the tone of the place' by fishing with trout rods, 7-pound tippets, and very small flies.

So there I was, at 8.25 a.m., eight hours and 25 minutes later, connected via a Fenwick eight and a half foot trout rod, seven-weight line, 7-pound tippet, and a size 14 bastardised Norwegian tube fly, to the 'bottom' of Iceland which, at the time, happened to be shaking its head violently!

How do I get myself into these predicaments? I had plenty of time to think of the answers because the 'bottom' held position behind the boulder, totally in control, effortlessly shaking his head and sometimes moving a foot or so in any direction. He just wanted to let me know he was a fish, and a fish in total command of the situation.

At 8.45 a.m. he slowly left his rocky home and moved out

midstream for his morning exercise. I could do nothing. I've never felt quite so helpless. Then he allowed the water to ease him slowly back towards the waterfall, shaking his head more aggressively, and stopping just short of the brink, to demonstrate his strength. After a further 10 minutes he allowed himself to drop over the falls then, with a rocket-propelled burst, shot down the long pool as I stumbled over the rocks trying to catch up while dacron backing came howling out from the little trout reel.

With nearly 70 of my 120 metres of backing beyond the tip of the rod, the fish turned and finned the current. I kept the pressure up, regained most of the backing and started to move downstream to get below him. It was just after 9 a.m., 40 minutes from hookup, when the fish thought I should see what I was up against and leapt. Fifteen? Eighteen? Twenty pounds? Who knows? Who cares, because in crashing back into the water he broke my silly little 7-pound tippet and I immediately upped him to an estimated 22 – he deserved every bit of it.

Kristian helped me to recross the river as I mumbled incoherently about 25-pound monsters; I think he had probably heard it all before. Anyway, I stopped fishing then, gave Kristian my final two rod hours of that session and returned to the lodge to lick my wounds. As ever, I shall later recall all the details of that fish in Iceland; at the time, I couldn't remember even the number of fish I had caught the day before. This fish had undoubtedly joined my private Hall of Fame, along with the Rakaia Monster, the double-figure brownie near Adaminaby in the Murrumbidgee, and the 'Fossen Monster' from the falls on the Forra in Norway. He had joined those who had beaten me resoundingly. Victory and size were their only common facets; in all other characteristics they were truly mighty individuals.

The 4 to 10 p.m. session was a cold zero for me, bringing home once again the extraordinary ups and downs that make fly-fishing so alluring. But I did manage one success that day; the lodge chef, who fed us magnificently, agreed to Graflax my salmon so that Gini could, indeed, take them back to London. I think his recipe is the best I've tasted and he agreed to part with it for publication:

Gudmundur Vidarsson's Graflax
3 cups salt – 1 cup dried brown dill – 3 cups sugar – ½ cup pepper –
2 cups dried dill – ½ cup fennel
Mix together and sprinkle on an oven tray. Place the salmon fillets

(skin-side down) in the tray, laying one on top of the other with a good
sprinkling of the mixture between the layers.
Leave standing in the kitchen for 24 hours (assuming a temperature of
about 20°C). Then place in the fridge for at least 24 hours.
Serve with the following sauce:
1 cup sweet mustard – 1 cup vegetable oil – 1 cup hot mustard – ½ cup
honey – 1 cup brown sugar – 1/4 cup cognac – 1 cup dried dill
Mix together all except the oil and cognac and allow to settle. Then stir in
the oil and the cognac and allow one hour to settle before serving.

My final fishing session lasted from 6 a.m. to 1 p.m. on Wednesday, 15 July, using the home beat on the bank opposite the lodge. I started at the Laxfoss end, with the Frenchmen across the river from me, trying unsuccessfully to find the secret spots that I had fished two days before. I fished without success until I was below the lodge. Kristian and my German mates had worked from the bottom towards me, also without result. Around 11 a.m. I moved to the very bottom of the beat where the water runs fast through a rapid and into a long, deep pool before entering the canyon. One of my French friends was on the other bank fishing the lower part of the rapid, so I climbed into waist-deep water among the boulders at the head of the white water to thrash it with another homemade Blue Charm, this time using a 12-pound tippet. I maintained a set position because movement was extremely difficult and, anyway, the salmon had to pass within 8 metres of me if they were to continue up the river. After a number of casts, I was firmly connected to a good fish and faced the problem of getting both of us clear of the rocks and white water and into a position where I could play and land him. But it was wonderful weather again, I was back on top, and 10 minutes later I beached the 5-pounder without difficulty.

As I was redressing my tackle, my French friend hooked up opposite me; it looked like a good spot. Unfortunately, however, his hook pulled out moments later and I had to sympathise with him; every time we fished near each other, he seemed to bring me good luck while I brought him bad. And this theory took on an absurd reality when, having returned to my rocky rapid, a few moments later I hooked another 5-pounder on the second cast. So, as I landed it, remembering Bernhard's philosophy, I suggested to my friend that he take over the top part of the white water which had been so good to me, an offer which he readily accepted, unfortunately without success.

Thus I concluded a fabulous fishing period with two more fish which I gave to Kristian. And I was very pleased to add that, on the next day when I was no longer fishing, my French friend landed a 12-pounder.

After celebratory champagne and lunch, and in the knowledge that I had fished hard for three days in one of the world's best fisheries, I fell onto my bed and slept until dinnertime. Meanwhile, Gini had covered some interesting territory in the car and had probably seen a lot more of Iceland and, indeed, read more about its fascinating history, than I had. But my business was to fish and to describe it and, in that, I was well content.

I worked throughout my final day at the lodge; a necessary song for my fishing supper, but it was by no means an easy song to sing. As I worked my eyes kept drifting to the window, to the lava cliffs, and down to the river where other lucky fishermen were chasing the elusive lax. We left the lodge rather sadly on the morning of Friday, 17 July and returned to Reykjavik in time for lunch. Ingo dropped in at lunchtime to give us flight details for the evening and, in the afternoon Gini took in more local culture while I had to stay at the hotel catching up. One day I'll get it I together but, in order to do so, I'll never try to combine fishing with anything else again; certainly not sightseeing and touring with writing about fishing!

We took off in the little Piper Cherokee at ten that evening; a beautiful Arctic evening with multicoloured clouds occasionally hiding a blood red sun as it dodged between the mountain peaks. I wound the Nikon into manual and played with the scenery as best I could through the distortions of the scratched perspex canopy. Ingo chatted on about the scene below, his knowledge increasing as we crossed rivers and diminishing when we flew over country not immediately related to the lax. The high point was 10 minutes, almost at ground level tightly circling Gullfoss – the most famous waterfall in Iceland. The sheer power of that milky, glacial water, as it thundered over the abyss into an incredibly narrow canyon which it had carved over the centuries, was simply breathtaking. To see from 200 feet up, and from every angle, was something even I hadn't planned for in my 2 years of safari research; it was a view which will live with me for a very long time.

Ingo invited me to fly the Piper back to Reykjavik circuit, a thrill at the end of a week of thrills for me, although it must have been pretty obvious to him that I hadn't flown for some 30 years. Thoughts of Lossiemouth and Tiger Moths went through my mind, invoking a sense of both history and peace; a great deal of fly water had passed under the bridge joining Scotland in the 1950s to Iceland in the 1990s.

It was the perfect finale in another country of my travels which I personally rated as Heaven on a stick, and a fitting point from which to go on, through Greenland, to Baffin Island for the next Arctic adventure. Sadly, Gini had to return to London (with the Graflax), and to Europe, where she would meet our daughter, Katharine, for more eastabout travels before returning to Australia at roughly the same time as I would, travelling westabout.

CHAPTER 20

Kamchatka

Monday 5 June: Now we are coming down to earth. The cute hostie at the check-in for Kamchatka accepted a note the Russian Ambassador in Canberra had given me about excess luggage and gave me a smile rather than a bill. She also gave me seat 1A ... as she did every other passenger, and we fought for seats in a very grubby and smelly IL-62. But she came with me to the plane and made sure I got a seat. I must have looked more obvious than I thought. After only three Aeroflot flights and four Russian airports, I'm convinced the Russian hostie is a little like the 1960s Australian hostie – attractive, if not alluring – and nothing like the union-driven matrons that ply Capricornian skies today.

The descent into Petropavlovsk–Kamchatsky almost beat that into Greenland from Iceland in 1992: ice- and snow-clad mountains, volcanoes (Viluchinsky, and those north), and more and more rock, ice and snow. I used reels of my precious 35mm supply. It was worth every frame.

We landed at Yelizova near Petropavlovsk in 'cold war' scenery – bunkered pits for military aircraft, radar and microwave aerials, military barracks, the lot. We were passport-checked inside the aeroplane by a 100-kilo, short-cropped female and ushered through an iron grille to meet our luggage (if lucky), and our host(s) (if more than lucky).

You guessed it: 'Meester Krees', as they call me, had no one to meet him, 50 kilos of luggage (five articles) in tow, snow on the higher ground at 9.30 at night, and an unappealing prospect for the next 24 hours in an alien, once believed to be hostile country. Fortunately, as I talked to an official about my problems, a man named Yuri said that not only was he an ex-fisheries inspector, but also he could help because his wife spoke excellent English. Forgetting, for a moment, about steering clear of strangers in Russia, I accepted his kind offer of a lift into Petropavlovsk to ask his wife (she left even Aeroflot hosties for dead) to ring telephone numbers I had in the hope that we might achieve something; and all this at 11 p.m.

Nothing seemed to work, despite his kindness. Three laps of the block looking for the Fisheries Office found nothing, phone calls went unanswered and, around midnight, I persuaded him to leave me at a hotel to lick my wounds, clean my teeth, terrify my luggage, and sleep until the rising of the sun, when I might be prepared to 'kick some ass!' 'Kicking ass' in Russia, of course, has been a pastime for centuries; and who the hell was 'Meester Krees' to tell them how to play their own exquisitely-orchestrated game?

Tuesday 6 June: I phoned my USA mates at Kamchatka Adventures in Washington State (partners with Purga, a commercial company that owns a sportfishing lodge in Kamchatka) the next morning at seven o'clock. Later, at office-time, I spoke to Vladimir Burkanov, Director of the Federal Department for Protection and Reproduction of Fish Resources and Fisheries Regulations, Russian Federation in Kamchatka, who started to get cogs into motion.

Initially, the commercial sportfishing contact was difficult. That was probably my own fault; I'd relied on telephone and facsimile contact too much. Last-minute faxes and details had gone astray, as they do in Russia, and we had to achieve a starting point. The commercial side was also very involved in the inaugural Anchorage to Petropavlovsk direct flight by Alaskan Airlines, and any ideas I had about being involved in salmonid observance in this incredible part of the world were, understandably but not intentionally, put on their backburner.

The day progressed. I'd soaked up 20-odd hours in Petropavlovsk (the top-secret submarine base of the 1960s and 1970s) and had still come up with nothing … perhaps I was meant to. Then, at last, I made contact again with Vladimir Burkanov in Kamchatka. The commercial contact, Purga, had given me a driver/interpreter named Valery, who took me to Fisheries headquarters for a 2.30 p.m. meeting with Vladimir and his staff. The result:

1 A state helicopter and fly-fishing guide/interpreter would be put at my disposal;
2 They would take me to a Fisheries camp to write up Sakhalin (and fish) from Wednesday to Friday;
3 We would raft the Schapina and Kamchatka Rivers on Saturday and Sunday;
4 The program would be flexible on Monday and Tuesday;
5 We would return to Petropavlovsk early on Wednesday in time for me to visit the big sportfishing business, Purga (Toby Sprinkle, their USA contact, was in the country) and their lodge on the Zhupanova River;
6 I would return to Petropavlovsk late on Wednesday 14, for departure Thursday 15 June for Khabarovsk as planned.

Thanks to 12 months' research and Vladimir Ikriannikov in Sydney, I had the full support of Russian Fisheries and had really fallen on my feet. Moreover, Purga were happy to show me their lodge.

At 4 p.m. I checked into a much cheaper – and better – hotel for the night, ordered dinner (and breakfast and lunch for the next day), sorted out my gear and brought my notes up to date. After dinner and half bottle of vodka, I had a big banya [a bath] and fell into bed. Once more, this time surrounded by snow-clad volcanoes (last eruption 1994), I was back on track with an exciting week ahead.

Wednesday 7 June: Breakfast at 7 a.m., then 4 hours' writing and painting before lunch and packing my gear.

Thinking about the last 36 hours, I just wonder how much of this extravagant sine-curve existence my system can take. As far as writing the book about Russia goes, I think I'll have to take an entirely new approach; a tourist book is simply not on, yet the experience must be recorded and shared – a published diary maybe?

Eugene, my guide and safari operator, and his Fisheries companion Igor collected me at 5 p.m. (three-hour delay) and we drove to the heliport just out of Petropavlovsk. When we return next Wednesday, they will land me at Yelizova, where I'll transfer to the Purga helicopter to visit their lodge on the Zhupanova for a few hours, before spending my final night and day at the hotel (which, incidentally, did all my laundry, and gave me a bed and three meals for US$60).

We took off in an ex-Aeroflot, twin-turbo MN8 with a crew of three, plus Eugene, Igor and me, a girlfriend (to cook) and another young man. It wasn't good for morale to inspect the helo too carefully, but it did its job – without seat-belts, and with the windows open for photography – very well. The trip was out of this world: flying over snow-clad mountains, past ice-covered lakes, and dodging in and out of active volcanoes. I used another precious roll of film and will try to get Valery to find more when we return to Petropavlovsk. Two hours later, the ice and snow cleared to a birch and spruce-covered plain, with eight A-frame hunting cabins and a natural sulphur creek with steaming water at bath temperature. We unpacked, settled in and lit a fire for dinner. There is no fishing nearby, so I can work through Thursday and Friday before we take to the rivers on Saturday. A good start on one of the world's most spectacular stages.

Thursday 8 June: I slept in until 7.45 a.m., then had a glorious hot sulphur bath – stark naked in a natural hot sulphur pool with shaving cream on my chin and falling snow on my shoulders – then breakfast. Stomach faintly upset, so I had a few 'Dr Morgan's specials' from my first-aid kit and started a working day. The others loaded the helicopter to pre-position the gear for our river drifting and fishing, which I said I'd be happy to start after lunch tomorrow. I find it hard to work in this dramatic mountain scenery; it is all I can do to keep this diary written and illustrated in the wild, and occasionally do a mud-map painting. There is so much more to see, do and understand. I see four days in a dacha at Lake Baikal, and ten in Moscow, as the only possibilities to do the book-writing part. Otherwise that may have to be delayed until I'm at home, when I can devote my time to it.

When the team were about to take off in the helicopter this morning, they forgot to remove the tail support. As they revved up to lift off, the support was blown clear, but a piece – a three-foot square of 5 ply – flew up into the tail rotor and was reduced to instant Red Head matches! They had to shut down, of course, to inspect for damage. The pilot declared all OK and off they went. I went back to my scribbling and painting, thankful I was not on that 'test flight'.

Later, at 3 p.m. I heard voices. Eugene, Igor and Lena (the girlfriend) had left the helicopter drop zone and walked back via the top of a volcano to the northeast of us ... just for fun, they said. I didn't realise it was so late, and we stopped for lunch. Then they told me the helicopter had crash-landed and the only things left were themselves and my waders! Big Russian Joke ... they climbed no volcano, the helo was OK and they only brought my waders back because I would need them to walk through a swamp tomorrow. I'll get even!

I worked for the rest of the afternoon and evening, and often one or two of our party would drop in to watch.

Friday 9 June: Up at 8 a.m. and Eugene wished me a 'Happy New Year!' I asked if it was Russian New Year, and he said: 'No, just wanted to practise sayings.'

Snow was falling gently again as I had my sulphur bath and shave – a delightful experience. Then breakfast and back to work, which I'll cut short … it is time to go fishing.

Well, we packed to leave camp and that is when I realised there had been a misunderstanding. The helicopter was not coming back until next week to collect us and we had a three-mile walk through deep, permafrost tundra to the river and the boat, carrying all my gear, including my huge case and other items. 'Nyet problemski!' the two Russian men announced and slung it on a sapling between them. In single file, we set out in wet snow for the river; it took over an hour, resting every 10 minutes.

When we arrived and I saw the 'boat', I had another mild attack of hysteria. It was nothing more than a big Rubber Ducky with a steel frame, built for white-water rafting! How we got all our gear into that boat, let alone ourselves, I don't know. I insisted that my gear was packed in a heavy-duty plastic sheet that was carried as a camping groundsheet. Anyway, we set a target distance to cover, had lunch, and launched ourselves into the fast-flowing but dirty river at 2.30 p.m. We made steady, wet and cold progress for an hour or two and then struck the first major rapids. Eugene and Igor took the boat down the rapids while the rest of us travelled inland to meet them at the other end – me carrying a trendy leather briefcase through the Russian mountain jungle because I had my diary, tickets, passport and money in it and I had thoughts of it being washed overboard, down the Kamchatka River and out to sea.

We all made it safely, wet and cold, to continue downstream without further drama until 7.30 p.m., when we stopped to make camp. There was a primitive hunting cabin nearby which I was invited to use while the others put up tents, despite fresh bear tracks in the sand. We were soon warm and dry, with a huge fire burning outside for cooking and a heating fire burning in the 'one-bed' hut to dry our clothes. A good dinner, a bottle of vodka, and a promise of clear weather, clean water and fishing tomorrow sent us to bed at midnight quite contented. It is amazing what the body will withstand temporarily with a promise of relief in the end. I only wish I could have been better briefed about all of this, particularly about my luggage. I should have left most of it at Petropavlovsk.

Saturday 10 June: Up at 7.15 a.m. Ablutions in the river, breakfast around the fire at 8.30.a.m., and wrote up this diary on my knee while sitting on a log. Packed up and started down the river at ten o'clock.

It was an easier day in fine but cold weather, and no rapids. We had to stop on many occasions to chop fallen birch and spruce trees from our path! The water was still murky. I tried fishing when we stopped for lunch but had no joy. After lunch we came across a cabin in the middle of a bubbling sulphur thermal area. Without hesitation Eugene and Lena shed their gear and jumped in. Lena is an extraordinary woman – they are all outdoor types in the mould of Sir Edmund Hillary – and I found out that the young boy, Rossland, is her son, although they would easily pass for brother and sister.

Further down the Schapina we found a clear-water stream joining the main river, where I asked to stop and fish. At last, my first success in Kamchatka, a fat, 3-pound rainbow to the Peter Ross. Igor also took one on conventional spinning gear before we continued downstream.

At dinner last night we discussed fishing politics. Apparently the Americans started coming to Kamchatka when it opened up in the early 1990s, hunting and skiing. At first they saw it as a natural extension of Alaska for the lucky and adventurous few, and later as a goldmine for sport-tourism companies. Already there are 30 tourist/guiding companies in Kamchatka, and five helicopter companies (there is no other way of reaching the sports playgrounds). A few, such as Purga, with their access to good accommodation, in-country facilities and staff, have American partners like Kamchatka Adventures, who have enormous marketing expertise and connections with good airlines such as Alaskan. They can offer the best wild sportfishing and guaranteed comfort to the free-spending internationals. The others, who offer much more fundamental stuff – rafting and camping (as I am doing) – are left literally and figuratively out in the cold. The free-spending sportsman likes his comforts at night, and having experienced both, I don't blame him.

We stopped to make camp on a gently-shelving (easy fishing) sandy beach at 8 p.m. When we unpacked the boat I found that, despite the plastic, my case was wet. Fortunately, nothing of consequence was damaged, but it emphasised the point about the right gear.

No success with fishing, so dinner and off to bed.

Sunday 11 June: We got underway at about ten o'clock. Because the Russians keep such advanced time zones, last light and bed are about 11.30 p.m., so nothing much happens until 8.30 the next morning. This morning there were fresh bear tracks in the sand close to the camp.

It was a pleasant enough morning, rafting with very few obstructions through the mist, firs and birches, with snow-clad mountains in the background. But very, very cold; especially when sitting quite still (you can't do much else) on a raft, travelling at about ten knots with the current and creating ten knots of cold breeze. It is so cold that things slow, then one starts to get drowsy.

We stopped for lunch at the confluence of the Right and Left Schapinas. The fishing potential looked good but, again, we had no success. So off we went, knowing there was one more gorge to negotiate before miles of flat country and the confluence with the Kamchatka River.

Some 15 minutes from the gorge there was a strong and deep drumming sound in the air. Five minutes later it was a constant roaring noise, and when we entered the final long, wide run before the gorge, it was almost deafening. What's more, that final run seemed to have no outlet. Then we saw it – a tiny passage maybe 20 metres wide, the only outlet for miles and miles and mega-megalitres of Schapina River in snow melt. It was an unbelievable maelstrom; a witches' cauldron; white water that made Meryl Streep's *The River Wild* look like a Sunday school outing to the brook! We tied up to the bank 50 metres short of the entrance and Eugene and Igor went to investigate, with me following some distance behind taking photographs. An hour later they returned to report it was too dangerous. I could have told them that 59 minutes earlier. It also explained why there were so few fish further upstream – they simply couldn't pass the gorge.

We towed the raft back upstream to a rocky beach where we could set up a comfortable camp and wait for the helicopter. Borscht and bread for dinner – again; we've had it for breakfast, lunch and dinner for three days now. If the helicopter can find us and put down (by no means certain), and if the fishing is poor once we are lifted out below the gorge, I'm going to call for a halt and a return to Petropavlovsk to try the Purga alternative. The scenery may be out of this planet, but this

Davey Crockett existence – 22 hours' slog for two hours' fishing with no fish – isn't helping my examination of fly-fishing in Kamchatka. What's more I need 24 hours, apart from my Purga trip to the Zhupanova, to sort out my wet and dirty gear, get some laundry done, catch up with my notes, visit Mr Burkanov and, most importantly, have a hot shower, put on some clean clothes and have a hotel meal.

Monday 12 June: Up at 8.30 a.m. (the others after 9) and wrote up yesterday. I had to stop every ten lines and thaw my hands by the fire. It is obvious why international fly fishermen stick to Purga Lodge when fishing in Kamchatka.

I think we are running out of food, and there is only one bottle of vodka left.

At ten o'clock the sun burnt through the mist to reveal a truly glorious day. At least the helicopter could get in – if it could find us. We packed up the camp and the boat and played a steady game of Russian poker while we waited for the noise of rotor blades. I cleaned them out. About 11.45 a.m. Eugene thought he heard something, so pulled out an alarm pistol and shot a red flare. Nothing. They were looking for us downstream of the gorge, not realising how bad it was. Finally, 30 minutes and six poker hands later, the helicopter hove into view. To me that bashed-up old MN8 looked like an Anglo-French Concorde.

It landed and shut down, whereupon ice-cold beer and warm fresh bread were offered all around. After loading, we took off and flew northwest to intercept the Kamchatka River (muddy and high) then followed it north to Kozirevsk, where we landed and refuelled. The central Kamchatka plain is in direct contrast with the mountain regions. It was warm under the clear blue sky and we all shed layers of clothing down to jeans and open-necked shirts (all grubby).

In the air again and we headed northeast, past Kluchevskoy, the highest and most famous smoking volcano, to the Elovka River, a clear fast-flowing tributary of the Kamchatka where there might be a chance of a Chinook. We landed and people disappeared in a multitude of directions on different tasks. I wandered down to a stony bank and started fishing a storybook run, but with no success. Returning to the others, I found they had extracted a Rubber Ducky and 40hp Yamaha from the helicopter, and pumped up the boat. They invited me to come and fish. Would wonders never cease?

But though the guys were good at rafting, they weren't that good with an outboard motor. At the first indication of the propeller touching a rock, the driver seemed to panic and open the throttle wide. The prop looked like a broken corkscrew when we got back. At one stage the motor stalled and couldn't immediately be restarted. As we raced downstream with the current I suggested we should tie up to the bank to fix things before we reached Alaska.

Nevertheless, it ended well: the motor was restarted, we caught some fish (five Russian char and two 4-pound rainbows to the Peter Ross for me), then had lunch at 5 p.m. on the river bank, and returned to the helicopter at 8.30. Eugene said: 'Just bring sleeping bag', which I did. I followed him around a hill, and there was a very pretty Russian hunting cabin where, after dinner in the twilight, we spent a very comfortable night.

I haven't mentioned the mosquitoes. They've been around in squadrons since day one in Sakhalin. They are about the size of a Mk V Spitfire but less noisy, and are only put off by smoke and sub-zero cold. They start at about 8 a.m. and put in a very busy 14-hour day. Their main diet is insect repellent, DDT and blood, and the Russians tell me they are the same all over their country.

We had fish soup for dinner last night and the vodka supply was topped up with a 90 per cent spirit bottle which, when mixed with water, produces six bottles of standard vodka. I mustn't get so critical when tired, cold and wet; they are doing their very best for me, and I must stay throughout tomorrow as planned, as it is apparent that the fishing gets better at lower altitude in the tributaries.

Tuesday 13 June: An early start and old fashioned noodles for breakfast. Away in the boat at 8 a.m. The river had risen a foot as the good weather melted the snow, and it was discoloured. I managed four good grayling to a Red Doctor, then we packed it in at 11 a.m. and dismantled the boat.

I also identified the predominant trees and colours on the river bank: dark green – spruce firs; medium green – alders, larch and some birch; light green — willows, poplars and most birch. Then, while the team were busy 'doing things', I made some sense of my clothes and luggage and caught up with my notes. Don't know what is in store for this afternoon yet.

We packed up and took off after lunch, and I found we had been fishing the Rossoshina, a tributary of the Elovka, not the Elovka itself (it was our unsuccessful first stop that afternoon). Next stop was further downstream on the Elovka and then on to the Kamchatka

River, where we dropped Igor and Rossland to do Fisheries research. I was genuinely sorry to see them go. We'd had a hard week together and I had come to like them both very much; Igor as a competent guide and hard worker, Rossland as a cool, crazy 15-year-old. I gave Igor a fly painting and Rossland my Pierre Cardin ballpoint (courtesy of Singapore Airlines), as he had been lusting after it since day one.

Last stop we snuck upstream on the Zhupanova to find it grubby with snowmelt. A nearby feeder was clear, however, and we camped at its confluence with the Zhupanova. First attempts were unsuccessful, but later I managed two 3-pound rainbows to the Red Doctor. To bed at midnight.

Wednesday 14 June: A very cold night and not much sleep in the tent. Up at 7.30 a.m. to have a good clean-up beside the river and fresh clothes. Then the rain started. I'm lying in the tent writing this. I don't know whether we will get out because of the weather, or if I will get to Purga Lodge today.

At 9.15 a.m. the skies cleared, we packed my personal transport and an hour later we took off for Yelizova, where we arrived at 12.30 p.m., 30 minutes ahead of schedule. I said my thanks to Eugene and Lena, and gave them a fly painting each. It seemed appropriate, even though I was to see them again. I gave the aircrew one of the koala bears to hang on the instrument panel and they thought it was just wonderful. Then I walked down the strip with just my cameras (Eugene's team were going to take my other luggage and laundry to the hotel) to meet Oksana Klimenko, company secretary and interpreter for Purga. Good timing. Toby Sprinkle from the Alaskan connection was also there and we had a quick but fascinating discussion … salmonid politics again. Toby had work in Petropavlovsk and left with a promise to meet at the airport before I leave tomorrow night.

Oksana gave me a tour of the Purga complex – which included their contribution with Japan and USA to the 'Save the Aleutian Goose campaign', and a look at the geese for which the Russian connection is the caretaker. Then lunch, courtesy of Purga, then a meeting with the big boss, Anatoli Kovalenkov. Anatoli then flew me and Oksana north to the Zhupanova again, via the river mouth where his company (Wolf Company) has a commercial salmon enterprise producing thousands of tons of Pacific salmon for smoking each year.

We flew on to the Purga lodge, Cedar Lodge, arriving around 3.30 p.m. Oksana gave me a guided tour of the complex, which is well up to world standards. There is a main living building with six bedrooms (four beds each) all with ensuites, a lounge, a laundry and a fly-tying room; a recreation centre with bar, banya and billiard room; a separate dining/kitchen building, and various staff and machinery complexes. They run a squadron of six top-quality, 110-Yamaha-powered fly-fishing boats, four guides, and a domestic staff of about ten. The business has been in operation since 1991–92. It meets world standards for a great new sportfishery and I wish them luck. They have a contract with Katmai Lodge/East Russia Adventures (Toby Sprinkle etc) to produce the clients for their Purga operation, and all parties were keen for me to promote them in the Southwest Pacific.

After the tour I was taken fishing for an hour or so by the head guide, Valare, but with high and discoloured water I was lucky to take one 7-pound rainbow on a wet Sculpin. We had dinner – and vodka again – before we flew out at 8 p.m. We were accompanied by Valare, another guide, and the chef(ess) who were on their way to Alaska (courtesy of Toby) for further 'instruction' before the season starts on 1 July. As with Sakhalin, I was in Kamchatka too early. Although the Chinook run starts in June, the rivers are still too full with snow melt to get decent visual fishing. July is better, and August and September better still; when the Coho run, double-figure rainbows are regular, and the autumn steelhead start to run into the west coast rivers. Again, I had no choice, but I enjoyed the fishing I had in some of the most beautiful scenery in the world, and badly want to return late one summer. I'm told it is even better than Alaska.

I said my farewells at the Purga helicopter base in Yelizova and Anatoli said I must come back as his guest when the salmon are running. They gave me a car and driver back to Petropavlovsk. I arrived at 9.30 p.m. at the hotel to find my other luggage had been delivered by Eugene's team, and my laundry was being attended to. Their hospitality knows no bounds.

I sorted out my 'mess' and disappeared into the banya for an hour to become totally squeaky clean ... and so to bed.

Thursday 15 June: I met a couple of BHP Australians and Brits last night; all they could talk about was the bloody rugby tests in the UK. Considering the unique nature of this country in which they are billeted, and its extraordinary history, I found their attitude parochial to say the least.

Eugene is to collect me in 15 minutes for a farewell meeting with Vladimir Burkanov at Fisheries headquarters. I'll give him a copy of *Heaven on a Stick* and, if I'm any good at conning, I'll get them to photostat this diary and fax a copy to Gini (22 pages – big con job). It would be nice to hear Vladimir utter that international saying: 'Nyet problemski!'

STEVE MORGAN

STEVE MORGAN, at 33 years of age, is the managing editor and a director of the Fishing Monthly Group, which includes *Queensland Fishing Monthly, NSW Fishing Monthly* and *Victoria Fishing Monthly*. He also finds time to run ABT Fishing Tournaments and produces the AFC TV show. A keen saltwater fly fisherman, he has held two world fly-fishing records for longtail tuna.

The following article appeared in *The Australian and New Zealand Flyfisher's Annual 1998* and is reproduced (with photographs) with the kind permission of the author.

CHAPTER 21

Her Pool

He was only one of many. The pool contained several of his kind.
He lived at one end, with two others. They had all been here since
the last flood, from the time their lives began, five seasons ago.
They all knew not to spend too much time in the middle of the
pool. Even though the water was deeper, safer, darker and slower,
they had learnt not to go there. They would be chased and beaten as
they had been before. The big fish of the pool was not their mother.
Even if she was, she wouldn't tolerate their presence at this time –
not for another eight or nine moons. She lived there in the darkness where the log met the towering boulder. Out of sight but never
out of mind.

She had been in the pool for the same number of years but had
hatched more than twenty springs ago. After the last flood she
had stopped there. Since then she had survived on the pickings that
her new home offered. Small silver herrings teased during the day
but were easy victims at night. Sharp, summer storms brought food
from the land, and she had feasted in the past on small marsupials
and slithering snakes. Cicadas and ducks had also met their end in

her cavernous mouth. Lately she had fed well. Her territory was secure and the water lazily warm.

From his position, he could see a lot. The water in which he lived was crystal clear and there were not many creatures that passed through it that escaped his attention. He was particularly interested in the current intruder that splashed down and floated near the bank. Curious, he eyed the potential meal, himself under the watchful eye of his brethren. It pulsed rhythmically over the entire width of the pool and then mysteriously disappeared.

Another of its ilk noisily landed on the water's surface, this time on the border of his territory. Hesitating, he again approached, one eye on the morsel and another scanning the shadows. He didn't want to incur her wrath.

The foam popper chugged and gurgled back towards the angler.

Caught in two minds, his movements became erratic. Darting for the fly. Stopping.

Charging headlong at his fastest speed. Waiting. He'd entered her space and didn't care. Eat it. Crash!

Charging back to his own territory he could see that she had emerged. Her presence supercharged his efforts, but his progress was curtailed by the tension in his jaw. Powerful tail beats consistently propelled him towards the bank. He was terrified by the threat from behind and the unknown threat somewhere ahead. His surges lessened and he was dragged into the shallows.

'Nice fish, but did you see the one that was following it?'

'Must've been thirty pounds!'

After his escape from the mysterious pull and the bright flashes of light, more of the morsels beckoned in full view. He could see them from his refuge in the crack between two rocks. Mostly they swam through her territory, and he was happy to leave them alone. He would spend the next day cowering under his log.

'Ready to try the next pool?'

'Yeah – we'll try for that big fish again on the way back.'

FRED
DUNFORD

A DEDICATED broadwater fly fisher, Fred Dunford works tirelessly for the betterment of fly-fishing and the environment.

His profession as a high-school teacher of biology, agriculture and junior science supplemented his desire to study, among other matters, the *Hemicordulia tau*, which in turn led to the development and dressing of the well-known 'corduliid' trout fly.

Fred was, and still is, active in the Monaro Acclimatisation Society (MAS), initially as secretary and later as scientific officer. He was also involved in the Monaro Shire Council Environment Committee, the Monaro Conservation Society, the Upper Murrumbidgee Catchment Management Committee and many other working groups.

He has been given several awards: Life Membership (MAS), based on service; the Victorian Council of Flyfishers (VCF) Conservation Award 1996 – this was the only time the VCF went outside its own state to make the award; and the Jack Ritchie Victorian Fly Fishers Association (VFFA) Conservation medal. He was awarded this last on 29 August 1997. This was the only time this award has gone outside Victoria. The award was commissioned by the Governor General of Victoria, and has only ever been awarded three times – the first time was (posthumously) to Sir James Youll, 1864.

It could be argued that he is best known for his ongoing Australia-wide efforts as convenor of the 'Save the Eucumbene' campaign to stop development along the shores of Lake Eucumbene. More recently, Fred mounted an intensive five-month campaign to have stocking bans on various rivers lifted; as of December 2002, stocking bans on four of those rivers have been lifted.

Somehow, in his later life he has also found time to write a book, *Face of the Broadwater Trout*.

CHAPTER 22

Three Bits of Cardboard

There were three special pieces of cardboard that I searched for when we went through Dad's effects in April 1998. His Wingham to Cooma railway luggage label. The photo of him at age 70 with his 9-pound Tasmanian monster on the Corduliid. And the end-of-year business notice that appeared every Christmas in the window of his second-hand furniture shop.

It was Chris Geelan, after the funeral, who reminded us about the annual sign in the window. Scrawled on a sheet of greying card, without explanation or apology or 'Compliments of the Festive Season to All Our valued Customers', were two simple words: 'Gone Fishing'. And that's exactly what he did. Eucumbene, Tantangara, Jindabyne, Oberon, and even the fabled new Lake Pedder in its glory days: we camped beside and fished them all.

I still see with total clarity how it all started that 1940s summer on the Bulga. Dad and Pa have returned from the Dairy Pool just on dark with a vivid silver and scarlet rainbow trout of nearly 2 pounds. 'I was just a bit lucky,' says Dad as we crowd round the kitchen table under the yellow lamplight. He is trying to make Pa feel a little better about missing out. But we kids are absolutely agog. We have never seen anything so exquisitely svelte and beautiful in our lives.

Not to be outdone, Grandpa Coleman crept out of the house next morning at dawn. Later I see him coming up the track from the Dairy pool, haloed by the early light that clips the distant ridge tops and filters down over the paddocks. There is a rainbow of just over 2 pounds swinging jauntily at his side.

The full onset of my own trout obsession around 1961 was eventually to bring the wheel full circle. Well before Dad finally retired and looked like being stuck in town for the duration, brother Max and I got him back to his roots again, teaching him fly-fishing and getting him out there at every available opportunity. In the process, we were to share with him times and experiences not reserved for even the most wealthy or famous.

The memories spread before me like the snapshots that go with them.

First comes December 1964. We are at Tantangara Reservoir in its short-lived glory days. From our red Fiat van, looking out over the creek mouth bay to the ankle-deep shallows on the far side, we see backs and dorsal fins sticking up out of the water like conning towers. I pretend to drive straight past without noticing anything, but our rear passengers stamp their feet and beat a tattoo on the walls. I fear someone may actually explode out through the back. Even the bold-as-brass bow-wavers can probably see the whites of their eyes.

Max, with Dad in tow, storms down the near-vertical face of the road bank cutting, both of them fumbling with knots and leaders as they put up their rigs on the run. They try to hotfoot it out over the Kelly's Plains mudflats, each in turn getting a fit of the staggers as they pick their way towards the snaky meanders of the creek. The bed itself is knee-deep mud, and the vertical banks are 3 feet deep in a sort of clayey quicksand that might swallow an ox in a sitting. The balletic duo try to step over the top ... The climax is wet, cold and extremely muddy, and the bow-wavers all discover they have urgent appointments at the other end of the lake.

But at length there is a happy ending to the day. I climb the hill to the van, with little to show for my efforts, to be greeted by Dad's happy face in the torchlight as he admires Max's magnificently conditioned 3½-pound rainbow. 'Maxie's just gone back again – he reckons he can get another one,' he says with a little cat-swallowed-the-cream grin, as contented as if he's caught the fish himself. Why should this little holiday scene stand out from all the others? I don't really know. But I'm glad it does.

Then comes the Great Oberon Fish Freeze Break-In of 1965. 'It's only poetic justice!' I rationalise as we survey the locked doors and shutters. 'We told the fellow we were going home today, and he didn't even send over his offsider.'

Dad's serious countenance changes to one of dawning realisation. 'I suppose a bit of self-help wouldn't go astray in the circumstances,' he drawls with his half-sheepish, half-quizzical lopsided grin – a grin which had probably got him out of a fair bit of trouble with grandmother in days gone by.

So without another wasted word, we break into the establishment. My current best trophy trout of over 6 pounds mysteriously signs himself out. We ogle a few of his even heavier classmates, leave the money on the counter – this is, after all, an honest Break and Enter – and get out of town as quick as we can!

Now we are at Pedder in January 1978. Dad brilliantly solves the problem of what to do with your long-dreamed-of trophy trout when there's no deep freeze or taxidermist within cooee. The Dunford Field Method is easy. Just have half a bag of casting plaster at hand. Leave the finished product under your rig to harden and dry, then catch another 12½-pounder to go with the first! Which I do.

Pedder again, this time on 20 December 1980: a clear evening of abating winds, one night before the full moon. I have very strong suspicions about the monster Dad is allegedly playing. I have had them from only a couple of minutes from hookup. But I let him go through the motions for a good 12 or 15 minutes, and I am completely unrepentant. He is animated and enjoying himself, so who am I to tell him that his big fish had already broken and gone in about half a minute flat?

The canny Pedder monsters really know the ropes. Not for them the long dizzying runs into the middle distance. They merely drop straight down onto the drowned tea tree, the nearest branch, double back for the perfect half-hitch and use the extra purchase to snap the connection with an impatient little shake of the head. To add insult to injury, once you are firmly half-hitched round a springy tea tree branch and separated by 30 yards of fly line, one immovable object feels much the same as another. Dad doesn't know the difference, but he's not the first or the only one.

But then the triumph. Less than an hour later, fishing a Corduliid dead drift, he hooks and lands a 9-pounder. By the leviathan Pedder standards of the day, it is 'only' a baby monster, but not too many venerable 70-year-old fly fishers can boast of better.

Pedder a third time, a little over a year later. 'Just as well we're getting the fresh stuff straight out of the sky,' says Dad as he surveys the tannin-stained waters. 'I could never drink that dirty brown stuff out of the lake, like Ted and them.' He has spent countless happy hours in the rain, minutely adjusting the canvas rigging and dickying around with all the leaks and drips, until they are channelled into orderly little rivulets that run off the awning and plink into the camp water tank. No small boy could enjoy himself more.

What he doesn't know is that all the time he's rejoicing in nature's purest drop, 'Guess Who' is quietly supplementing the supplies with that 'dirty brown stuff' straight from the lake.

Then there is the night at Buckenderra when Dad's return is long overdue. Alarm bells are well and truly ringing, and the search is on. Way down the Middlingbank Arm I think I see something in the dark. One of the rocky shadows seems to detach itself, and for a moment a slight, spare-framed figure is silhouetted against the light of a makeshift moon. As I draw closer, I can hear the sweet unmistakeable music of a double-taper fly line.

Dad has simply not budged from the little sandy spot where I left him in the afternoon. With up to nine times the volume of water in Sydney Harbour to choose from, he is still flaying the same cubic metre of water! 'It was just like the beach,' he enthuses before I have a chance to chastise him. 'They just kept coming in at me.' Indeed, considering his normal lack of conversation, he is as talkative as I can ever remember him. We stand there in the torchlight admiring his catch, emphatically the best of his life: five spanking rainbows and browns all taken in one frenetic half-hour, when the rest of us have struggled to get even one.

Another moment comes into view. It is the end of another summer's fishing, and we are taking him to catch the train back to Wingham. There is a handshake and a simple, 'Thanks for everything.' It makes all the hours of camp cooking, tying his flies and undoing his countless 'windknots' seem worthwhile. 'Don't forget to write and tell me what the lake levels are doing,' he says. Now, after finding so many of my old letters filed away in his drawer, I realise he was talking about a lot more than just water levels.

. . .

Fifty years after it all started, I returned to visit the shrine where Dad and Pa caught their famous brace so long ago and far away. We found the very place where we once lay on the bank and watched the rainbows idling along in the crystal depths of the prodigious Dairy Pool. We found what was left of the watercourse. But the pool itself was gone.

Where once there was a brimful sandy-bottomed meadow pool up to 8 feet deep, the whole floodplain that it occupied had been swept away. The stream itself had cut its way down to the original bedrock, and there was only a languid ankle-deep flow over bare rock. It was as if the whole thing had been only a dream.

But it was not. The Dairy Pool and all that it meant, and everything that it started, is deep in my psyche. The fact that it is not there today only adds to the mystique.

Once again Dad reappears in my mind. He is talking with his friend Don, who wants to know how it is that he doesn't seem to get lonely spending all that time on his own in the flat. 'Yes,' says the master of understatement, 'but don't forget – I've got the memories.' And so have I.

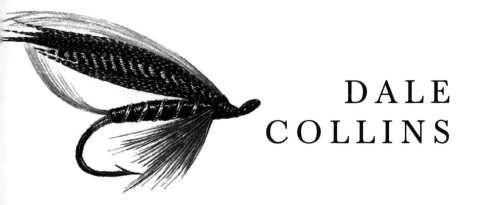

DALE
COLLINS

DALE CUTHBERT Collins was born in Balmain, Sydney in 1897, the son of a doctor.

He began his career as a journalist, working for the *Melbourne Herald* newspaper and *Table Talk* magazine. He also contributed stories to the weekly *Bulletin* magazine. In 1922 he accompanied A.Y. Gowen, an American millionaire, on a world cruise on the latter's motor yacht, *Speejacks*. His descriptive account of this voyage, *Sea Tracks of the Speejacks Round the World* (1923) led to the best selling novel *Ordeal* (1924).

Dale Collins wrote a number of adventure stories for children but did not always use his own name. Sometimes he wrote as 'Stephen Fennimore', and at least one novel, *Sunset Plains*, appeared under both names. He also wrote novels for adults, using the pen-name of 'Michael Copeland', and a travel book, containing personal reminiscences, appeared as *Victoria's My Home Ground.*

He died in 1956, aged 59.

The following story is from *Victoria's My Home Ground,* and although Collins was not a fisherman himself, he paints a portrait of an era and of Fred Fry, a legendary figure on the Howqua.

CHAPTER 23

New Chum Rides the Range

If you are one of those wiry tan types born to the saddle, the expedition would have seemed quite commonplace; to this plump soft literary gent in his fifties – who, even in his youth, was more interested in books than physical activity – the invitation came as a challenge, and to accept it was both foolhardy and exciting.

When we were last in Mansfield we met Fred Fry briefly – the Forestry man who fished for trout from horseback – and I hazarded the opinion that we should meet him again as he had promised to take me out to the headwaters of the Howqua ...

Then came a letter from Chief Forester Jim Westcott announcing that he and Fred Fry were off up the Howqua, and would I care to be with them? It was one of the easiest trips they did, and though we'd be five days in the saddle, it was a packhorse job, which meant that we'd be walking all the time. We would sleep in shacks, camp out two nights and take our own food. What about it?

I remembered the country as stern and wild, I hadn't been on a horse since I was last there as a child of ten, and the climb up Collins Street hill was about all the mountaineering I cared for.

But oh, heck! If I didn't grasp the chance now I certainly never would, and you could only die once.

I caught the coach to Mansfield ...

The Rover lurched across the rocky ford and the waters of the Howqua splashed up. I tasted them on my tongue. The last time I had done so I was a child. Downstream somewhere was the site of the vanished Tarika. I had been here before. We were back in the gold country, and this narrow valley had once held a flourishing township. Howqua had had all the buildings I have listed in the case of other ghost towns. This very bit of rough track showed on the old maps as a proper street with a name. Today only the gums and the wattles and the lightwoods and Fred Fry's house, which he built for himself when the roof of the ancient office of the Grand Rand mine, where he used to live, blew off one night. The walls of that office are crumbling away, and soon the blackberries will cover the last traces.

Nothing will remain then of Howqua. Already, on the charts of walking clubs and the like, its name has been replaced by Fry's, and the miles upstream are measured from Fry's. Soon it will be Fry's on the official maps. Years after you and I and he aren't here any more, some bright young thing come to catch trout – for I feel that the fetish of the trout is so deeply ingrained that it will survive even when interplanetary weekends are available – will wonder how such a lovely spot came by the prosaic name of Fryston. There'll be nobody to explain.

'Hullo, Dale.' Fred came to greet us, his leathery face wreathed in smiles. 'Hullo, Fred.' I thought I had forgotten him, but I hadn't. These real men of the bush are personalities. Fifty-eight, tall and powerful and muscular, Fred has lived hard all his life. He has no time for the cities. He dwells alone, and when he leaves his home – apart from an occasional visit for stores to Mansfield, whither he rides on horseback – it is only to go further into the ranges. He has eighteen horses and two dogs, and finds them company enough, though everybody lured by trout to those parts calls on him and relies on him for help.

He takes them in and brings them out. (I like those phrases.) If they're of a mind he can take them up on top. His callers range from Field Marshal Blamey down to Bill Smith. Some boy scouts he befriended presented him with a visitors' book. The intervals between the dates may be long, but it holds some interesting names.

There can't be many other men in this mechanised age who ply the old trade of operating a pack team.

The house he built himself has a large living room, two bedrooms and a workshop and a store. The feature about it which fascinated me were the great beams across the roof. These were the size and thickness of large telephone poles. Twelve ran from end to end and as many shorter ones across between them.

When I marvelled that he had been able to get them into place Fred said it was easy. With the frame erected, you simply sat on top and hauled them up in the bend of a rope.

'Oh, I see,' I said, since it would have been silly to question such a simple and obvious explanation, but I still haven't a notion how he did it.

Two cattle dogs lay with their noses on the doorstep. They never ventured in. Horses came to the door, grumping and snorting as they asked for bread. In most of the country I've been through the folk can tell you all about the performances of motor cars. Here was the old bush where horses still mattered, and were as much individuals as any humans.

I met Mick, who was going with us as a packhorse. If ever an animal had personality, it was Mick. His eye was knowing and he wore on the end of his grizzled nose a neat white moustache, brushed out at each side in a sweep, like a brigadier's. Mick valued this unusual ornament, and wouldn't let you touch it. I was to come to admire the way he and his fellow toiler, Rose, carried their clumsy 200-pound packs through the bush, missing trees infallibly, even with only inches to spare, their great hooves treading as neatly as a circus pony's. They came between heavy draughts and cart horses, but somehow they looked as big and sturdy as elephants.

On the other side of the stream was a tin shed where, in the days before Fred entered the employment of the Commission, Forestry men slept on occasion. Jim remembered it as a place full of scampering rats.

'And it still is,' said Fred. 'That's what makes me so wild that some fool went and killed my snake that lived there.'

'Did he in our time?' asked Jim.

'Suppose so. He'd been there ages.'

'Was he poisonous?' I enquired.

'I suppose so, but he was death on rats. Silly idiots! Why couldn't they leave a man's snake alone?' Fred took out a stone and began to sharpen his knife. He felt its edge fondly. 'Could shave a mouse sleeping,' he said. He had a bushman's turn for a phrase, and lyrebirds were pheasants to him, wombats badgers. 'I shod all the horses last night, Jim.'

We sat late talking at Fred's place. The night was warmish, but it seemed natural to have a fire blazing in the big iron fireplace. Fred brewed tea as black as tar. It tasted good, though after a week of it I was to wonder whether I hadn't heard of something called tannin poisoning ...

The day came in blue and gold, parrot's jewels against the cloudless sky, kookaburras laughing.

The horses were saddled up. One, irritated by the attention of the crotchety 12-year-old dog, Storm – both he and his mate, Digger, became wildly excited whenever the time for departure drew near, and made nuisances of themselves – gave a fine exhibition of pulling away, lashing out and general cavorting.

'Not ... not mine, I hope, Jim?' I asked anxiously.

'Mine, worse luck,' said Jim. 'And I'm relieved to see that Fred is taking some of the sting out of him.'

Indeed, Fred did so. His animals meant everything to him, and were always his first concern, but he would stand no nonsense from horse or dog. The way in which they obeyed, respected and loved him suggested that discipline is a good thing in the family.

Fred had filled and buckled the heavy packs and now carried them out to the front. And when I say heavy, I mean just that. They were made of solid black leather and were built for strength without any attempt at weak compromises in the matter of saving weight.

I tried to lift one, but it seemed to be nailed to the ground. Mick eyed them with his wily eye as he walked into the lane between them. The saddle he carried was also built for strength and would have been weight enough for most horses. Fred picked up the first pack and swung it high into the air. Its steel rings slipped over steel hooks on that great saddle on that great horse. He repeated the operation on the other side. He might have been handling feather cushions. Then he piled cunningly on top bags of food for men and beasts, and the tent. The whole was strapped in place with great bands of black leather with heavy buckles – all again made for strength. The mountain balanced perfectly.

The younger Jim made well-meant efforts to assist. They weren't appreciated. Whatever he did was wrong. Fred was the expert and proud of it. He would rather do the job himself. Now I am quick to learn a lesson like that. I stood aside then and throughout the trip. This was not only wise, but much more comfortable.

Rose's turn then. Fred wasn't even short of breath when he finished. 'This is Molly,' he said. 'She's yours, Dale. Leave it to her, and you won't go wrong.'

I fell in love with Molly on the spot. She had a kindly and liquid brown eye, her coat shone with content, and even if amidships she bore some resemblance to a barrel, that gave her a comfortable look.

'I am a complete mug, Molly,' I said, stroking her white blaze. 'Look after me, like a good girl.'

She gave a little reassuring whinny. The racing writers of the moment always refer to a certain Chicquita as the glamour mare. They can have Chicquita and all her glamour. Me, I'll take Molly.

Assisted only by a hoist from Fred similar to those he gave the packbag, I leapt lightly into the saddle and presently my feet found the stirrup irons.

Aboard a horse for the first time in over 40 years I sat at ease, recovering my breath, whilst my companions mounted. Then with Fred leading Mick, and the younger Jim, Rose, and with Jim bringing up the rear – I had a feeling that he was there to pick up the pieces should anything happen to me – our little cavalcade moved off into the blue.

Clip-clop! Clip-clop! How well I was to get to know that sound, and the gentle sway as Molly ambled on and on, her small and pretty hooves tapping and tapping.

I have confessed my love for old Mother Murray, but Miss Howqua was the sweetheart of my childhood and she had not aged a bit. She was still young and fresh and beautiful and laughing. She sparkled crystal clear over the polished stones and boulders with never a trace of silt or sand. The smallest pebble was visible 10 feet below; the trout with fanning tails were clearer than those in an aquarium.

As if to strike a high note for this reunion, two great wedge-tailed eagles flew down the stream at treetop height and, perching on a branch, stared at us along their patrician noses.

Eagles as close as that were something to a city dweller. 'We're just coming to the first ford,' said Jim.

'Good!' I said – though perhaps that wasn't exactly what I meant.

'Molly will cope with it.' She would have to.

The bank was fairly steep, and a drop of a foot or so. With a confidence her rider didn't share, she stepped down into the stream, and lowering her head a little to look into the depths, picked her way across. The iron shoes rang on the stones, which shifted sometimes; she stepped neatly away from the bigger boulders or over them; the spray went up in a glittering shower and the laughter of the waters rose loudly. Nothing to worry about in this: it was exhilarating, refreshing. 'There are twenty-three more during the morning.' 'That suits Molly and me.' And I meant it. The bush had closed in all about us, and the world of men was far away.

All at once a great factory chimney rose out of the green, towering up a matter of 60 feet, and 12 feet square at the base. All about a tangle of gums and wattles. No need to be told what had set it there. Only gold could have been responsible. And so it proved, for this had been the battery and treatment plant for the mines. Once there had been a great water wheel, too, 63 feet in diameter with a 30 foot shaft a foot in diameter. When the gold petered out, this had been dismantled and dragged out by horse teams. The shaft became the propeller shaft of a ship which was in need of one down in Melbourne. It fitted its new purpose to a T. That was no mean feat of haulage, seeing the country through which the teams and their great loads had to pass. And yet the labours of the miners of the old days remain even more remarkable. Along the hillside wound a water-race which ran for 3½ miles. A big tunnel 300 yards long had been driven through the rocky hillside with dynamite – or more likely only gunpowder and pick and shovel. In this way the power was brought to the wheel to send it threshing round.

Perhaps we are right to bow down to silly gold. It certainly makes men work wonders. Clip-clop! Clip-clop!

The narrow red track – just wide enough for single file – climbed steeply until we rode along a ledge 200 feet high with the glinting river and the glinting treetops far below; it curved and wound, and sometimes its stony surface canted sharply towards a sheer drop. (Well, I'm not doing badly. I should be scared, but I know I can trust Molly.) Then down to another ford leading to a flat of dappled sunlight and shadow, the breeze lost. Again a splash through the cool waters where the red cliffs shut down on our side and the flat was now on the other bank. It was all so beautiful that the grime of the world, the murk of the years fell away, and World War I had yet to be fought. Yes, Miss Howqua ever was the river of perpetual youth.

At the Four-Mile, exotic among the darker colouring of the bush, the bright, fresh greens of English trees burgeoned suddenly with a suggestion of a northern spring. A clearing had been made on the slope of a hill and on a sheltered flat snug in a curved arm of the river, men had planted these strangers – a whole plantation of New Australians which had taken sturdy root and were flourishing. A neat one-roomed white shack stood in their midst. Fred had had a hand in building it – as he has a hand in most everything in these parts. Plans are afoot for the addition of another room with a connecting verandah. That old chimney will provide some of the brick work, and in his weekends Fred is gathering material.

Clip-clop! Clip-clop!

At the Eight-Mile we paused for lunch at a Commission shack. Nothing pretentious about it – just a log hut with an iron roof and fireplace and a single row of bunks round the side filled with dried bracken. An earthen floor. But the door stood hospitably open, and all travellers were invited to make free use of it. To the few who passed that way it was a boon.

Only assisted by Fred's firm shoulder and strong right arm I sprang nimbly – well, more or less nimbly – from the saddle. The horses were tethered in the shade, and Fred went to work with the manner of a man who has a pressing engagement. The heavy packs and saddles were swung to the ground with practised ease, and Mick, with a twitch of his white moustache and a shrug of broad flanks, said that that was much better. They munched the sweet grass, and did not need watering, for they had drunk often enough from the stream as we waded the fords, always careful to wait until any disturbance had subsided and the drink was crystal clear again.

'Now I think I'll get some trout,' said Fred.

He had carried his precious rod slung in a canvas case over his back. It looked like a rifle, so that in his slouch hat at the head of our little column he had suggested the pictures of a Boer leading a commando group. Now he fitted the rod together, attended to the line, chose a fly, smiling happily in anticipation as if this were a most unusual treat instead of almost a daily occurrence.

Ted, his wonder horse, who was more than human – said Fred – wasn't with us. He had reached a span of years which in a human life would have made him seventy. He was a bit under the weather, but was coming good again. Yes, thank God! He'd be as good as ever in a few weeks' time. Jim said it was a marvel to see him in action. Even if a trout hit him on the face he didn't move a muscle, and on one occasion, whilst the rest followed the track, he had taken the angler miles upstream, like standing in a gallery looking down from high above.

In respectful silence we followed the expert, and I was specially hushed because I realised I was about to be initiated into a great mystery.

Fred was in no doubt about where to go. He knew every yard of the Howqua. Pushing through the scrub he emerged by a deep, dark pool. He had forgotten all about us. Stepping out on a rock he sent the thin, light yards of line dancing through the air just wherever he wished. He was more sturdy than graceful as a general thing, but now his movements were as flowing as a ballet dancer's. At the second cast a trout leapt in a little silver flurry and took the hook. Fred played him and brought him in and dropped him in his bag. He wasn't a world-beater, but a rainbow a foot long. It was a beginning.

Disdaining waders, wearing riding boots and pants, Fred marched into the stream. The line flicked again and again, reminding me of the delicate proboscis of a butterfly probing a flower, though in truth it was even more pliant and nimble than that. His brown face wore a new expression of absorbed interest. This, I saw, was a science and a spell, a kind of enchantment. If somebody had told Fred at that moment that his house had been burned he would have nodded absently and made no comment.

I began to realise what Hal and the others had meant. Here was a healthy and happy drug of escapism such as mankind rarely finds and so often needs.

The ten fish the law allows a day were in the bag in about twice as many minutes. I should be able to add that now Fred lent me his rod, and at my first cast I landed a 4-pound brown trout.

This, however, is a true record. Fred wouldn't have lent me his rod if I'd gone on bended knee, and if in a moment of insanity he had, all I should have caught would have been a blue gum or the seat of my trousers.

He might make it look delightfully easy. It wasn't. We took the fish back to the hut and cleaned them out reverently in the little creek, being particular to take out the black strip down the inside of the spine. Then we wrapped them tenderly in bright green fronds of bracken, and spoke in happy anticipation of supper that night.

To be honest, I wasn't sorry to reach the Fourteen-Mile in the late afternoon. To you chaps who spend your days galloping over the great open spaces, 14 miles in a day on horseback would be a bagatelle. To me it was enough, quite enough. True, we had done it all at a walk, but the way had been up hill and down dale – I spurn the chance for a pun there – and a novice at least had not been able to relax for a moment. My borrowed leggings were so tight that they had stopped circulation; my old grey flannel bags had chafed; the saddle no longer seemed the proud throne it had been that morning.

'How do you feel, Dale?' asked Fred, extending his arms as if to a baby.

'Fine, fine, Fred. Perhaps a shade stiff.'

He planted me firmly on the good earth, and with an effort I kept a balance on my gent's tan town shoes.

Another shack at the Fourteen-Mile perched on a little rise by still another creek, looking out across the river at a densely wooded and sharp hillside which was beautiful in the golden light. So that there should be no mistake, a large trout taking a fly was painted on the door. I was told that the artist first hooked his fish then painted it. I wonder was it really as big as that? What a temptation for a little modernistic elongation!

To one who had just received his water rate demand, it was shocking to see that the last people who'd been at the cabin had left the tap turned on. Then it struck me that it was odd to have running water at the Fourteen-Mile, and that there wasn't any tap. The stream just poured out of the end of a piece of green plastic hose. That was stranger than ever, for the Howqua was quite 40 feet below, and there was no sign of pump or windmill.

Fred explained. He had had a hand in building this house, too, and, indeed, it had the same smooth logs up in the roof. Something about the hillside opposite struck him whilst they were at work. He investigated and found a creek which even he had never known was there. Easy to lay 350ft of hose down the slope and through the river and up the other side, providing perpetual running water by gravitation. An outdoor shower bath was installed.

That water, too, had some peculiar quality. I've never tasted better. We kept a mug on the stones nearby and it was seldom out of use.

In the fashion of the remote bush, though there was a large bolt on the front door, it lacked a padlock. Within was a stock of tinned food, ranged on shelves, which must have been worth well over £50, from my experience as a husband who sometimes takes the string bag and does the shopping. The floor was made of slabs, and four bunks in two tiers occupied one end, with the fireplace at the other. A table, sideboard and chairs completed the furnishings. We admired the piece of perspex let into the roof as a skylight, and were impressed by provision of a proper lavatory, fenced in with brush.

But again it seemed strange to me, for this property belonged to Bob Ritchie of Delatite Station, and from what I've seen of station homes, he would have been much more comfortable there, and as for the trout, he probably had a stream on the estate.

Still, we were well pleased that he'd taken the fancy to build at the Fourteen-Mile, for he provided us with comfortable lodgings for the night.

Whilst Fred saw to the horses, we went down to the river, but not to fish. Armed with soap and towels we walked 50 yards and found a perfect pool where we stripped off and slipped in. The nearest I shall ever get to a bath in lightly iced champagne, and never was a bathe more appreciated. I lay in a frothing cascade and all the aches and pains and sweat and toil were washed away. I've swum at Port Sudan in the Red Sea, and in many other places in the tropics, and welcomed the benediction of the water after the steamy heat. But that water was tepid and usually muddy. This was chilled and clear and bracing. You could cup your hands and drink your bathwater.

My respect, and affection, for Molly was increased when I discovered how slippery those rocks were. Even with bare feet it was difficult to stand on them. One would have thought her polished iron shoes would have skidded in all directions.

Dear Molly! Dear Miss Howqua! I felt so fine when I climbed out that the fears for tomorrow vanished away.

Up at the house it was time for young Jim to fling his aerial over the bough of a gum and contact Mansfield. Oh, yes, we could do that with the aid of a box of tricks about 6 inches square which fitted neatly into a canvas haversack.

When would you have liked to have been born? I sometimes think I should have made my entrance 50 years earlier, written my books in a much less competitive era, lived through the days when Britain bestrode the world and the lion's roar set that much simpler jungle all of a tremble, and have been safely buried now. On the other hand, 1897 wasn't a bad choice. My children and yours will have no sense of wonder. They will not be able to conceive a world without cars and planes and radio and all the other marvels. When television comes to Australia they will accept it as a matter of course. Yet in my little span I can remember when one stood to watch a horseless carriage and the telephone on the wall with the handle at the side was a device which made many panic when they attempted to use it.

Our children wouldn't have stopped their play when they saw young Jim squat down by his set in the sunset hour and begin to intone:

'This is VL3CK calling VL3AE – VL3CK calling VL3AE. Are you receiving me? Over.'

'Radio,' the children would have said nonchalantly. 'Yeah, a walkie-talkie set.'

And that would have been that to them.

But to me – dear old buffer – Jim knelt before a magic shrine and by an incantation summoned a voice out of the empty blue. Had heavenly choirs come in out of space it would have been natural enough. Instead Florence from the office in Mansfield reported that a small fire had broken out near Merrijig, caused, it was believed, by lightning in a local thunderstorm. Bill and Fred had gone out – no damage – fire under control.

'We're at the Fourteen-Mile, Florence. Nothing to report. Did you send that telegram for me? Over.'

Florence had. Over.

Not sensational tidings to exchange, perhaps, but surely it was dramatic to be able to talk to Florence across all those miles of tumbled hills through which our little cavalcade had crept.

Within the hut another priest was busy. Fred was grilling the trout. He performed his office with care and love, and when we ate it was in seemly silence and with due appreciation.

'Ah!' we sighed – grace after trout, amen …

[On the party's eventual return to the Fourteen-Mile, which had seemed primitive a couple of days earlier:]

Someone had left the water running, and we stayed in the Howqua for an hour, and Fred caught trout and there was nothing ahead for the tenderfoot but a simple ride which was child's play, though it had seemed quite an adventure once. The focus had changed. The shack spelt civilization now.

Did I ever think I was rather good to do this bit of the ride? Why, you could have put a babe in arms in the saddle, and he wouldn't have been troubled.

Some of the trout Fred had caught overnight we'd salted down, and at the Eight-Mile he went out again to gather more for the people back at Mansfield who hadn't had the luck to be with us.

He returned with nine, but no big ones.

'I dunno,' said Fred, 'but I'd like your English wife to see and eat a real trout. There's a pool down a bit where I fancy I could find one.'

And off he tramped, tireless in the quest.

'Only a tiddler,' he said when he came back, and produced a 4-pounder, which is quite a length of fish. We rejoiced and cleaned it and made it ready for the long journey.

Clip-clop!

Just too easy.

Suddenly a shout from Jim: he'd found my pen lying by the trackside …

Fred, though he didn't show it, was a bit huffish that his bushman's eyes had missed that tiny spear of blue. (Personally, I'd forgotten I'd lost it.) But honours were even soon, for Fred leapt down and picked up my handkerchief. Queer to think of these trivialities, lying out in the sunshine and the moonshine, sniffed at by wombats, pecked at by magpies, and finally found again.

Back at Fry's we took stock of the stores. Jim had been right.

The food which had seemed to me enough for a regiment had dwindled away. Owing to the plentiful supplies of trout, however, we hadn't needed as much meat as expected. My silverside was still intact. We left it with Fred, and housewives may be surprised to learn that, after a week of being carted about in a flour bag in blazing sunshine and dumped on and off the packs and generally mistreated, it was still as good as gold.

Maybe in the country the meat starts off fresher than we get it in the city.

My parting from Molly was a sentimental moment.

'Old lady,' I said, 'I couldn't have done it without you.'

She spurned a piece of barley sugar, so I gave her the last of the bread, which wasn't as stale as one would have expected.

'Been a real holiday for Miss Molly,' said Fred. 'She usually carries packs, but she's the surest, safest mare of the lot.'

Rather a shock to find that my steed on other occasions was assigned to such a humdrum role, but she'd carried her live pack faithfully and well and I still wouldn't change her for any pampered, spoilt thoroughbred.

She nuzzled my shirt with her soft, damp, black nose, and her brown eyes were affectionate.

Three hours later I was saying I wished I was riding her again, for the lightly laden truck wouldn't grip on the rough, steep road over Timbertop and we had to cut down trees and load up with stones to get to the summit.

Molly and I would have taken it in our steady stride.

Clip-clop! Clip-clop!

This story, like most true stories, ends in an anti-climax.

We put the precious trout in the refrigerator overnight. Various locals, called by telephone, gratefully came and took their gifts with salaams. Five over for me, in addition to the big one. They were packed most carefully and next day the coach chap put them underneath so that they wouldn't get the sun. He, too, realised that trout weren't like ordinary luggage. I didn't bother to mention that I hadn't caught them myself, and he treated me with more respect than I usually receive and gave me a cigarette.

'Envy you,' he said. 'Wonderful sport.'

'Quite fun,' I agreed in lordly fashion.

Whilst I was waiting for the coach to start a quiet kind of cove asked me where I'd been. I told him.

'How would you like to take 800 cattle up that last pinch?' he asked.

I declared flatly that it would be utterly impossible, but he said he and his brother did each spring. Well, it takes all kinds to make a world …

We cooked the famous trout as soon as I got home. It tasted like slightly sour putty.

M.E. (BILL) McCAUSLAND

1894–1974

THE FOLLOWING article from *Fly-fishing in Australia and New Zealand* (1949) is reproduced to give the reader some idea of fly-fishing over 50 years ago. The book went through three editions between 1949 and 1957, indicating its popularity in those days.

He also contributed articles to the *Herald and Weekly Times* publication 'Wild Life and Outdoors', edited by naturalist Philip Crosbie Morrison.

The article is reproduced with permission from Lothian Books, Melbourne, and is exactly as it appeared in the 1st edition.

Editor's note: When reading the monetary values described in the article, it should be compared with an average man's wage at that time. A figure of £5 per week would be normal.

Selvyt: A polishing cloth for silver.

Cerolene: A hard paste, pink in colour and similar to mucilin etc.

Amadou: A dried fungus, brown in colour and very absorbent, used to dry flies by placing the fly in a fold of amadou and gently squeezing.

CHAPTER 24

The Genesis

Much has been written on the use of artificial flies for the capture of Trout, and although some very comprehensive books have been published, they have been mostly written by English and American writers concerning the conditions obtaining in their own countries. While the principles of this sport remain the same the world over, it is, nevertheless, a fact that no book dealing comprehensively with Australian and Tasmanian conditions has yet been written. It is with the object of assisting the local angler that the writer offers this book, and also to give a modicum of assistance in encouraging that grandest of all hobbies, the luring of the Trout with the artificial fly.

To those men who have crossed the equator of their lives and to whom the retiring age already appears on the horizon, I would say: 'Take up fly-fishing.' Reasonable proficiency in the casting of a fly is not unduly difficult. It is never too late to commence, and the sunshine and the open air, the sweet music of a stream or the soft stillness of a lake or lagoon, together with the whole-hearted interest in nature that follows inevitably, offer the best recreation the world has to bestow. To the family man it fills a long-felt want. The week-end picnic venue can be chosen near Trout water and everybody is happy. When the day is reached that a fish fiercely rushes that fly tied and cast by yourself, then indeed is life complete.

To the experienced fly fisherman there is little help one can offer. He has doubtless reached the point where only the controversial matters are unsolved, and far be it from the writer to join issue on these matters. Whether the Trout is colour conscious or not is something we may never know, and if perchance we do know and it should make easier the catching of fish on artificial flies, it may not be entirely for good. It is in the difficulty of the art, allied with those odd days when everything goes right, that lies the essential charm of this fascinating sport.

The Beginner

The person who has decided to take up fly-fishing, but who has never handled a fly rod before, should bear in mind that fishing with the dry fly is an art to be approached with some reverence. It is essentially not the 'chucking of bait' into the stream to catch fish. When the light is off the water I know of no freshwater fish that is easier to catch with bait than the Trout. The man who sits up all night fishing with wattle grubs or oysters and proudly displays his string of fish has nothing to boast about. Schnapper are probably just as hard to catch with bait as Trout after sundown, and he is only murdering some of the most sporting fish extant. Fishing a river with a spinner and automatic reel, in my opinion, is little better; it displays greater energy, that is all.

Rod

It is extremely difficult to convey in writing the essential points that one looks for in a fly rod.

The average angler endeavours to make one fly rod suit all purposes, from casting for ½-pounders in the Kennet and the Wye to the playing of the wonderful rainbows of Tasmania's Great Lake. A good rod presents a kind of paradox, insofar as it should possess resilience and yet be on the stiff side. Lightness and strength are desirable. In brief, your rod must have a quick recovery. A floppy rod in a head wind can be irritating enough to drive an angler almost to distraction. My suggestions for an all-round utility rod are as follow:

Description – split cane of super quality.

Weight – 5½ to 6½oz.

Length – 9 feet (approx.).

Split cane, or, to be correct, bamboo, is made either single or double built; the double built is more expensive and has better lasting qualities, but we have used single built rods for years with the most satisfactory results, and with proper care your rod will have many years of life.

The cost will naturally be governed by your pocket, but do not be misled by the would-be expert who suggests that you buy a cheap rod to commence. You cannot hope to learn to cast with an inferior rod, and the net result will probably be that you will give up in despair after the first few attempts, and decide that fly casting is too difficult. Good rods can be purchased for as low as £8, but a first-class maker will probably want from £10 to £15 for his product. Whilst rods by J.M. Gillies may cost up to £25, remember that the best of our local makers' products compare more than favourably with any of the imported rods, and you can hold your local man responsible if a fault develops, which is not always possible with an imported article. In any case, if you are buying from a local maker, he will take pains to see that you get a rod suited to your casting capacity, and will generally put you on the right track; if you are buying from a store, then endeavour to secure the help of an experienced fly fisherman before you make your choice. Most shops have experienced men in charge of their department.

Line

A fly line is generally tapered at both ends, so that when one taper is worn out or broken the line can be reversed and the other taper brought into use. Your line must be of good quality. A fly casting line is made in lengths of either 30 or 35 yards and of varying weights. The price ranges up to £5, and the maker of your rod will tell you what weight of line will best suit your rod; but, failing that, it should be borne in mind that it is better to have your line too heavy than too light. With a following wind, the light line will be quite satisfactory, but one cannot always get the wind one desires, and in the case of an adverse wind the heavier line is easier to cast.

Reel

The reel must not be too heavy or too light for the rod, otherwise the balance will be destroyed and your wrist will become unduly tired after a long day's casting. If you intend going after large fish in big water, you will require a reel which holds about 100 yards of backing, as well as your tapered line. Any reputable store will stock suitable backing, which should be neatly whipped on to an end of the tapered line with fine waxed silk. If you have been fortunate enough to have had your backing immersed on several occasions, it is advisable to secure new backing at the commencement of the following season – for remember that if your backing becomes rotten and breaks, you will probably lose your expensive tapered line.

Ball bearing reels are expensive and, in our opinion, unnecessary; a good centre-pin reel will give you good service and is much cheaper. Have your reel selected by an expert to match your rod.

Casts

Tapered casts are sold in different lengths from 6 feet, but there is little doubt that 9 feet should be the minimum length for you to use. Calibration of gut is important, and much has been written regarding the necessary fineness, shadow, glitter, etc., of gut, but if you buy a few casts tapered to 2x, 3x and 4x respectively, you will be equipped to tackle most waters. In gin clear water with strong sunlight, you may use as fine as 5x, but you will be fortunate to catch many fish with any cast in such circumstances.

Flies

Do not rush in and buy a conglomerate assortment of flies. If you have purchased your rod from a local maker, he will advise you as to the type of flies you will want, taking into consideration the particular water you are likely to fish.

When you land your first Trout with a dry fly, then inevitably that fly will have no equal to you for a time; but as you progress, your natural observation and experience will assist you in selecting the right fly to use for any particular occasion. However, you may find it hard to obtain advice on a selection, and the following is a list of good utility flies for Victorian waters:

March Brown	Red Tag
Wickham's Fancy	Coch-y-Bondhu
Furnace Brown	Red Spinner
Whirling Dun	Red Spinner (spent)
Orange Quill	Black Gnat (Halfords)
Coachman	Royal Coachman
Cinnamon Sedge	Dunne's Brown Ant
Greenwell's Glory	Greenwell's Glory (spent)

Flies are tied on various sized hooks, but, generally speaking, you will want them tied on hooks numbers 1, 2 and 3. A few smaller sizes, either 0 or 00, should be obtained with the Whirling Dun, Black Gnat and Royal Coachman.

Dressing of Line

To keep a line in good condition, it is essential that it be dressed thoroughly and often. During a long day it may be necessary to dry and dress a line more than once to keep it afloat, and at least once after each outing. Several excellent line floatants are on the market.

To dress a line it is first run out and dried, and the dressing well rubbed in. A piece of soft chamois leather is as good as anything for applying the dressing to the line, but a piece of dry clean flannel or rag will serve. The more friction that is applied while dressing the line the better the result. Friction imparts warmth, which opens the pores of the line and allows the dressing to penetrate. When the dressing has been rubbed in, the line should be lightly polished with a selvyt brand, polishing cloth .

Try to avoid putting the line away on the reel for any length of time while it is wet. It takes little time to run the line off the reel on to a line dryer, or even on to a hearth-rug, and it will not take long to dry if the room is warm. When the fishing season is over, the line should be run off into some receptacle free from dust (an old pillow case is excellent) and put away till the first of September arrives again, or wound on the reel and the reel put in an airtight container, together with a Gillies dehydrator.

Gut and Fly Dressing

Everyone is aware that gut must be soaked thoroughly before using. If the cast lies on the surface in curls, it is your own fault. It simply has not been soaked long enough. A thorough soaking depends on the temperature of the water. Lukewarm may soak the cast in 10 minutes, whilst icy cold water may take an hour or more to achieve the same purpose. It is advisable to take at least two spare casts in the cast damping tin with you, but when the day is over, remove them, as continual soaking tends to lessen the life of a cast. If you are in a hurry, warmish water may be used to soak casts, but be careful that it is not too hot, as this will weaken the cast. If you are fishing on still water, it will be necessary to smear a very fine coating of line floatant on the cast, and this is sometimes necessary on a river if the cast shows a tendency to sink. In this regard American Trout fishing books advocate sinking the cast to make it less visible to the fish and to avoid shadow. I have always found that it has a tendency to drag the fly under with it. It is extremely difficult to strike a fish with the fly floating and portion of the cast or line submerged. Some fishermen leave a few inches of the cast near the fly free from floatant, but we have found no advantage in this. The grease should be applied to the cast with the fingers, which are only lightly smeared for the purpose.

In oiling the fly the oil is generally applied with a small brush or feather fixed into the cork of the bottle containing the oil. Several good fly dressings are on the market, but you can make your own as follows:

Fill an aspirin bottle three-parts full of petrol and add cerolene in the ratio of one part of cerolene to ten parts of petrol (a little more or less will not matter); shake the bottle for a while and place in your cupboard. Next day it will be ready. If any cerolene is still undissolved, a further vigorous shaking will soon remedy this. Cut off portion of the web on both sides of a stiff feather and fix the butt into the cork by first making an incision in the cork with a penknife. Now cut off the feather until a length is left that will fit comfortably into the bottle, and the fly dressing equipment is ready. Apply the oil sparingly to the hackle and body of the fly. When a fly is dressed with a raffia or quill body it is unnecessary to oil anything more than the hackle and wings.

Attaching Gut to Line

There are two ordinary methods of attaching the cast to the line: either whip a small loop on the end of the taper, and, placing the loop of the gut over the loop on the line, draw the end of the gut through the line loop; or else make a single knot on the extreme end of the taper, bend the line in your fingers to make a loop, and proceed as before and draw tight.

Attaching Gut to Fly

There are several methods of attaching the fly, the two most used being the figure of eight knot and the turle. The turle is the better knot, but the figure of eight is a safe tie, so long as the top loop is forced over the eye of the hook before drawing tight, and is made as follows:

Draw the end of the cast through the eye of the hook, cross the end under the cast to make a circle, now bring the end back over the cast, making a figure of eight and bring end through first loop. When drawing tight, see that the loop is brought over the eye of the hook.

The turle knot is made by drawing the cast through the eye of the hook and allowing the fly to slide down the cast. Now make a running knot round the cast, leaving a loop. Bring the fly up through the loop and place the loop over the eye of the hook and draw tight.

Repairing Cast

Occasionally, through one's fly getting entangled in a tree or other object which is out of reach, there is no alternative but to break the cast. First, however, make every endeavour to knock the entangled fly off with a long stick, and if this cannot be accomplished, point the tip of the rod at the fly, pull the line and then break the cast by a slow pull, trying to break it as near to the fly as you can. Packets of cast points are sold at a reasonable cost, and when you have time you will find it quite practicable to put new points on the casts yourself. The two methods used are either the blood knot or the barrel knot.

Although as a general rule one fly is quite enough to deal with, some fishermen use two. The second fly is attached to the cast by a dropper, which should not be more than 3 inches long and should be placed about 3 feet from the end fly and tied against a knot in the cast, so that it will not pull along the cast if a fish is struck on it. Tie a single knot round the cast, then make a half-hitch also round the cast, and draw tight.

Landing Net

Collapsible landing nets, although having some disadvantages, are the easiest to carry and will work efficiently when one becomes accustomed to them. Choose one with a deep net, as most nets shrink considerably, and a deep net is safer with a big fish. The net should have a clip on the handle, so that it will readily fix on to a ring on haversack or belt. The haversack is better, for if the net is slung on the belt it will catch on sticks, etc., while walking along, and always at the most inconvenient moment. The haversack or bag should be light and strong, with front pockets to take the fly-boxes. A properly equipped bag will contain the following:

Fly-box, line floatant, fly dressing, cast damper, spare casts, sharp penknife, nail scissors (necessary for clipping off the end of the gut after tying on a fly) and amadou for drying the fly when it has become waterlogged, preparatory to re-oiling, or for a quick dry when a fish is rising and the fly, cast or line is sinking. Finally, a 'priest' or 'killer' to knock on the head that great sporting fellow, the Trout that has been landed.

When you find 'the fishing coat' you will doubtless affix some or all of the above articles in various arrays in and around it.

Waders

Full waders are necessary if you are to fish in water that is likely to come above the thighs, but otherwise they are cumbersome, heavy and tiring. Care must be taken to see that you do not get out of your depth when wearing them, for, full of water, they can become a danger. Stocking waders are comfortable, but do not always allow sufficient depth of water. The best waders are undoubtedly the American style of trouser waders, finishing with a belt at the waist.

Wading Boots

Boots specially manufactured with felt soles are the best obtainable, but as the soles wear out rather quickly they are expensive, and heavy hobnailed boots give a good grip for river work. For lake and lagoon work, where the bottom is clay, grass or mud, ordinary sandshoes are light and comfortable.

DON GILMOUR

DON GILMOUR was another of Tasmania's fine authors. His works included *The Tasmanian Trout, Trout Fishing in Australia,* four books on the trout fishery of Tasmania and many articles.

Gilmour was a life member of the Northern Tasmanian Fisheries Association following service to that organisation both as president and patron.

He was also involved in the Victorian Fly Fishers' Association, the Tasmanian Fly Fishers' Club, and was vice-president of both the Australian Freshwater Fishermen's Assembly and the Australian Casting Association.

He wrote a weekly fishing column for *The Examiner* for 15 years and for the *Weekly Times* for 8 years, had a radio program for 6 years and presented a weekly television segment for TNT9 for a decade.

He also taught an adult education course on the principles of fly-fishing for more than a decade. It was no surprise when he was inducted into the Tasmanian Hall of Fame!

The following article from *Trout Fishing in Australia* is reproduced with kind permission from his family.

CHAPTER 25

Alpine Country – The Streams

Dew still sparkled in the wispy grass fronds, while spider webs strung between tussock clumps closeted droplets of moisture soon to be evaporated by the sun climbing up into a clear sky, as I casually approached a small stream winding over the highland moors. I had to cross this stream to reach my chosen fishing spot, a lagoon renowned for the huge dun hatches it fostered.

Within metres of reaching the stream I heard a splash, surely a trout rise. Another splash. This needed investigation, so I carefully crept closer to the little stream, parted a clump of tussocks, and looked down at the shimmering waters. I blinked incredulously, for there lying beneath me and slightly upstream was a fish of 2000g (2kg) at least. To hold it in position against the current, its tail was beating firmly, yet slowly, not in the gentle rhythmic beat of a resting trout, but in that firm determined beat of a feeding trout, poised and ready to dart after its prey. What a magnificent highland monster.

Suddenly there was a splashing roll, 10 metres upstream, followed by a concentrated wave disturbance from just around the next bend, then downstream a resounding smack on the water surface. It was one of the most amazing sights I had ever encountered while fishing.

My hands shook and my knees trembled as I gently lowered myself to the ground. It was unbelievable. As I put my hand on the grass to take my weight, however, a feeling of revulsion coursed through me as a crushed animal spread over my extended palm. Looking down, I now realised why the trout were 'boiling' in the stream – the grass grubs (or army caterpillars) were on the move. Why hadn't I seen them before? I asked myself, but of course it was still early and the dew was just disappearing from the midsummer dried grasses. It was not until the dew disappeared that the grass grub continued on its restless crawling journey, ever onwards, looking for fresh pastures to strip of their foliage.

The grubs in their forward quest, moving with their roll-up, uncurl, roll-up movement, followed out a grass stem or tussock blade to its very end before dropping off on to the ground and proceeding forward. In conditions like these, where a river has tussocks interspersed with dried grasses overhanging high-cut banks, the grubs provide the fish with a wonderful feast.

A once in a lifetime experience was ahead of me, for today, feeding on the surface, were the big, previously unknown denizens of the stream, waiting poised for the grubs to drop regularly and continually into the waters.

This was a typical alpine stream with deep, undercut banks, the odd shrub growing at grotesque angles due to the strong harsh winds of this elevation, ribbon weed beds and watercress islands breaking the surface, and narrow enough to jump over in many places. Indeed I had crossed this stream many times, not bothering to fish it for the odd little 300g fish found rising here under normal conditions.

Most anglers are loath to fish these narrow streams because of the effort involved in placing the lure in the narrow confines. Now what would I use? What would any angler use in similar circumstances?

The answer to that is the theme of this whole book. No particular manner of fishing should be rated above any other – an angler splashing down a woolly worm fly, or a spinnerman lightly dropping a brown devon lure – neither one is any better than a natural bait angler flipping forward a natural grass grub bait.

There is little difference in lure presentation in the above example – no difference in the stalking skill or positioning of the angler – no difference in the severe handling of a hooked trout necessary in these awkward confined conditions which favour the escape of a hooked trout.

Throughout this book the skilful art of all types of fishing for trout will be equally applauded. A master of all techniques, not afraid to change his feathered hook for a bare hook on which to place a natural bait, or exchange his 2.75-metre rod for one of 1.5 metres with a threadline reel attached, the man who can fish under all conditions, not worried because the water is too low and clear, the wind too strong, or that there is too much undergrowth to cast, he is the man who can adjust his way of fishing to suit the conditions he finds himself facing and he is indeed the man I consider can truthfully be called an angler. I will doff my topper to him.

After all, it was either parental teaching or friendly advice, or mere chance that started you fishing with a particular type of lure. If you started fishing with natural bait, progress to the art of fly-fishing; and if you started fly-fishing, progress to the special thrills of natural bait angling. Be inquisitive and adaptable, and eager to learn new ways; that is the prerogative of all great sportsmen.

Summing up the situation I was placed in when faced with these grass-grub feeding fish, I quickly changed my 3X dry fly cast for a heavy version leader, even breaking this back to a 4kg point. Stripping off the feathers and silk from an old wet fly, I made ready to impale a close handy live grub on the hook. That was easy, but now came the more exacting task of how to deliver the grub in a natural way to the waiting trout.

Experience had taught me that to wave my rod over the edge of the bank would scare my quarry deep down into their cavern homes, for these large trout do not usually show themselves on the surface during daylight; they have grown big and fat from night feeding, when there was the least possible exposure to danger, and thus they would be continuously wary.

To get below the fish and utilise the 'blind' spot in its vision, that area directly down the backbone from eye to tail, was impossible because of the crumbled edge and insecure footing obtainable along the bank. In any case, intervening tussocks and small shrubs would interfere with an upstream cast.

A kind of once only dapping appeared to be the only method, but this would be extremely hard, for it required first a wriggled careful approach to the bank to see ahead exactly where the fish was lying, then a retreat back far enough to kneel-cast without being seen by the fish. With the soft natural grub on the hook it was impossible to false-cast out sufficient line from the reel without flicking off the grub, so I had to peel off line and coil it by my side. I estimated about 4 metres would be sufficient and as much as I could expect to shoot forward in a continuous action cast.

Preparing myself in this way, I now faced the problem of how I would know if the fish took my bait. This I felt I could do by taking several upright kneeled steps forward, so that I could look quickly over the bank, just after I had made the cast. Tensed and anxious, I swung the rod back, shooting out the line and instantly kneel-stepping forward almost at the same time.

The grub hit the water with a small splash. The next second was a blur as the water erupted. My rod jarred down hard against the bank and continued tugging down with a growing pressure till twang … all went limp, leaving a length of hookless nylon to float skywards.

It took the loss of another fish, again of majestic weight, to drive home the message, but then it came through loud and clear. First I must let the fish hit an upright rod, a rod that will bend and fight the fish for me, a rod that will take the rolling lunge, yet hold the fish's head up, not allowing it to charge down under the bank and break me on some obstruction. The rod must be held up at 12 o'clock and grasped firmly as if it were held up in a vice.

Secondly, when the rod had taken the initial strike it had to be held upright until the end, for the lunging pull of a fighting fish tends to tire the arm and cause the angle to drop, so that the fish gets closer and closer to a direct pull from the reel, making the spring-like action of the rod ineffectual.

With these things in mind I walked upstream looking for another fish to try my newborn knowledge on. Here again I learned a lesson, for in these highland streams the banks are eroded and undercut; thus the fish lie close in under the banks, actually in underwater caverns. The vibrations of a person walking overhead must make a noise like a drum beat in these caverns, for as I approached I could see fish after fish go down and disappear. This brought out all the stalking instincts that I possessed, so tiptoeing slowly upstream I rounded a bend to see halfway up the next strait a rolling splash rise. Determinedly I said to myself, 'You are mine, mate!'

I carefully edged into position, first spying over the bank to be sure just where to drop my grub, then shuffled back into position, peeled off the right amount of line, and the battlefield was declared.

Dropping the grub over the bank with a plop just above where the fish was positioned I rose to my feet, taking a pace forward, and keeping my rod right up. As I looked over into the stream I was just in time to see the white lined cavity of the trout's mouth before it slammed shut in a charging roll swirl.

Bracing my feet and holding the line firmly with my left hand, I took the shock strike. The splashing, lunging, head-shaking trout tried every way possible to get his head down into his cavern. I was just as determined he wouldn't. Then the fish decided that flight was the better part of valour so with a surge it headed off downstream.

Still holding hard so that actually little, if any, line was pulled off my reel, I followed, half into a weed bed and then out again. A dive under a shrub growing on the bank and overhanging the stream provided an extra hazard, as I had to stretch around the shrub to free the line. A dive for another cavern under the far bank was held by the creaking rod. Then it was nearly all over as a crumbled edge of the bank gave beneath my weight, nearly upending me, yet the flight continued with the trout leading the hectic way.

Reaching a sloping bank going down to a reasonable-sized hole, I determined that this would be the place to end the battle, so bracing my feet I stopped the downstream race and started to reel in line. The ensuing fight was hard, but eventually I slid my net under 3100g of magnificent trout, dark brownish black in colour with few red spots, but in first-class condition.

Now that I had mastered this type of fishing I continued on through the rest of the morning until the grass grub had disappeared, or at any rate the fish had stopped rising to them. By this time my bag had grown to five lovely fish, all close to the weight of the first specimen, although he was the best fish of the day.

Perhaps to start a book with an actual true personal exploit is unusual, but this event happened to me more than 25 years ago and seemed an appropriate place to begin, for since then I have had many opportunities to enjoy fishing in many parts of Australia, yet this early experience has taught me always to treat with respect these often overlooked alpine streams.

Although it is hard to generalise with these alpine streams, the majority do have sections of narrow deep waters with heavily undercut banks. Often the same stream will become shingly and the width will extend as the waters become shallower before again constricting. Usually there is a determined flow all the year in these streams. A boulder may turn the flow, but few stones break the surface. In fact it is more likely that the banks have caved in or partly crumbled to concentrate the water flow under the adjoining bank.

Tussocks and grasses grow right to the water's edge, with the odd small shrub haphazardly growing there, but there is always weed in the stream bed – patches of watercress or wild mint, ribbon grasses wavering back and forth in the current flow, coarse snow grasses filling the slacker back eddy waters.

These alpine streams hold some of the best fish in Australia, so perhaps it is appropriate that we start our story here. Some of Australia's mightiest rivers are born of streams which in many cases you can jump across.

Seldom do you find the big fish out of their caverns; only the grass grub or the flying grasshopper provides enough incentive to bring them up to the surface during daylight hours.

My remarks have been centred on the permanent resident fish of these streams, not the spawning runs of fish that often pass up these streams at the appropriate time, particularly in some Snowy Mountain streams, where these spawning fish completely take over a stream and alter the fish behaviour and composition of the fish population.

You can be lucky, as I well remember I was one beautiful balmy day. While fishing a lagoon with a light 3X cast on which I had attached an Orange Quill dry fly on a size 13 hook, I decided the conditions this side of the lagoon were not ideal – there was barely a ripple on the water and the cast lay over the surface like a steel hawser. The far side, however, did have a slight ripple and looked a much more likely place to catch the spasmodically rising fish. So I made for the stream flowing out of the lagoon. I had to cross this to reach the other side of the lagoon. It was too wide to jump and too deep to wade, so I wandered downstream looking for a suitable spot.

It had the typical steep banks, which in places had crumbled, making it awkward to negotiate. I was in no hurry and did not notice how far I had gone until suddenly I realised that I was several hundred metres downstream. What a pest, it would be quite a walk back.

With this in mind I determined to cross, but just at this spot the stream turned, and at the turn there was quite a deep, clear hole, almost a sizeable pool. Weeds grew out from the bank in the slack water away from the current, while the fly life was humming over and alighting on the pool surface in droves.

I stopped and admired this little pool. What a lovely home for a trout, what a food supply, I imagined to myself, but not a fish in … wait … there was a neb, just for a moment, in a runnel near the slack weed bed. Then the increasing wavelike action from the rise confirmed my suspicions.

Squatting down, I watched and waited, noting the brownish shadow moving up the runnel, disappearing for a few moments, then again moving up the little pathway. As he went the neb appeared once, twice more. This was not the neb of a 300g fish which we all expected to find in this little mountain stream, this little waterway that anglers for years had scorned, preferring to fish the nearby lagoon. This looked like a good fish.

The longer I watched this feeding fish the more excited I became. But how on earth would I land such a good fish in this narrow overgrown water, especially as I would have to leave on my frail 3X cast and dry fly to have any hope of even hooking him. Well, if I did lose him I would only lose a fly. This was my philosophical approach.

Re-examining the problem, I realised that I could expect to have only one cast, for with weeds both sides of the runnel the fly would have to land in the centre of a 15cm strip of water, with only a few centimetres of float before drag would reveal the unnatural fly to the fish. I did it! The fish stuck his neb out and took the fly beautifully. The fight was on.

Don't ask me to describe the next quarter of an hour. It was all a sweaty haze as I dug the fish out from the weeds with my net handle, pummelled him out of hidden caverns, held my rod up to get around giant tussocks, stumbled, fell and crashed my way downstream in hot pursuit of the hooked fish.

It was at least 200 metres further downstream, in a weed bed of a miniature pool, that after I had probed with my net for the umpteenth time, the fish floated to the surface, all draped in broken off weeds and belligerent to the end. Half on his side he lay there while I, fearful of a further rush downstream, strained out the open net and scooped him shorewards.

One of the best stream fish I have ever taken anywhere – a beautifully proportioned golden brown female of 3700g.

I, like many other anglers, would have laughed if someone had intimated that there was a fish anywhere near these proportions in the little stream, bypassed by dozens of anglers each season. As I said earlier, you can be lucky.

The natural bait angler has the best chance of success in this sort of stream, for the few pools are usually too small to float a fly, and the excessive weed adds hazards galore for the spinnermen. The semi-dapping grasshopper exponent, the fisherman with a mudeye, grass grub or in times of spate a worm, has much more chance of success, especially if he recognises that his footsteps along the bank are drum beats in the caverns, making necessary the very cautious approach outlined earlier.

Mike, one of the best natural bait experts I have ever met, described to me the way he fishes these streams, and for real action he recommends it. His bait is the lizard, the 6-to-9cm size, soft-bellied, and with the habit of dropping its tail in times of stress.

By attaching the lizard to a number 10 long shanked hook in through the bottom jaw, he literally drops it over the edges of these streams, in places he has previously decided could hold a cavern dweller and, more importantly at night, when the trout are on the prowl.

Using a stiffish rod and a 5kg breaking strain line, he reckons he could hold a whale, and needs to be able to, for the tremendous slashing strike in the pitch black evenings, as this wriggling bait alights on the water, is enough to give the weak-hearted man a seizure.

The subsequent fight in the confined, darkened conditions is a shin-bruising, exhausting test of strength and luck, as you can well imagine. The lizard, just cast out into a lake or pond, is very effective bait, so Mike says. I have not tried it, but the reptile squirming in the water would be sure to attract the big fish, in a slashing strike. Although it is not the intention of this book to single out any particular water in the continent, there are a few areas that deserve special mention.

One is the Eucumbene River in the Snowy Mountain region of southern New South Wales. Lake Eucumbene, at 1160 metres [altitude], is one of the largest bodies of fresh water in the world, with a shoreline almost 350 kilometres around.

The Eucumbene River is unique, and is the only river entering this vast lake. Tunnels discharge water from other catchments into the lake depths, but the river is the only major stream flowing naturally into the lake.

The population of fish in the lake is colossal; some say two million fish. No one really knows; neither do they know the exact number of fish that run up the Eucumbene River to spawn annually. Some say one million fish make the pilgrimage.

Numbers as such are not important, for there are thousands upon thousands of fish in this river from mid-January through until the following spring, and during this time anglers have some magnificent sport in its short length.

The river is not large, being gravelly, shingly or stony-bottomed over most of its length. From where it starts in a moss bed depression a few kilometres south of Kiandra, it winds through mountain snow grass plains, in a slow meandering course, gathering in a few side streams on its way.

Below Kiandra it would be 7 metres across at a maximum width, coming into 4 metres in the deeper constricted areas. Where the river is wider and shallow, thigh waders will allow anglers to crisscross the river at most places quite comfortably without getting wet above the knee; however, there are holding holes, or deeper areas in places throughout its length; one in particular I will mention later is known as the 'Tank Hole'.

After leaving Kiandra the stream constricts to a narrow pass between some very large boulders in a gorge. Here the stream careers madly downwards for a few metres in a white foaming turbulence to the base of this cascade known as the 'Suicide Hole', where anglers using all sorts of lures take hundreds of fish throughout the period mentioned, for the fish lie in this hole gathering strength to fight their way up through the maelstrom of the pass.

Below Suicide Hole the stream drops gradually down through a gorge until eventually it enters the lake itself. However, through this gorge there are pools and glides which hold some lovely fish for both the fly and spinner enthusiasts.

It is the manner of fishing the Tank Hole which I feel needs enlarging upon, for from this hole, which is estimated to be 6 metres deep by 15 metres long and 8 metres across, anglers extract hundreds upon hundreds of fish each year.

To many people the manner of taking fish from Suicide Hole, and the concentration on the Tank Hole, is obnoxious. However, let me reiterate what I said a few lines back: there is no other major water that fish can move into from the lake except this river.

The reduction of the numbers of fish by angling, no matter how it is done or what lures are used, as long as it is legal, is preferable to forced killing by authorities, and force killed they would have to be if the size and quality of the fish in the lake is to be maintained. Experience has already shown that when the water level of Lake

Eucumbene drops, then the trout have a tendency to become slabby, possibly through lack of food to keep them healthy, and to offset this the population must be kept under control, to guard against over-population with numbers of small slabby fish.

The Tank Hole is fished by all kinds of anglers. The least productive method appears to be spinning, for then the lure will not go right to the bottom and still work efficiently. The natural bait man using a mudeye, so long as he has a delicate touch and is thus able to feel the lethargic fish as they nibble the bait, enjoys quite good sport.

Fly-fishing upstream with a fast sinking line appears to be about the best method, and last March, I went with Ron for an afternoon and early evening exercise in this way of fishing.

The flies we used were a big Mrs Simpson or similar heavily hackled wet. This, Ron explained to me, was so that the feathers could literally tickle the trout into some sort of reaction; but he warned me that I was not to expect any violent snatches at the fly.

We walked the few metres from the car to the river bank, where Ron selected his favourite stand, a jutting out section of the river bank just large enough for him to stand on and cast up the pool. I was directed to go down, cross the river, and come up opposite him at the foot of the pool.

Together we started to work out line, for a long line was essential; the heavier sinking line made the long line casting all the easier to accomplish and I soon got out a few metres more than my normal length of line.

When we eventually shot the last metre or two of line forward, the flies landed directly upstream and past the top of the pool, into the shallower water above. The line quickly sank, offsetting the current coming towards us carrying the whole cast and fly into the deeper, very top of the pool. Down, down it kept going.

'Don't let any slack develop,' Ron said. 'Just let the line sink to a reasonably taut line with the reel.' So for up to 2 minutes we just waited for the whole line to sink.

I could imagine what was happening: the fly was beginning to settle among the fish, which were lying in tiers, head to tail, right over the very bottom of the pool, where it would be almost dark. There was a slight edging movement to one side by a fish as the unfamiliar feathered fly moved in among them.

It was then that I started to retrieve very slowly; gingerly I handled the line between forefinger and thumb, ever aware of the slightest obstruction to the retrieve, imagining at the same time the fly working along the side of a fish, then bumping the snout of the next fish lying downstream, then along its side and on to the next.

Ron, with his years of experience of the area, had estimated there were over 5,000 fish in this hole, for recently there had been a minor spate in the river.

Suddenly Ron started to wind like mad, his rod bent and line cutting down into the depths. A resting fish had sucked in his fly and was well and truly hooked. It exploded from the surface like a submarine missile and Ron resorted to handlining to catch up with the fish, now spearing for the bottom to regain the companionship of its mates.

Ron, experienced in such tactics, soon had the fish under control, and after several high-flying manoeuvres he slid his net under a nice brownie, 1500g or so.

As soon as Ron had landed his fish I again started the long cast, slow retrieve way of fishing, but I must admit the patience needed for this is not part of my makeup – I prefer a little more action, so after an hour or so I sat on the bank and watched Ron.

Periodically our nerves would be shattered by a huge boiling swirl as one of the resting hundreds of fish barged to the surface, possibly to oxygenate itself or rid itself of some irritation. One fish that did spear to the surface for no apparent reason really excited me. It must have been all of 3000g, and just to prove he really was that big, he rose twice in the space of a few minutes.

Dusk was now coming on so Ron and I went back to the car for a meal, and at the same time we changed our line to the high floating variety, and put on a medium 2X cast, for we had also planned to fish another part of the Eucumbene River, after dark, with a muddler minnow.

To me this was much more interesting; there was some real action here all the time. An hour or so later, when it was pitch dark, we left our car at the new position and edged our way closer to the river bank. Periodically we had to use our torch to orientate ourselves, but we soon switched off completely, allowing our eyes to become accustomed to the dark and the almost indistinguishable surrounds.

Our muddlers had been well oiled, in fact almost bathed in oil, to ensure that they floated in the moving current. This heavy oiling was essential, as we would be unable actually to see the muddler while fishing, and it is essential that it floats.

It was now necessary to worm and edge our way to the very brink of the river, grasping hold of a handful of tussocks for support, moving one foot carefully after the other, so that a wombat hole or river cave-in along the edge would not bring us crashing down full length.

The spot I selected was the head of a long pool, an area which I knew was deeper in the centre as well as along the far bank, which was slightly undercut in places, the spot where during the daytime resting fish could edge under the bank overhang and expect reasonable protection. This spot also allowed the fish to move out into the centre during the dark, and feed extensively. At night they do feed ravenously, rising to anything that passes in front or over them, for they have little if anything to feed on during daylight hours.

Estimating the distance to the far bank, I stood upright and cast the heavy dangling muddler upstream, into the fast frothing water where the river was breaking out of a constricted glide. It landed in the rapid, only the slack appearing in my line as it came down towards me indicating its progress. Judging this cast to be unsuccessful and the lure almost at my feet, I this time cast up and across, right into where I judged the far bank to be.

After several more casts I was able to hear the slight splash as the muddler hit the water on the far side. Absolutely essential are intense concentration about the area you assume the muddler to be, a taut line, and the readiness to strike at the slightest noise or disturbance near your fly.

The tension in this type of fishing builds up to a crescendo. It is dark and you are only vaguely aware of where you are. The river you know is almost at your feet, and also you are semi-aware that a false movement as you edge downstream along the pool edge could result in a wet uncomfortable ducking or a sprained ankle if it is a wombat hole. The tussocks are tall and troublesome, so you have to keep your backcast well up in the hope that the heavy muddler will not become entangled in their snatching heads. And all the while you are hoping your muddler is working on the surface and floating enticingly.

Suddenly a splash is heard, and seen at the same time near your fly – perhaps the word 'heard' is operative, for it is on this signal that you strike, as I did then.

The water fountained in a shower of spray as a fish leapt skywards, then my reel handle spun around in the fisherman's song as an 1800g fish tore off line going upstream. For quite a few moments I was busy fighting for control – getting a good footrest was the first thing – then I alternatively let out or took in line rapidly according to the whims of the hooked fish.

Not having seen the fish, and not knowing exactly what the conditions around me were like, I felt I was really up against the elements. Would there be a patch of water weed for him to tangle in? A stone to cut my cast on? Was there a cavity under the bank for him to tear under? Was the water level close or would it be far down the bank, thus making it hard to get my net eventually under my catch. All these questions and more went through my mind as I fought the strong careering fish.

A slight pause, as he rolled and beat the surface in a frothing, cavorting session of catherine wheel twists, enabled me to slip my torch from my pocket, switch it on and jam it into my mouth, and so by moving my head I could pick up the fish's twisting torso in the light beam. The light obviously frightened him; with a screech of the reel he again made upstream, but not so far this time, as he was tiring badly.

Now that I could see my surrounds I picked a sloping bank section, and from there started to work the fish towards me. Frightened, he kept swimming back and forth in a semi-circle around me, held by the line to the restricted arc. But the fight was almost over, and shortly I swam the fish over the extended net and slid him up among the tussocks.

During this time I had tried not to let the light beam shine downstream too much so I would not scare any other fish in my pathway, but even so it was in my opinion wiser to spend the next 10 minutes relaxing with a quiet smoke on the bank beside my flapping fish and let the darkness of night again spread over the river.

By the end of the evening, or about two hours later, I had three fish all around the same size and all caught in this exhilarating manner in the black night.

I don't know any comparable stream in Australia where such good fish can be taken in this same way as in the Eucumbene River. The muddler is good in many streams, but for real excitement I am a true convert to this type of fishing.

These alpine rivers have some very heavy fly hatches: nymphs are prolific, beetles become attached to the surface film in dozens, while grasshoppers in late summer create real feast conditions for the trout. Hackled Hopper, Ginger Dun, Geehi Beetle and Red Tag are some of the main dry fly patterns used on these waters in their wider middle reaches; as the angler works further upstream the patterns used are smaller and more intricate, more in keeping with the fly life available as natural food.

As the high elevation of the few streams in the continent that fall into this category is taken into consideration, it can be appreciated that the water temperature does not rise as rapidly or as high as streams lower down the mountain sides, and this results in a more prolonged period of fly activity.

The further south one goes, the more caddis, mayfly, midge, and stonefly hatches occur, so that fly-fishing in the island state of Tasmania is an angler's dream and delight, extending right through from October into March.

The midge hatches in all their various species, combined with the tussock caddis – that fawnish white moth prevalent throughout the whole of Australia – create good rises of fish towards dusk. Add to these two beetles and you have the most common activators of trout moving on the surface.

My first choice when spinning these alpine rivers is a small revolving blade lure, the type that has a firm body with a metal blade revolving ahead of the body. However, the colour is the important ingredient – action and placement are vital, but these come from practice and experience. In the clear, often snow-fed waters of these alpine streams, the basic colour should be silver – making the combination either silver and red or green or blue. The slightest discolouration in the water, however, would cause me to change to gold as the basic colour. There is a long established lore among anglers: a dark lure for darkish discoloured waters or a light, bright lure in clear sparkling waters.

Spinning one of these clear waters is a joy. My short rod is whippy, yet has a firm resilient feeling, and by using a 2.25kg line the smaller lures can be cast quite long distances. One thing I am very particular about is my reel: this is the only mechanical part of my whole equipment, and like any other mechanical device, must be regularly serviced and kept full of grease, with the moving parts liberally coated with oil.

These alpine rivers mainly have the same characteristics in places that create good spinning: water-beds of weed in the slack away from the current, high banks with the odd crumbling breakaways that have fallen down into the stream to divert the water current, thus making ideal coveys for resting fish, nice sweeping bends with big pools surrounded with water grasses, and tussocks along the banks, some being waist high.

Sections of the river banks are often lower, creating shallow saucer-like depressions, ideal spots for trout to forage over at dusk after nymphs. As well, the odd shrub grows along the bank, in many places leaning right over the stream and making good hiding places for trout on the fin.

Trout love to lie on the centre side, the deepwater side of weed beds. Here they lie under the undulating weed fronds, and where the stream flow is diverted by a bank crumble or a large boulder, the little slack back eddies create many places well worth a cast or two.

You must creep carefully along the bank, taking advantage of every shrub, tussock or boulder to break up your solid silhouette against the skyline. But most importantly, you must keep your rod moving all the time, either casting or retrieving, for the old saying, 'You can't catch a fish without a lure in the water' is true.

Place your lure delicately and accurately, not 9cm from the weed on either your side or the other side of the stream. Three or four quick turns of your reel as soon as your lure touches the water, followed by the retrieve alongside as close as possible to the weed bed, will ensure there is no slack in the line.

This upstream spinning allows you to cover a lot of territory if you so desire, but I have found that long distances covered do not necessarily mean more fish. A thorough exploring of all the likely spots within casting range is more important.

This thoroughness and complete knowledge of likely trout resting or feeding spots is known as streamcraft. Many times it has put fish in the bottom of my creel and those of other thinking anglers when more energetic fishing partners have travelled metres upstream with an odd cast here or there and certainly without thinking why they are casting in that spot.

Again, in this type of river fishing you are likely to catch good-sized trout, so the same rod position as in the grass grub episode earlier is essential – rod up to take the strike of a heavy fish, perhaps a lake fish up the stream with spawning intentions – although it restricts the area your lure can come through the water at each cast.

Under normal river conditions, where the fish are generally smaller, it is the angler with the rod held down and the spinner fished right out who catches the fish in the last few turns, but where there are big fish in an alpine stream your rod must be able to take and absorb the initial plunging strike, then take control and manage the fish immediately.

After casting first up your side of the river, centre side of the weed bed, I would then proceed to lodge my little lure at the head of any small backwater which sometimes lies between the weed bed and the shore on my side (here during the retrieve you will often get weed, but it is worth a trial). The next cast should be close to the weed on the far side upstream, followed by one across to the weed on the far side downstream, with the final cast from this area downstream into the clear water of the centre. For this last cast I make a distinct pause after the lure enters the water, allowing the lure to sink deeply before starting a slow, uneven retrieve, moving the rod tip distinctly as I slowly wind. Fish in the caverns under the bank often do not have weed completely covering their doorway, which leads out into mid-stream, and often as they are waiting there they will come charging out to take an enticing deep swimming lure passing by.

The two sorts of alpine streams I have mentioned, namely the small jump-across size and the wider possibly spawning fish carriers must be considered the cream of these alpine waters, and they are well worth searching for. Whenever you are crossing a highland plain or moor and you come across a slow-moving section of stream that has slowed between the peaks nurturing its existence and the next rapid, rock-strewn descent, approach it carefully, for should it have plenty of weed, undercut banks, deep holes here and there with mud or shingly bottom, you could have found your 'Mecca'. At any rate it is well worthy of close and careful attention.

The majority of the streams in the alpine country fall under the heading of burns, for they are rocky cascading rivulets – their steep, rocky topography ensures the waters are turbulent, frothing flows, pouring full pelt down the mountain sides. These rivulets occur in many of the wildest regions of mountainous Australia, and they combine to form the main rivers of our continent.

The acidity of the water in most of these waters prohibits the heavy growth of weeds necessary to succour food life in any great quantity. Stone flies and caddis flies, however, often hatch prolifically in some waters where the conditions suit them, but the majority of the food mainly comes from land-based insects, who from misadventure land on the water surface.

In some isolated streams, where their headwaters are based in limestone regions, acidity is not a problem. Weeds grow and these waters are really good fish producers.

Before a burn is of interest to anglers it must contain fish that are at least pan-sized, therefore normally the burn must reach about 3 metres or more in width. The water will doubtless be fast flowing, tumbling over rocks, swishing around shoreline boulders or obstinate moss-covered earth clods, hissing down glides, rotating around miniature whirlpools, lapping continuously against pebbly beaches with the small quiet backwater haphazardly placed down its edges.

Spinning these waters is a real art only mastered by a very few, those who can use the smallest thumbnail spoon or the very tiniest revolving blade lure.

There is little room to move the lure through the water and a miscast will often knock off one of the treble barbs – in fact these burns cannot be recommended unless you have mastered the very intricate facets of the art.

Natural bait anglers, adept at casting a grasshopper, come into a different category. Here the artist with the long swishy rod, who can adroitly drop his hopper, live beetle, cockroach or similar lure at the very head of the little pools or runs will have a lot of fun.

To the fly fisherman it is like the burn fishing of Scotland. Some Australians have adopted the sparsely tied flies of Scottish origin that sink quickly and are taken underwater with little time to create drag, while perhaps the majority like the high floating Red Tag type of dry fly, bobbing momentarily on the surface before the current swoops it further downstream. Whichever way you fish these burns and boisterous waters, the fishing is fast and furious. Beautiful in their spotted red and brown colouring, the fish are not usually large – say around the 300g average – no matter where you fish in Australia.

A variation on the above is provided in some of the wider turbulent streams, where the evening fishing can be very enjoyable. Let's look at what the anglers of Tasmania used to enjoy before 1967, for it was then that the famous Shannon Rise ceased, due to a diverting of the Great Lake waters away from the Shannon River.

The 1-kilometre-long Shannon River from the Great Lake Dam down to where the released waters entered the Shannon Lagoon created one of the greatest fishing events in the world, for every year during a period of about 6 weeks from early December, a caddis fly known as the snowflake caddis hatched by the countless millions in this river section. The flies hovered over the fast-flowing, crashing waters like a white cloud.

The fish from the placid waters of the lagoon worked up into the maelstrom to gorge themselves on this moth feast – in fact it used to be claimed that you could walk across the jammed backs of the assembled trout.

Having fished the 'rise' for over 15 years, I feel honoured and humble to have such marvellous personal memories of this great event, and if the famous Brumby's Weirs had not developed to provide such worldwide fishing by utilising the same Great Lake waters, I would really feel thwarted.

When the thrill of the daytime 'rise' was over, and following an early evening meal, we would reassemble on the banks of the river for the dusk fishing. I can remember some really exciting times in the semi-gloom.

Many fish did not leave the river and head back to the lagoon each night; they stopped in their selected feeding position and waited for the following day. It was to these fish, plus the resident fish, that we cast our flies, and the success of this kind of fly-fishing has stood me in great stead in subsequent outings.

At that beautiful time of day when the colours of nature are brightened and magnified by the last rays of daylight, we would attach a small wet Alexandra fly and ply the swirling waters of the stream. The Alexandra fly, with its brilliant peacock side feathers, is a deadly evening fly; in fact I have heard that it is banned in certain private waters in other countries of the world due to its deadliness. At any rate it caught many Shannon fish. You use it somewhat differently to the usual wet fly-fishing; instead of the 45° down and pull across, it is 45° upstream, drift down, then across. The idea is that it represents the floating nymph while coming down with the current before it reaches the end of its drift, then when being jerked across the current it represents something else.

This manner of fishing relates to upstream nymph fishing, which I will mention later, but to emphasise the point here as well, the majority of the strikes will occur as the fly alters direction from the drift to the retrieve, so that is the time to be particularly wary and careful.

To close this chapter on the streams of the alpine country, I will mention a type of fishing that under the circumstances really floored me. In fact I doffed my topper to Old Bill.

The occasion was several years ago, when Old Bill said to me, 'Son! Do ya wanta see how to do this fishin' game?'

Old Bill was a family friend who was getting on in years, and I found out that his father was actually a convicted poacher sent out from England in the mid-1800s. He had been assigned to act as gardener/groundsman to one of the wealthy families who had built a glorious English manor house type of home, many of which are now so prized by the National Trust, and so enrich the Tasmanian landscape.

Old Bill had learnt his fishing from his dad, so this would be interesting, I thought, and I agreed to take him up to one of those swiftly flowing streams covered earlier in this section of the book.

As he did not want to be there much before dark, only long enough to 'get me bearings', we duly arrived on a moonlit night in midsummer – a warm glorious evening. I assembled my fly gear, then stood mesmerised by Old Bill.

From his old moth-hole-riddled rod bag he extracted first one, then four lengths of bamboo. Not matched cane, just bamboo like a surf rod; old brass ferrules joined these lengths together to make a really long, almost double-handled fly rod. The rod rings were held on with waxed string, while the old Mallick-type level wind reel had slide reel fittings all made of brass. A genuine museum piece, I would have called it all. The level floating line was the only item not 50 years old, I estimated.

Pulling a 2-metre length of level heavy nylon off a spool, he knotted it on to the line before attaching a brown cod-type hook of about size 1. What he was going to put on the hook he refused to tell me until it was darker. Instead he brought out his old briar pipe and sat down, back on to a tree, to wait.

Go and 'flip' the fly about for an hour or so, he chided me, so this I proceeded to do. Returning as the sun's rays were disappearing, I proudly showed Old Bill two very nice trout for this river, about 500g each – then I literally challenged him to do likewise.

'Tha she come, son,' he said, (he called everyone 'son') as the big golden moon began to appear over the distant hills. 'Give 'er a few minutes to get up further, then I'll show yer.'

Like all men of the soil, Old Bill could enthral me with his stories, be they about fishing, hunting or just plain living, so the few minutes' wait certainly did not drag, despite my curiosity about what he would use as bait.

Then, with a toothless grin, Old Bill pulled from his pocket an old strip of white cloth – a strip of sheet or pillowcase, a piece hem-sewn along the edge – from which he cut off a length about 7cm, which he carefully began to bind around the hook. .

He started from the centre of the strip of cloth, at the bend of the hook, so that when he reached the eye he could tie off with a granny knot, leaving the ends to stand out at right angles to the hook; these ends were about 1.5cm long after he had trimmed them up.

'Looks like one of them white moths, don't he, son?' I gulped agreement. Old Bill weaved his way to the river bank, where he ducked his lure into the water before he said, 'All right me spotted beauties – come and get it.' With that he lay back and heaved the piece of damp cloth almost directly across the white-flecked rapids in front of him, before adopting a type of rapidly moving up and down movement with his long rod while he wound in his line with a quick jerky motion. The white lure appeared to skip from ripple to ripple, slide across any glide and disappear in each swirling waterfall, quickly to reappear and skittle across towards the shore.

After four such casts, slightly downstream from each other, a swirling, rocketing lunge signified a fish, obviously attracted to this skittling surface jumping lure.

The trout was carefully played into the bank while the old man bellowed, 'Set yer net right under her, son.'

In one hour he had six fish equally as good as mine on the bank. He said that was all the fish he needed, so I could take him home now. I did.

Even now I can hear his last remark to me as I dropped him off. 'I told yer, son: it takes an old man to make a good fisher – and yer don't need any fancy gear neither, do yer?'

Editor's note: At the time when Gilmour was writing, many forms of fishing were legal on the Eucumbene River. Today, regulations have changed: anglers must make themselves aware of the current fishing regulations before fishing this blue-ribbon water.

DOUGLAS
STEWART
OBE AO

DOUGLAS STEWART, prolific poet, playwright, author, and devout fisherman, was born in New Zealand in 1913. He worked as a journalist in New Zealand before moving to Australia in 1938. He became the literary editor of the *Bulletin* magazine and literary adviser to Angus & Robertson publishers.

In his charming collection of nature pieces, *The Seven Rivers*, he evoked an Australia and New Zealand that will appeal to anglers and nature-lovers alike. With each piece sparking off the next, the book crackles with life as the author bravely confronts wild pigs, wayward wombats, kiwis and water-rats, as well as that ever-elusive trout ...

Douglas Stewart was awarded the OBE in 1960 for his services to literature; he was later awarded the AO as well. He was married to artist Margaret Coen, whose drawings appeared in his book.

He died in 1985.

Though there is a chapter about swordfish, another about snapper, and even a piece about pig-hunting, it is mostly a book about trout-fishing in Australia and New Zealand.

I wrote it simply for the pleasure of going fishing again in retrospect along my favourite rivers.

Douglas Stewart, Foreword, The Seven Rivers

This chapter, 'The Duckmaloi', is reproduced by courtesy of the estate of Douglas Stewart and agent Curtis Brown (Aust.) P/L.

CHAPTER 26

The Duckmaloi

There were good trout in the Duckmaloi and it ran through beautiful country; but I must say the first time I saw the place it gave me the horrors. The trouble was, I was a newcomer: doubly a newcomer, for I had not been long in Australia, and I had never before stayed at the guesthouse from which we fished. It takes a few years to learn to cherish the more formidable particularities of Australia; and it is a truly terrible experience to arrive for the first time at any guesthouse, even so kindly an abode as was Richards'. You don't know what time the meals are, and where the lavatory is. And all the other guests seem to have known each other for years; and when you arrive they look at you. Looking at newcomers was, in fact, a favourite occupation for those who did not ride or fish at Duckmaloi. They used to sit on the veranda all day, on those ancient leather armchairs, and stare at all the guests who came hopefully down the red road in the Richards' car or the mailman's rattling cart. It gave them something to do; and someone to talk about.

Then there was the heat. The valley of the Duckmaloi, 100 miles from Sydney over the Blue Mountains and 20 miles out into the ranges from the bleak flat township of Oberon, lay folded between the mass of Mount Bindo to the right and the lower hills rolling away from the Fish River Creek to the left. The sun hung over it like a white eaglehawk and struck down mercilessly. There was no escape from it – except perhaps in one awful retreat under the high-propped weatherboard house where there were some broken chairs, a broken iron bedstead, and usually a few fowls expiring in their dust baths. Once, when it really was too impossibly hot to fish, I spent some days under the house, reading *The Fortunes of Richard Mahony*. I never really got through that dismal masterpiece; but I did, in desperation, try ... On the veranda, if you preferred sitting and watching for the mailman – he came about three o'clock every second day – you slowly and steadily cooked. Out on the long slope down to the river where a friendly garage-man from Sydney took me the first day to introduce me to the fishing, a mile over ploughland, bare grass-roots, and fallen timber, it was hot enough to knock you down.

There were also the flies. Duckmaloi was a great place for flies. They were those little bush-flies that ride by millions on your back and leave you with a concerted buzz of disappointment the minute you enter a house. I never thought them as unsanitary as house-flies; and just as well, for if you ever grilled a chop in the open they swarmed upon it from all directions and, no matter how vigorously you waved it in the air to make it at least difficult for them to perch on it while you snatched a mouthful, you generally ate, on an average, at least two or three dozen a day. They had a habit of flying down your throat and choking you if you opened your mouth to speak and, in a pardonable search for moisture in that dry country, they loved to nestle in your eyes. The horses thrust their heads into the bushes to escape them and so, often enough, did we. If you wore a fly-veil you could not – or so I have always thought – see the snakes properly.

For Duckmaloi was also a great country for snakes – brown snakes, black snakes, tiger snakes.

We met our first, a nice medium-sized black snake, among the fallen logs on the track down to the river. I daresay there was a snake under every fallen log, and the brushwood fence, over which we clambered warily into that final paddock, was certainly infested with them. The serpent took refuge in a hollow, burnt-out stump; and Horrie, the garage-man, who was also an expert bushman and afterwards taught me many things about the small creatures which inhabited that apparently lifeless countryside and empty water, cut a forked stick and neatly pinioned it. Then he proposed to seize it by the tail and crack it against a log. I suggested – sensibly, I still think – that it would probably bite him. Horrie, after some cogitation, agreed that it probably would. So after various futile attempts to get at it with a stick, we left it to bite us another day.

We hadn't been 10 minutes at the river before another snake came slithering through the tussocks, and later in the morning there was a really beautiful black snake with a red belly coiled and sleeping peacefully in the long water-grass at the stream's edge. Next day, down near the crossing by Gearon's, forcing our way through the straggling wet undergrowth after a thunderstorm that had soaked us to the skin and sent a fresh current of life through the baked landscape, we saw, simultaneously, three snakes quietly weaving their way across our track. It was good weather for hunting frogs, I suppose; but they looked very much as if they were hunting fishermen. To a newcomer from New Zealand, these were quite an appalling sight. The three stray specimens on the first morning were enough to make it almost impossible to walk. And how fish without walking? What is to be done with rod and fly – or I am afraid it might have been rod and worm in those days – when one is standing paralysed with fear on a tussock heap?

In a sensible stream you could walk the clear shingle at the edge and at least see what you were treading on. Afterwards on the Duckmaloi (the same day that my wife sat on a black snake in a tussock when she was settling down to paint) I did see a tiger snake stretched in full view across a clear grassy patch, drinking from a little pool. But the Duckmaloi had few clear patches of grass and no shingle at all. In a sensible stream, again, you could avoid the snakes by wading. But the Duckmaloi wasn't wade-able.

And in the end it wasn't the heat or the flies or the snakes but the nature of the river itself that so disgusted me that first day. For if you are a fisherman you love water: and what was there to love in that lukewarm brown trickle, sluggish and muddy as a drain, creeping through the ragged grey tea-tree or somnolent in big brown pools? Where was the dance of a rapid? Where, in that hot silence, broken only by the low roar of the flies when you disturbed them from your back, was the music of running water?

And where were the fish?

I don't know how many days Horrie and I tramped that useless, ugly stretch of water between the sandy swimming hole and the bigger hole upstream beyond which, dwindling to a yard in width, the river disappeared in a tangle of willows; how many times we sat at these pools futilely dangling a worm or dropping an equally hopeless fly, investigated the inch-deep snake-infested rocky runnel between them; how many times we wandered downstream to where below the ruined old pisé homestead of some early settler, the stream turned wide and shallow and laid its flat waters to sleep amongst quite unfishable bulrushes; how many times, filled with new hope, we slithered down the mountain across the road from the guesthouse to the willowy valley where the Fish River Creek (in which never in my life have I seen a fish) ran green and clean at least, but just as useless as the Duckmaloi, from pool to pool among the tall grasses; how many times, down the clay road in the heat, we trudged the 2 miles to the foot of the ridge where the Creek met the Duckmaloi and became – with a most resounding falsehood – the Fish River (a most hopeless place to fish, anyhow, because the miners from Lithgow used to camp there at weekends and, so it was rumoured, slay any fish that were there with dynamite); or how many times, to make an end of this catalogue of hot, blank, useless days, we pushed further down the Fish River through the scrub and the briars to the pool below Gearon's farmhouse where the dogs rushed down and bit us and the snakes slithered all round us. The one thing certain is that in all those peregrinations we caught only one trout, a small one of about a pound – and the man who caught that was (I suppose I should have rejoiced; but I do not remember being particularly pleased with his good fortune) Horrie. It is difficult to be sincerely enthusiastic about other people's fish, until you have caught one yourself.

Yet there were fish enough. The Duckmaloi teemed with them, in fact. There were thousands of them. Down at the junction of the two rivers, where we usually finished at night because we were fishing from clear paddocks or from the roadside, and didn't have to trample on so many snakes, the water, as fishermen say, simply boiled with trout. After the long hot days, when the fish were too stupefied to eat, the evening rise was superb. Everywhere you looked there were hungry trout gulping down the white moths that swarmed out of the tea-tree, the big blundering hawk-moths, the lacewings fluttering past like miniature aeroplanes with their double wings, the buzzing beetles, the long-horned caddis-flies, the gnats, flying-ants – the myriad insects that, waking like the trout in the dusk, stirred that languid riverside to life. In the shallows flickering with sunset, small fish leapt clean out of the water. Every yard or so of the long pool downstream, bigger fish, or fish that reasonably seemed to be bigger, broke the still surface with their rings of light. In dark places under overhanging bushes there were mysterious and alluring splashes. The only problems were what fly to use and which fish to fish for. It was bewildering and stupendous.

And it was also beautiful. The sunset lay rosy on the pool, and under it, as the dusk deepened and the ridges changed from blue to dark blue to black, lay Mount Bindo's gigantic reflection. Bats wheeled in the glittering air, and all along the river, with the boomping of the bullfrogs calling to each other underwater and the innumerable shrilling of the tiny red and green and brown and bronze-coloured frogs that lived under every stone, in the wet grass and under every river-loosened clump of clay and tussock, began the most remarkable frog-chorus I have ever heard. The last wild calls of the kookaburras rang from the ranges; from the tips of the tallest grey ringbarked trees, gilded with the last of the light, the magpies sounded their sweet flutes. The infuriating bush-flies went to bed. Whatever had seemed drab and dry and commonplace and nondescript about the river during the day changed utterly with the night. It was deep wild mountain country, the valley full of birds and frogs, the Duckmaloi full of trout.

It would have been better, of course, had we been able to catch those trout. It is possible, being a fisherman, to be so maddened by one's inability to hook a single fish when there are dozens rising all round you, as not even to notice the sunset; and those fish were very hard to catch – impossible, in fact. It may have been that phenomenon which fishermen so often encounter on the most promising and exciting evening: that of all the myriad insects upon the water there is only one species which the fish are taking, and that is one you cannot find in your fly-box; but I rather think that these were nearly all very small fish – too small to take a fly. We used to see them nibbling the feathers of the Coachman or dragging it underwater in a quite futile attempt to swallow it. No fish. No good. What was the use of the country's turning beautiful at dusk if you still couldn't catch a fish?

And then at last, inevitably, for if you keep on fishing you must sooner or later get a fish, triumphantly I caught a trout: about a pound and a half, or let us say 2 pounds; a little bigger than Horrie's, anyhow. 'I thought you were about due to get one,' said Horrie generously. I thought so too: due and overdue. But there it was: and, flapping on the grassy bank, it gleamed in the dusk like the moon.

Extraordinary how one small fish can change the universe!

Even knowing the reasons, I have been puzzled from that moment to this how I could ever have found the Duckmaloi – or the prospect of trout fishing in Australia – unattractive. That I should actually have found it repellent moves me to the most profound apologies. The valley of the Duckmaloi was the most magnificent country. Golden and brown and lit with the green of oats and willows, it lay basking between its mountain ramparts. The soft blue heat haze smouldered among the ironbarks. Eagles patrolled it by day. At night the plover flew over, uttering their sharp, metallic cries like the sound of a knife on steel. The gum trees around the guesthouse glittered with dew and stars.

I wonder now that I could ever have felt uncomfortable in that house – except for one night when I shared a room with a deaf dentist from Sydney, who snored so loudly he nearly blew the house down. But it really was the most hospitable place. The food was excellent, and there was always fresh cream.

If there were a lot of people there, as sometimes there were, and they were not fishermen, which is a disadvantage, that had its compensations, too. You mostly had the river entirely to yourself. Only once, though occasionally I took out amateur fishermen and even girls, who walked ahead of you and scared the fish or stood behind you and got hooked when you were casting, was I ever really bothered by a rival fisherman at Duckmaloi. This was one of the times when Horrie and I had yet another shot at the tiny Fish River Creek – it should have had fish in it, that captivating little water with its deep unexpected pools and its clear straight tunnels through the grass. There was even a fisherman's guesthouse on it, Porter's Lodge. Maybe Mr Porter's patrons knew how to fish it. Anyhow we caught no trout in it the day the intruder was there, nor were we likely to.

He was a spinner-fisherman – not that I could scorn the spinner-man in those days – whom we had actually brought down from Richards' to spend the day with us: a bristling, bullet-headed man who wore the most enormous boots; and my most abiding impression of him is of these great boots plod-plodding rapidly and determinedly past us while we tried to keep ahead of him. For we, that day, were fishing dry-fly, and a spinner-man, heaving his great hunk of metal into the water and churning up the pools, must keep behind the delicate fly-man, or he will scare all the trout. We tried to keep him behind us; he would not stay. We tried to keep him with us, fishing each pool after we had put our flies across it; he forged ahead. We tried to make him take pool and pool in turn; he raced ahead. So we tried racing through the tussocks to get a quarter of a mile ahead of him; but plod, plod, plod on those vigorous boots, swinging his beastly spinner, every time, after we had had about 10 minutes' fishing, he caught up and forged ahead, so once again we had to take to the tussocks and run for it. It was a very athletic afternoon.

Now I come to think of it, one other of the guests from Richards' whom I remember with the same vividness, must also have been a fisherman; but he was a nice fellow, this stocky, straw-headed, newly married young man with his nondescript small bride, and found his own stretches of water to fish in, and he stays in my mind for a particularly delightful dream he innocently related to us one morning at breakfast. I don't know whether any of us – there were half a dozen men there at that time, and only the one woman – had really been eyeing his wife; I shouldn't think so. But he told us he dreamed that all of us had hooked the one trout, but he was the one who landed it, because he 'had it by the tail'. A rude story, if Freud is right; but I liked its innocence. That same young man had his sturdy, middle-aged father staying with him at the guesthouse, a farmer or some kind of tradesman, I think, and he remains memorable, too, because he used to thump insects.

Those were the nights when we all used to join in a game called 'Up and Down the River', a most appropriate game for fishermen, which consisted of a combination of just about every card game you could think of, from poker to five hundred, sitting all together round the long table in the lounge-room while the mopokes called across the valley and every kind of insect imaginable swooped in out of the night to try to commit suicide in the soft white petrol-lamp in the centre; and every time a moth or a beetle landed within range on the table, thump went that old gentleman's middle finger. I suppose he killed fifty a night, not that that made any appreciable difference to the insect population of Duckmaloi. It may have been a kind of sport, like fishing, but I think he felt, rather, that the insects were impudent. Beetles should be kept in their place. People are people, even if they are not fishermen.

There was a lot of human nature to be observed at that guesthouse; and a lot of merriment, too, as on the night they tied a bell under the bed where a pair of honeymooners were to sleep. To this day I share the misery – and wish I had done something about it – of the spinster from Sydney (thirtyish, dark-haired, pale, obviously longing for her holiday) who arrived one baking hot afternoon, took a swift gulp of the superficial discomfort of the place and, as I might well have done myself on my first arrival, departed next day with the mailman: sitting up so straight in his cart, so proud, so pale, so distressed, so inconceivably embarrassed, as slowly, like a tumbril, the vehicle floated her down the road and out of sight. If only she had stayed two days – one week – to get the feel of the place!

Of all the nights at that pleasant, homely establishment, one stands out supremely. But that was a different matter from 'Up and Down the River'. It was too beautiful to stay indoors; and, very likely, too hot. But the fierce glaring day had gone. The air was soft and warm, and the full moon was up. It was a night so full of enchantment that the whole world refused to go to sleep. There were the frogs, of course, filling the valley with their melodious uproar that, now deep, now shrill, rose at intervals to a scream of batrachian delight. The crickets trilled by millions. But that night, while my wife and I walked along the road through the radiant countryside, the cicadas, too, who ought to be singing only in the sunlight, woke and clamoured in every tree. The kookaburras blew their trumpets on the mountain, and, with notes as sweet and fluid as the moonlight itself, the magpies sang on the bare timber. How magical the day's birds sound by night; and how fantastically beautiful this earth becomes when every cranny of it is filled with soft light, and all its creatures sing!

It was on such a night, on a good many nights of moonlight or starshine – though never another quite like that – that, coming home late over the saddle across the mountain, we used to watch the flying possums, the phalangers, dropping silently through the air into their favourite blossom-tree, a yellow-box, I think it was. Their fur was silver when we turned the torch on them; their eyes, a soft opaline blue if you see them by day, glowed red like rubies. They never showed the slightest fear of us. They seemed to keep the same timetable not only night after night but year after year, coming at the same time in the same season to that one tree out of all the thousands that grew there; for they were always there as we came up through the bush, and we saw them for three or four years in succession. Once, near the guesthouse, the great tabby cat slew one and left it on the roadside; a dreadful crime, yet forgivable because that cat was a mighty hunter and used to come marching proudly back to the house early most mornings with his head high and a rabbit in his mouth. A very proud cat he looked, though it may have been partly the necessity of holding up the rabbit that made him hold his head so high.

There were fireflies, too, along that track to the saddle: not many; not often; but sometimes just two or three, green and ghostly, moving like tiny stars between the trees.

The truth was, of course, that there were miles more of that countryside to explore and to fish than we had investigated in that first disappointing fortnight. It always takes two or three trips for you to get to know a place, and always – for some mysterious reason, for surely you always know how to fish – two or three trips to the same water before you really begin to catch trout. Even in those dull waters we fished the first few days, there were, had we but known it, things besides snakes worth seeing, and fish worth catching.

There were bass. Everyone called them bream. These were a surprising fish. One expects to catch trout in a trout stream, or at least I did, not having been trained to find anything else, except, in New Zealand, eels, which fortunately were usually too slow to take a fly or even a worm if you kept it moving. But here, even in the swimming pool, were these curious bass, up to 2 pounds in weight, covered with an armour of big golden scales, and looking like a rather ugly snapper. They were good eating, too, with clean white flesh. The locals said that if you caught one you would catch a dozen or twenty, for they moved and fed in schools; and so, perhaps, if you fished in the local technique, lighting a bonfire at night, to the light of which they would be attracted, you would. I never fished for them that way, never having cared for night fishing, but it was very pleasant to dangle a worm for them in the shade of a willow or wattle on days when it really was too hot to move, catching two or three in a morning and sometimes, by a most regrettable accident, picking up a trout at the same time.

For there were trout as well as bass even in that uninteresting stretch of water nearest the guesthouse. The first I saw in the swimming pool darted up through the water behind a wall of tea-tree and took an enormous Coch-y-bondhu I was trying out in desperation – so startling me that I instantly pulled it out of his mouth. In a little runnel below the pool, flowing sweetly past a grassy bank, I watched a small trout of about a pound snap up a yellow butterfly; and put on some yellow fly myself, and got him. In the next pool upstream there was another trout

I remember well, because it required an intricate and really rather pretty bit of fishing to hook him – a backhanded looping cast to put the fly under the tea-tree where he was rising.

Once, in flood, that despised bit of water became captivating, because in every pool from the old pisé house to the swimming pool and on through the willows to the big bend around the foot of the spur, platypus – sometimes two or three to a pool – were swimming, floating among the froth and fallen willow leaves and watching you with their beady black eyes or diving in the brown water with that oily swirl that so often misleads you into thinking that the father of all trout has risen. The floodwaters must have been bringing them a feast of worms and drowned insects to tempt them from their burrows. Nothing is better in fishing than those moments when the river displays its secret life to you; and the platypus, lying flat in the water and watching you, fearless unless you move too abruptly, is the most delightful of all its creatures – though I have enjoyed meeting wombats in odd places and once spent one of the happiest mornings of my life, on the Badja River, near Cooma, watching a pair of yellow-bellied water-rats playing chasings around a half-submerged log: in and out and round about, rippling and gleaming through the sunlit water like an incarnation of its fluid delight.

It was that same flood in the Duckmaloi that gave me, too, one of the most curious and remarkable days' fishing I have ever experienced. A couple of days earlier I had had an amusing morning on the river with a fisherman from Sydney, upstream from the platypus pools, near where the old fossicker lived alone in his hut. Under the threat of imminent storm we were fishing that enormous pool where some scoundrel had a wire-netting fish-trap (which, alas, never had any fish in it when you pulled it up to take advantage of his scoundrelism). The Sydney visitor was a very dismal little man with a large, vigorous wife, leathery and weather-beaten, who professed – and with reason – the greatest admiration for him. 'If there's a fish about,' she said, 'my husband will catch it.' And her husband would have, too. Silent, small, finicky, inconceivably brilliant in his technique, he was standing at the foot of a high bank that made normal casting impossible. A trout rose right across on the far side of that great green pool.

The fisherman's fly, instead of uselessly banging against the cliff behind us, as any ordinary mortal's fly would have done, rose spiralling straight above his head, up and straight up with every flick of his wrist, until he had enough line out to reach the fish, then down, delicately down, straightening as they fell, the long delicate spirals sped across the pool to the trout. For some reason or other he missed the fish, but it was a wonderful piece of artistry.

Then five minutes later, accompanied by a mighty crack of thunder, down came the rain. And it rained and it rained and it rained and, as we crouched for shelter against the cliff, the river swelled and turned muddy before our eyes. 'Oh,' said the Sydney man dismally, 'there'll be no more fishing for a week.' Useless to tell him that at least you could fish for bass; useless to say that perhaps it would clear in two or three days. He was an impassioned pessimist and, true to his convictions, packed up and departed that night. I hope that, wherever he fled to, it stayed fine.

The Duckmaloi was a bad river in the rain – and you always get rainstorms at one time or another on any trip to the mountains. A river that runs high and clear in flood remains more or less fishable; a river that turns to mud like the Duckmaloi is useless. The trout go down to the bottom and stay there. But the Sydney visitor was wrong all the same. Within two days, though still full and discoloured, the stream had cleared enough at least to be worth exploring, and all along the edges, in a way I have never seen before or since, the trout were feeding voraciously, lying with their dorsal fins out of the water and gobbling the drowned insects. All you had to do to catch them was to drop them any kind of fly at all. It was most interesting fishing, though, dropping the fly among the froth and fallen leaves, right against the bank where the current, slower at the edges, flowed among rushes and tussocks and bushes still half-submerged by the flood; and it was strange and intriguing thus to be fishing over what was normally dry land. The trout, when eventually I cleaned those I had caught, were full of little water-snails. That is what they had been eating those two days when the river seemed unfishable; and so perhaps you could still get fish, even in the height of the flood, if you used a sinker and something that looked like a water-snail, or a big wet fly, or a worm …

It was, in fact, on that same stretch of water between the fish-trap and the platypus pools – and a noble stretch this was, too, close, rocky and wild, crowded between a high round shaly spur on one side and the mass of Mount Bindo on the other – that my good friend Dr Bruce Hittmann cured me for ever of the worm: an appropriate enough feat for one of his profession.

A little too high up in the world – he was a Macquarie Street specialist – to stay at a guesthouse where you might meet people who weren't fishermen (or who fished with worms), Dr Hittmann took a room at the hotel at Hampton, on the rim of that plateau from which, filled with miles of blue light, opens the superb chasm of the Jamieson Valley. With him came Harry Andreas, who had been a pioneer of both the trout fishing at Taupo in New Zealand and the swordfishing at Russell. Andreas was a fascinating fisherman to watch. He had reached the stage of perfectionism, of meticulous attention to technique, which all good anglers should attain in old age, where the right fly, the right gear, and the right and proper way to fish were infinitely more important than merely catching trout. He carried an iron tripod for boiling the billy in the correct manner. He had his line wound on an elaborate line-winder to let it dry out properly. He had some special gadget for undoing the knots in his cast – both nylon and gut will snap if there is a knot. He wore, as Dr Hittmann did, too, correct riding-breeches and leather leggings to ward off the snakes. He had the most dazzling array of dry flies, something to match every conceivable insect that might be on the water.

The trout were rising when we got to the Fish River – striking across country from Hampton to the big waters downstream from the Duckmaloi country – but by the time poor Andreas had erected the tripod and started the billy boiling, and unwound the line from his line-winder, and greased it, and unravelled the knots in his cast, and selected his fly, and got himself dressed to fish, the rest of us had brought in four trout and the rise was over. It is a mistake to be too finicky. All the same, I don't think any of us would have got any trout that day had it not been for Andreas's expertise, for it was he who suggested, the river being high and discoloured, that something large and bright was indicated – an Alexandra or a Butcher – and both of these flies did the trick. From that day to this, when I have to fish a flooded river, I remember old Andreas and the Alexandra.

I have cause to remember Bruce Hittmann with gratitude, too, for he used to tie his own flies and once gave me a large, impossible-looking bit of ginger fluff with which, one glorious sunny day over the saddle from the guesthouse, I caught – wading out deep in the warm summer water and casting far across the big pool to a trout that was rising in an awkward little nook under a grassy bank – a fine 3-pound brown.

With these two lords of the angle, the day after our excursion to the Fish River, I fished the Duckmaloi in the stretch between the fish-trap and the platypus pools. It was good fishing, too, though I kept losing fish because I had not then learned to tie the proper knot for a nylon cast – exasperating when you have worked out how to catch a big trout under the willow at the tail of the pool, by casting right across the current and letting the fly wheel round to him, to hook him and have him instantly snap free! But, losing them or not, the fish were there, and the dry flies snaked out prettily over the water. The sun shone, the water ran green and dappled under the willows or sparkled in the shallows. I had made friends that trip with some novice from the guesthouse – not a fisherman at all; just a bloke who had borrowed a rod and thought he'd have a go at the trout – and, taking pity on his inexperience, I had been instructing him in the art of the worm. Tom, if that was his name, was much too modest to fish with Hittmann and Andreas; in fact I had warned him not to dream of producing a worm in that majestic company. He just tagged along with us. But he was there – and so was I, and both of us wishing that we had dug a hole deep enough to disappear in for ever – when, coming to a grassy knoll at the end of the spur and seeing the excavations we had made a day or two earlier, the torn-up sods lying naked for the whole world to observe, Dr Hittmann said with ineffable disdain, 'Some fella's been digging for worms!'

Never, never again! Not the grasshopper, nor the witchetty grub (not that I have ever been able to find one), nor the freshwater mussel which I once tried out with no success at all in the Black Hole over the saddle, nor the cicada which sometimes served me so well in my misspent youth in New Zealand, nor the mud-eye, nor the drowned dragonfly (with which once in the Badja I caught nothing at all), nor the hawk-moth (which I tried desperately to make stay on the hook one night in the Duckmaloi below the old pisé house when the trout were so eager that they leapt into the tea-tree bushes after the big soft creatures swarming that night in thousands), nor the frog (which I never could bear to use anyhow, though deadly deeds were done with it on Taupo), nor the 'gentle' so beloved of Izaac Walton but scorned by all anglers of the Antipodes – never, never again any form of live-bait fishing.

Some fella, some fella, had been digging for worms! That is how dry-fly purists are made. The worst of it was – or nearly the worst of it, for nothing could surpass the horror of that accusation and the discomfort of the air of innocence we had both instantly to assume – was that Tom had been doing pretty well with the worm and had caught two nice trout in the first run he fished the first morning I took him out: while I caught nothing. It is no doubt because he got me into that awful scene with Dr Hittmann that I recall with a slightly malicious amusement the occasion, a few nights later, when Tom got himself lost on the spur going back to the guesthouse from the same reach of water. At least, he thought he was lost. For some inexplicable reason, as we were climbing the spur in the dusk, he decided we must go in totally the opposite direction: down to the river again and across up the other side, which, as I stressed with increasing emphasis, would take us up the side of Bindo and into the wilderness indeed. We had one of those dangerously tense little scenes, on the verge of a quarrel and heaven knows what sort of a mess, that blow up so quickly in a panic, until I persuaded him to climb just 100 yards or so further to the top of the spur, whereupon, glittering before us like a lighthouse in a storm, shone the distant lamps of the guesthouse – right where they always were. It was just the sort of thing a worm-fisherman would do …

I am glad, all the same, that I had not been cured of the worm on that incredible day, a year or two before Dr Hittmann's visit to Duckmaloi, when Horrie and I caught twenty fish in a morning in one little pool of the Fish River. This was in that most beautiful country which we had learned lay over the saddle that rose from the junction of the Duckmaloi and the Fish River Creek.

Downstream from the junction, the Fish River, as it now began to be called, took a long elbow bend past Gearon's farm and round the base of a spur-ragged country, and not many fish so far as I ever found out: though one day, fishing (alas) with a spinner, I had an exciting 5 minutes with a 2-pound rainbow that dashed round the far side of a little island in midstream.

I also had in that same place an even more exciting 5 minutes with the most frightful snake I have ever seen – 7 feet long it was, so Horrie told me; I was too terrified to think of measuring it. It was a gigantic brown snake, looking exactly like the fallen brown gum branches it lay among, and when I nearly trod on it, it reared up as high as my waist and hissed in horrid defiance. I did not like it at all.

The good fishing and the good water, where the river ran clear and green and deep, with shingle banks and wadeable rapids, just as a trout stream ought to be, winding through timbered hills and grassy flats, paralleled all the way by the track of cobblestones where the Chinese fossickers in the early days had built a water-race to aid them in their search for gold, lay 5 or 6 miles from Gearon's, a full day's fishing before you got to it. But if you climbed the saddle as we learned to do, sometimes walking, sometimes riding on horseback, and later, when the engineers had made a road of a kind to construct a pipeline for the dam at Oberon, perilously driving over by car, you dropped straight down onto good fishing … and into that wild country where by night we saw the flying possums and the fireflies, and by day the bush was filled with the clear calls of the native thrush.

A country full of bright water and happy creatures – of small ticking locusts and louder shrill cicadas, and honeyeaters that sang along the river all day and dipped from the wattles to splash their green wings in the pools. I remember it best in one season of searing drought when the hills around the guesthouse were teeming with thousands of rabbits – quite appalling to see; the whole hillside, eaten down to bare granite sand, would move in one verminous mass as you came over the skyline – and when all the life of that stricken countryside had crowded into the river valley to survive. We would see, vanishing in the scrub along the far bank, the dark backs of wallabies in flight; or the black snake stretched out full length on the grass; or, snorting and crashing in the scrub, a couple of the wombats that had their great burrows in the sand there; or, most curiously, we would watch hundreds of exhausted bees crawling about on the wet sand at the brink of the water, waiting for water and the cool of evening to revive them. We listened to the high clear calls of the thrushes and the honeyeaters; and to the happy singing small locusts and the trilling of the grey warbler. Bushfires smoked on Bindo; the cattle stood knee-deep in the stream, chewing great strands of water-weeds; and the mad old bull, hobbled with a chain that never seemed to hamper his roving, used to come blundering and clanking through the bushes and frighten the life out of us. We grew expert, when it was too hot to fish, at observing the small life of the stream that rejoiced in the summer weather: the little bronze lizards-skinks – which would dive into the water at our feet and come up triumphantly with a tadpole gripped in their tiny jaws; and which, so we found, could be tempted and tamed with a crumb of cake, but better still with meat. There were mussels living their dim lives among the water-weeds; and the minute sticks inhabited by the larvae of the caddis-flies which you could see fantastically moving about on the sandy bottom and which, when gently squeezed, would exude a startled little insect's head; and most fascinating of all, there were the ugly small dark-grey mud-eyes, larvae of the dragonfly, that crawled out onto a stone and slowly, slowly, if you had all morning to watch, wriggled out of their hard skins, jerked out the soft silk of their wings to dry in the sunlight and then suddenly, in one dazzling crystalline flash, took to the air and were dragonflies.

The engineers making the pipeline had built a causeway over the river at one place so that their jeeps could cross and climb, for some mysterious purpose, the high far hillside; and in this season of low water, the trout, so we found, could not get through the tunnels they had left for them. I had always believed – and still do – that except in winter when they go upstream to spawn, trout always stay in the one place. It is a fact that, day after day and year after year, you can always find a favourite fish, if you can't manage to catch him, in the spot where you know he lives. But they must, nevertheless, do quite a bit of travelling, for the quite absurd concentration of trout in the shallow, insignificant, altogether unimpressive little pool below that causeway could only be explained by the assumption that migrating fish were blocked there. Perhaps it is the smaller fish that travel, while the big fish, secure in a good feeding-spot, stay put. Certainly, none of the trout below the causeway was more than about a pound in weight. But there, anyhow, they were, and all you had to do was to drop in a worm, hook your fish at once, pull it out as quietly as possible, drop in another worm and catch another. So there we sat on the grassy bank in the sun, dangled our worms and, that morning, caught twenty trout between us. When we seemed to have cleaned out the pool Horrie climbed into the branches of the willow tree that blocked the top end of it near the causeway, and, from a hole amongst a tangle of roots and driftwood, pulled out a nice fat bass. No fish in the Duckmaloi indeed! I think that was the most surprising little pool I ever fished in my life.

But this was disgraceful fishing. And so, too, was that most curious rainy day lower down from the causeway towards the Black Hole when, fishing with a spinner, I found that every pool was alive with big fish, all on the move and all apparently feeding, but the only type of lure which seemed to interest them was the swivels on my trace which, inexplicably, they would follow with intense curiosity through the water and then, not attempting to bite at them, knock them with their noses. The spinner – Devon, Wisden or fly-spoon – never seemed any use at Duckmaloi, though once I did see a local fisherman with an enormous spoon, a rod like a telegraph pole and a

5-pound rainbow in his bag. But it is possible that some smaller lure, the size of a swivel, looking perhaps like some tiny immature fish …?

We did, I hasten to say, have great days with the fly, too, at Duckmaloi.

It was in fact on that river that a girl, a mere girl, nondescript and anonymous, one without the slightest knowledge of fish or flies or insects, a Presbyterian minister's daughter who happened to be staying at the guesthouse and used to come fishing with me for the walk — for she was a nice soul, and athletic — made for me the great discovery of my life, the one piece of expertise which I can contribute to the art and craft of angling: Tup's Indispensable.

We were fishing, the girl and I, at a pool below the old pisé house in the waters I had thought uninteresting (the ruined house, too, had its charms, for once I saw a mother swallow whose fledglings were trapped in one of the rooms, fly in again through the door out which she had escaped, and lead her fluttering brood round the room and along the corridor and through the kitchen to safety). We were fishing, I say, this noble girl and I, in the pool below the house and, though trout were rising, I was not catching them. What were they taking? There were plenty of insects about but nothing that seemed of any particular interest. They were taking, said this most observant and intelligent girl, who had been closely watching the water while I tried fly after fly in vain, 'a small grey fly'.

The only small grey fly I could find in my box — and I didn't even know its name then — was Tup's Indispensable. I tried it. There were two nice fish rising in the centre of the pool, near where it curved round the tea-tree to the tail. They both ignored the fly, prettily though it floated on the surface right over them. Then, by chance, it sank. Instantly the first fish took it, and in a few minutes I had landed the second as well. As simply as that are made the discoveries which change the course of history!

I have caught, I suppose, hundreds of trout since then on the Tup's. I have taken, or lost, all my biggest fish on it. It is always the first fly I try in the morning and the last which, towards dusk, for it seldom seems to work in the evening rise, I reluctantly change for something darker or whiter. It is not always valid, for obviously there is no sense in fishing with a blue–grey Tup's when there is a hatch of white moths or hawk moths, red ants or black ants, caddis or the black spinner. I am not sure that it works in the very high country of the Snowy — though that may be because when I have fished up there it has usually been the grasshopper season and for that the March Brown or Hardy's Favourite seem about the most acceptable offerings. But by and large, any stream and any season, and at any time of the day except dusk (and even then occasionally), the Tup's will do the trick.

It is not a very distinguished-looking fly. Just small and grey, as its discoverer said; or rather, small and bluish grey, with a blue and fawn hackle (no wings) and a touch of yellow at the thorax, and an abdomen of soft pink. I am not well enough up in entomology to say precisely what insect it represents, but it is a creature that, if you watch closely enough, you can see almost every day on the rivers, small and grey and rising in spirals above the water, usually in the late (but not too late) afternoon. It is a kind of 'nymph' – that is, the newly hatched insect rising through the water to take to the air for the first time – and for that reason, though sometimes the trout will take it floating, is best fished wet, 6 inches or so below the surface. It usually seems to be tied rather clumsily and insensitively in Australia – the yellow and pink too garish – and when I was at the height of my Tup's Indispensable period, before I shifted my headquarters to the Snowy, I used to have them sent over from New Zealand: from my fishing days in which country that first astoundingly successful specimen at Duckmaloi must have been a survivor.

Then, too, there was the discovery we made about the Black Ant: one day when these excited creatures, dressed in their shining wings for their brief nuptial flight and the founding of the new colonies, were swarming in myriads over one of the big pools across the saddle.

Fish were feasting on them everywhere, ringing the pool from end to end as if hail were falling in the sunlight. It was a day to catch a great bag of trout. But not one trout could we catch, and both Horrie and I had plenty of Black Ants in our fly-boxes. Then, by chance, we found out what they wanted. It was a Black Ant tied with a red tag at the tail; that infinitesimal spot of red – and they say that trout don't see colour! – made all the difference. I forget how many we caught – half a dozen or so between us, as quickly as we could pull them in, until, in the tea-tree or in fish that broke the cast, we lost the only two red-tied Black Ants we had. Horrie caught one more fish on a Zulu, which also is a black fly with a red tag, but the Zulu has a striped body and they weren't really keen on it. It was one of those discoveries one stores in the mind for use ever after: when the black ants are hatching, use a Black Ant with a red tag.

One other fly we discovered at Duckmaloi was the Olive Green

Dun. It was a big winged fly and whizzed over your head like an aeroplane when you made a cast; and a pretty fly, too, very appropriate in colour for that country, over the saddle, of green pools and green honeyeaters. We did very well with it one changeable Easter season, but it was not as dramatic a discovery as the Tup's or the Black Ant, and what I chiefly remember that time for was the sudden cold rains, and how Horrie would light little fires all along the river to warm his hands, and how, drowned at the mouths of their tunnels, we found the enormous golden-brown pupae of the bent-wing Swift Moths that hatch always on a stormy night at Easter. Sometimes we came upon the bodies of the great moths themselves, with stiff translucent wings and brown bodies as big as sparrows. There was, too, one gloriously sunny day that trip when the Captain of Industry who had come to fish with us – an immense man who carried on his back an immense rucksack crammed with fresh lettuces, spare fishing gear, quart-pots and a glove for handling them – charmed us by wading naked all day in the shallows where only the tiniest fish could be. 'I've been having the fun of Cork!' he told us delightedly when we came back at lunchtime from fishing the deeper water downstream; and he had, too – he'd caught twenty little trout in the morning.

Great days, in fine weather or wet! The greatest, in a sense, was the day of the monster: for that was a fish indeed, and if it did not turn the scales at more than 4 pounds, that is a pretty fair trout; and anyhow I never believed those scales. I first saw him, on my second trip to the Duckmaloi, one sunny morning on my way down to the junction. He was at the head of a pool by the roadside where a little creek ran in, and in the mouth of that creek, in about a foot of clear water, he was chasing water-beetles; round and round the shallow little creek-mouth, a curiously pale, silvery fish, shouldering the water aside as he moved, colossal in the sunlight. I was above him on the roadside, in full view of him; I dared not move a step. It seemed impossible to cast a fly downhill over the stones and bushes, landing it, as it must be landed, without a splash or an error of any kind right in that tiny pool where he swam, yet it had to be done; and that, inspired, with just the right length of line out, the fly dropping gently through the air, neither falling short in the tussocks nor reaching a yard too far and hooking the tea-tree on the other side of the pool, I did. The great trout, unimpressed, swam under my fly and continued chasing water-beetles.

He chased them in the same spot for 4 years, and every year I fished for him.

Once, in the dusk, having sneaked down into the long grass at the edge of the stream, I fished for him in the company of a small snake which rippled across the pool to greet me and disappeared among the grasses at my feet – a slightly disturbing experience. And then, one other night, stealing quietly into that same water-grass and dropping a Tup's Indispensable gently over the brink, I got him. What a commotion in that little pool. What surging and splashing and what a weight on the thin cast as he leapt. What problems with the snag in the creek-mouth. What perils in that grassy island in mid-stream! And what a strange fat silvery monster in the water-grass when at last, bulging out of the landing net, he was captured. When I gutted him, I found intact inside him a large bullfrog.

It was a night, I suddenly noticed, full of the music of frogs, shrilling or profoundly plonking. It was a night of huge silver stars. The air smelt of cool water and dry grass. There were moths. Ahead of me down the road rose the saddle of the far magical country of the phalangers and the Olive Green Dun. To the left as I turned for home lay the great dark of Bindo where the eaglehawk towered by day and the white clematis hung its stars among the timber. On the ridge to the right, hanging above the Fish River Creek, the white sally-gums and the black sally-gums moved their glittering leaves in the breeze. And back at the guesthouse, up the long dusty slope of the road, there were, I knew, the most delightful people who would admire, and subsequently eat, my tremendous 4-pound trout. The Duckmaloi, you might say, had proved itself.

DAVID SCHOLES

REVERED AS one of the great Australian contemporary writers of books on fly-fishing, Tasmanian angler, author and water colour artist David Scholes recently passed away after a lifetime enjoying the things he loved best: fly-fishing and the Australian bush.

Scholes served in the RAF in World War II as a Lancaster bomber pilot and flew a tour of operations with the elite 5 Group Bomber Command (the Dambusters Squadron). He spent his 21st birthday dodging flak in a Lancaster over Dresden. He later wrote *Air War Diaries – An Australian in Bomber Command.*

He was awarded the DFC in 1944.

The following chapters, from *Trout & Trouting* (Kangaroo Press, 1993) and *The Way of an Angler* (Jacaranda Press, 1963) respectively, are included with the generous permission of David's wife, Patricia, and family.

CHAPTER 27

Philosophy

It is usual these days, I suppose, when on the road in many parts of Australia, to meet one of those huge, thoroughly objectionable trucks with its ugly load of logs. Two things instantly come to mind: are they saw logs or pulp logs and where did they come from? The other morning, en route to the river, I met one of these monsters coming in the opposite direction. Its load consisted of just two logs, the pitiful remains of two giant and stately gums that for the greater part of a century had looked out across the timbered valley towards the rugged, rocky hilltop beyond. The sparkling stream below tumbled over stones and flood debris, edged by musk and myrtle, fern and moss. Perhaps the two noble trees had grown close enough together to converse, doubtless discussing the forest and its condition, agreeing that the summer had been abnormally dry and how urgently a decent rain was needed. And who am I to say that these trees are unable somehow to communicate. Are they not alive like you?

They had often seen the pair of eagles riding the thermals over the range and also watched closely the smoke from a lightning-strike fire that passed too close not to cause alarm. For decades they had stood there towards the edge of the sky, with only the sounds of the wind and birds and possums. Occasionally an old dead tree might crash to the ground or thunder roll down the gully, while insects buzzed to and fro. They were an integral part of God's world and totally at peace with it. As Dante Alighieri said, 'Nature is the art of God.'

They had, of late, become aware of man's existence – vaguely at any rate – because of the aircraft that sometimes passed far above, leaving tell-tale vapour trails to drift slowly away. But not until several years ago had they had any close acquaintance, when a few kilometres away a road had been constructed by forestry workers, the grinding and clanking of their heavy machinery hurting the bush.

Thereafter their world changed, for every so often a noisy vehicle whined along this road, the dust hanging in the previously clean air to settle on the rocks and stumps strewn along its sides. Once there had been rifle shots and the voices of men. But the most hideous sound of all had been the staccato of chainsaws and the screaming of the trees and undergrowth as the saws sliced and hacked their way forward, with no care for the death they wrought or the tangled mess they left behind. But logging is always associated with utter disorder and destruction.

So they passed by, these two vast trunks, I think on their way to a sawmill. No ordinary sawmill, mark you; it would have to be a big outfit to handle them, as I would estimate their greatest girth at 6 metres, while heaven alone knows their weight. Solid they were, with true heartwood to their centres, their debarked sides showing strong, clean sapwood. And as I did then, I now feel a sadness as I think of the agony of the chainsaw tearing its way through their flesh until, at length, each lofty head shuddered, slowly gathering velocity, to fall crazily earthwards, smashing all before it. Then, beheaded, debarked and rudely dragged to the loading ramp, there to lie with other hapless logs until hoisted gracelessly to the trailer, they go to be reduced to beams and planks. What are we that we make such chaos of everything we touch on earth?

The upland slopes, where these and other trees have been removed, are now completely open to the sun. No longer is there a shaded, damp carpet over the forest floor; instead even the smallest native plants cry out for moisture. And, snaking their way in all directions, are bare earth snig or caterpillar tracks, dry and rough in summer but smelly mud ruts in winter. Saplings and some crooked trees are left amongst the maze of twisted dead branches and bark. No more the virgin bush, but a kind of half and half, with scattered stumps and bruised wildlife uncertain of the long distances between habitats. This is the scene when an area is logged.

On the return home that same day, in more or less the same place, I met another huge truck with its load of logs. But this time I had no doubt about its destination; the thirty or forty mixed trees that made up its tall cargo were bound for the chipper and then to Japan. Possibly the area they had come from had been clearfelled – in other words totally destroyed – leaving a mangled mass of earth, branches and bark which might then be burnt before being replanted with row upon straight row of quick-growing eucalypts; these in turn to be cut down, the moment they are ready, to feed the chipper. You and I may love old gnarled gums with drooping twisted limbs and jumbled low scrub, with hollows in them providing homes and nests for wildlife. This, for many of us, was the Australia we fought for, and some died for, in time of war. But since then we have progressed. But worst of all, when heavy rain comes these clearfelled slopes suffer sorely. Little trickles unite to form streamlets, that combine to cut deeper and deeper into the soil, washing it downhill to the stream below, turning its clear water into a muddy torrent. No more the straining and slowing effect of the forest floor. No more the wide leafy canopy takes the brunt of wind and rain. More of the hillside is carried to the river and on to the flooded flats, while the trout do their best to cope with the murky scouring spate. No longer does stream chatter and murmur joyfully over the pebbles and gurgle over the rocks in miniature waterfalls. Even in winter, after steady rain, while it surely rose in height and its flow increased, its water still remained clear. But now, fed by the uncontrolled input from perhaps several clearfells, it tears down the valley in wild confusion.

That day I also looked in dismay at the many irrigation sprays. In theory their abstraction is limited, but does anyone really know how many billions of litres are hurled over the crops in a single day? Or what this does to the natural ecology of the streams and their inhabitants? And what about the countless introduced willows that line the banks? I have written at some length before, in *Ripples, Runs and Rises*, concerning this threat. And in the intervening years their alarming spread has gone on regardless. In these two ways our streams are severely depleted while, at the same time, our woodlands are ravaged by logging. Theodore Gordon, that grand old backwoodsman, father of dry-fly-fishing in America and creator of the immortal Quill fly, was greatly distressed by timber destruction and artificial reafforestation in his time. And so am I today.

Stop now and ponder awhile. Dream a little and refresh your mind. See there's an angler sitting on that grassy bank, old Izaak himself, his tackle beside him, as he gazes across the pool. And what does he say?

When I would beget content, and increase confidence in the power and of providence of Almighty God, I will walk in the meadows of some gliding stream, and there contemplate the lilies that take no care, and those very many other little creatures that are not only created but fed – a man knows not how – by the of the God of nature, and therefore trust in Him.

Izaak Walton, The Compleat Angler

I have been trout fishing now for a long time, ranging widely in Australia and in a number of overseas countries. I have met many people of all ages and both sexes, from office boys to supreme court judges, from wharf labourers to company directors, the unemployed to state governor. Over 50 years have come and gone since my first outing on the Yarra River at Launching Place in Victoria – a one-shop town then with a railway station and small hotel.

Today, looking back over all the thousands of trout taken after even more thousands of casts, covering thousands of kilometres and thousands of days, what have I to say about fly-fishing? I will not attempt to resolve or define why I go fly-fishing or list its attributes and delightful virtues. I have done this in previous writings. No, but let me tell you that there is what I see as a definite spirit to fly-fishing, the essential stuff or heart and soul of it, that can only become an indwelling part of the fisher through experience. Add to this the personality of the angler and his skills. Without all three being on the credit side, the balance sheet is in the red. There is no other way. To have a minus in any one of the three requirements will not do. The company has not been many, it is true, but to have known them and fished with them has been a sheer joy. Most of those I have known have, alas, made their last cast, and unfortunately, amongst the new crop of fly fishers growing up there do not appear to be many who might join this great band. The old brigade has almost died out and fly-fishing is the loser.

Several times I have had the good fortune and memorable experience of fishing for wild brown trout on private waters in Britain. There is nothing snobbish or aristocratic about it; it's simply that the owner of the property owns the land beneath the river as well as the fields beside it. He may not own the air above the land or the water that flows over it, but he owns the fishing rights and it is trespassing to go on that land without permission. One cannot even go walking there, far less fishing, shooting or mushrooming.

Here in Tasmania the law covering stream fishing is somewhat similar, but not entirely clear. The popularly held belief that an angler may walk along the bank or wade upstream from a bridge provided he does not get out on the bank is simply not true. A landowner in Tasmania may lawfully deny access to the stream, but cannot charge a fee if he does grant it. The water and fish belong to the state, but without permission from the landowner an angling licence does not permit you to angle for them!

Our British forefathers brought many pests to Australia: rabbits, foxes, starlings, perch, thistles, blackberries, gorse and more. Unfortunately, they did not bring with them their angling laws, and there is a certain amount of confusion. But when I think, say, of the Kennet above Ramsbury Mill, or below Ramsbury Manor Arches, or parts of the Wyle, there just isn't any comparison. It's like trying to compare a Holden with a Rolls-Royce. Mind you, by the same token, there is nothing to compare with the screech of a rosella parrot, the crackle of dry gum bark underfoot or the unique scent of the Australian bush after rain. Nothing.

Fishing private water overseas is often by invitation, as has been my good fortune, there being no charge; otherwise the fee varies according to the length of stream available, the quality of the fishing, the time of year and the time spent fishing. Normally fly-fishing only is allowed, sometimes limited to the use of the dry fly. This will come to Australia bit by bit. At first there will be a wide range of public water, but as time goes by, where the landowner can control it and where the fishing is of a high enough standard, private water will be established, especially stillwaters and artificially excavated ponds. In the main these will be stocked with hatchery-reared rainbow trout and, according to the size of the fishery, the use of artificial lures will be permitted in larger reservoirs.

Angling competitions will take place between teams, rather like football matches, with teams sponsored by tackle makers, breweries and wineries. But just as surely, private fishing will be instituted, where you or I can go to enjoy the style of fly-fishing we prefer. Our daily bag will be limited, sometimes to a brace or two, or the fishing may be catch and release. In either case it will be a user-pays arrangement. You may not like the sound of it, but both groups of anglers will be catered for – the numbers people and those who desire the real thing. In addition, because money and competition are involved, fishery improvement will be undertaken to attract more customers.

There are one or two other possibilities: where, for example, water is discharged from a reservoir for downstream domestic use, hydro-electric generation or irrigation, if angling restrictions are imposed and policed, and the angler pays a small fee for his sport, there would seem to be hope for some kind of running water fishing. This fishing might, of course, be affected by the artificial raising and lowering of water level as flow rates allow. But beggars can't be choosers, and unless we own or have access to private stream fishing, lovers of this kind of angling must soon learn to beg.

So, another year is over. Another season dawns. I trust I shall be granted another interlude in which to enjoy the magic of the stream and the riches of good companionship. But it's not the same hope that once set me dreaming. With the passing of each year I grow more fearful that the lifestyle which I have enjoyed and laboured to protect may be snatched away and I shall be powerless to prevent it. The wilderness is shrinking and I am well aware that what I once knew as solitude, which I need in large and regular doses and without which I become fretful, is an illusion. Just over the hill I know there is a road, a telephone and a hotel with good food, whisky and private TV. In addition, the publican is genial, the waitress pretty and at the end of the day the bed is warm and comfortable.

I find one of the most pleasant facets of our art is being able to talk about it afterwards, especially on cold, wet, winter nights before the fire. Which is why I seek out the comradeship of like-minded anglers. The thought that this way of life might be ending is too soul destroying to contemplate.

But I was greatly encouraged recently, after talking about the future of fly-fishing with a close angling friend. He is younger and more in touch with current attitudes and is quite confident that anglers themselves will take care that futuristic devices and practices will not encroach upon or alter the jewel we have cultivated and grown to love. I do hope so, because there are large numbers of people out there who have never seen a trout and would not be overly concerned if they all became impregnated with mercury, or dioxin, or DDT. We fishermen need to be seen as environmentally friendly people, but fiercely unshakable in our beliefs, as well as harmless, unfathomable cranks.

CHAPTER 28

I Believe in Fish Stories

Every so often one hears a remarkable tale about fishing. Like most strange stories, those that are passed on from person to person sometimes become progressively more extraordinary. It seems to be quite beyond human resistance not to add on a bit, or turn things round slightly, just to make the story a little more flowery or a fraction more dramatic. That is the trouble about fish stories. After hearing the same one for the third or fourth time, possibly from as many different sources, one tends to become wary, because almost invariably, each version varies to some degree. This is particularly true when you know something of the actual facts. It is only natural that you become somewhat sceptical and inclined to take things thereafter with a largish grain of salt. This is all very unfortunate, since some of the fishiest stories are absolutely bona fide, strange and incredible as they may seem.

I was, until the spring of 1961, just as questioning as most anglers, but now I am likely to accept any kind of fish story as genuine, no matter how fantastic, the change being due to the fact that I was at this time involved in a most unusual occurrence myself. But although

I had a witness present and can support my story with others very similar, whenever I relate what happened to somebody else I can detect a faint but definite look of uncertainty on the countenance, a distinct shadow of doubt.

When fishermen hear that Bill Smith captured a ten pounder at so-and-so, they like to have reliable facts on the matter before becoming convinced. Too often they are misled by inaccurate reports concerning someone else's experience. They may depart hopefully and at full speed to where tailers are stated to be in hundreds on the shores of some lake, or to some river where fish are rising like fury, only to find nothing. Quite possibly the trout were in fact behaving as described the day before but, to those newly arrived, unless there is positive proof, it is quite understandable that a very real feeling that they have been led up the garden path can develop.

Fiascos of this kind do not help one's attitude toward fish stories, they only assist in the development of an increasingly suspicious outlook. But the personal experience of some extraordinary and puzzling happening has an immediate effect. How you change! How you look back over so many tales which previously were thought so highly unlikely, but which now appear in such a completely different light. You may even feel guilty of doubting your best friends and consider you should do some apologising or else pack up and leave the district!

Against this, however, you now have a marked interest in weird and wonderful stories. You still like to get things straight, of course, but instead of turning a semi-deaf ear, you become most inquisitive. You gather all the information you can, think it over and digest it. Whenever given the slightest chance you relate your own mysterious account, especially when you feel confident that it will outdo some other. The whole business, I have discovered, provides food for much thought.

Take, for instance, the story once told to me by the late Jos Sculthorpe, a keen and skilful angler, who loved the telling of a tale as much as he did listening to one. Now Jos was a Justice of the Peace, a good and honest fellow, yet his story, when first I heard it, seemed a little incredulous – a trifle beyond the realms of straightforward comprehension. I did not at all doubt that the incident had in some way actually taken place, but, since I had never experienced a similar rarity, I was not in a position to grasp or appreciate the situation as it must have appeared to Jos, or to Bre Lutwyche, his usual fishing companion, who was also present at the time. Today, however, I have a clear conception of their thoughts and feelings and can picture the whole peculiar occurrence quite plainly.

Briefly, it all transpired one day in the summer of about 1940 at Gunn's Lake on the Central Plateau. Jos was wading knee deep in the water, fishing a dry to occasional risers that came and went within range. Presently he beheld a reasonably large fish approaching from the right, swimming along slowly in a fairly straight line. Its whole manner, however, was most unusual, for the greater part of its back showed clearly above the surface, its dorsal fin standing upright like the conning-tower of a submarine. Nearer it came and nearer, it drew almost ahead of him. The fly fell short of the mark, but not that far distant that many another fish would not gladly have altered course to collect it. Another cast was made, this time slightly overshooting the target. The trout swam on until it touched the cast somewhere in the vicinity of its junction with the line. Immediately it stopped, as if in two minds what to do next; but in a few moments it turned towards Jos, inching its way along the floating line, against which the side of its back kept contact as if magnetized. The second cast had been of moderate length, so that quite a few yards of line lay upon the water, thus giving Jos and Bre time to converse about the phenomenon as it continued to take place before them.

Presently it became obvious that in a few minutes the fish would reach the limit of the floating line. Therefore Jos lowered his rod, thereby allowing as much slack as he could to lie on the water. Bre now suggested that an attempt should be made to net the fish, as soon as it came close enough. Accordingly, Jos prepared the net and held it beneath the water ahead of him. In due course the trout, still following the line, arrived directly above the open net, whereupon Jos lifted it out with the utmost simplicity. Both men momentarily stared at each other dumbfounded before bursting into a mixture of laughter and excited chatter as they waded towards the shore. Rare it is indeed, I should say, that a fish will actually swim unhooked into the net!

Part of the extraordinary affair was quickly explained when the captive was emptied out on the bank. It was blind in both eyes, or appeared to be so, caused by a fungus growth that had spread over much of the head. Blind or not, its shape and condition were quite fair, while an autopsy disclosed that sub-aqueous food had been recently taken, no doubt obtained purely through sense of smell.

Why this fish, weighing about two-and-a-half pounds, had swum along the surface in such fashion in the first place, and why it should feel its way so carefully along the line are not, however, so easily explained. This, to be sure, was a mysterious experience and one that I feel is probably unique.

To anyone who has never witnessed something like this, such a story may well leave them somewhat non-committal. About as far as they might go is to say 'Well, I'll be damned', or words to that effect. There is no real sense of understanding, or of being able to share the feelings of the other party. But once having personally set eyes on such a peculiar occurrence associated with the sport, there is all the mutual comprehension in the world, due in the main to a definite knowledge that these sometimes almost unbelievable things happen.

The oddity which gave me this insight took place comparatively recently. On Sunday, 24 September 1961, Colin Gibson and I were fishing in the Bronte area. About midday we decided to spend a short time on the lower section of the canal that carries water from the Pine Tier Dam pipeline into Bronte Lagoon, an interesting place from which I have always taken a fair total of fish each year. Colin took the left bank and I the right. We began polaroiding our way upstream, but due to a stiff breeze our field of view was limited. Moreover, the canal was well filled, and consequently there were few shallow areas where a trout could be seen, even under the best of conditions, unless it was lying near the surface. We soon agreed that the outlook was practically hopeless and therefore walked along fairly quickly, intending to go only as far as the first concrete fluming, where I would cross over the footbridge and return to the car with Colin on his side.

However, a few hundred yards short of this point, I noticed a healthy movement in the water ahead, a yard or so out from the edge. I prepared at once to cover the area, working out line as I moved a bit nearer, soon being able vaguely to distinguish the trout, which seemed to be only about a foot under water. Clearly it was a large fish, but I was not quite close enough to see it in great detail. My Black Beetle went out in good style and I had reasonable hopes that it might even be taken first cast, when the shape in the water made another conspicuous swirl. At once I was aware that something unnatural was afoot; the disturbance had an unusual look about it. Again I cast, moving still closer as I did so. Then I realised that the fish was slowly approaching me, not head on but backwards, at about half the speed of the current. My curiosity now thoroughly aroused, I walked carefully along the bank until I had a perfectly clear view from an almost vertical position, and here began a most remarkable string of events.

First I saw that my earlier judgment had been entirely correct. The trout was certainly big. At a glance I would have put him down at a good 6 pounds and felt quite justified, but let me tell you before going further that by the time the affair was done, during which I had ample opportunity to study him closely from all angles at a distance of no more than a yard, I finished up convinced beyond all doubt that just under double figures would have been a more accurate guess. Here then was this trout, a brown, swimming against the current, but slowly losing ground for the simple reason that in his mouth he held another brown trout of at least a pound and a quarter. Even more remarkable was the fact that this smaller fish was not held by the head, nor by the tail, but amidships, just as a dog carries a bone, its dorsal fin inside the larger one's ugly hooked jaws. I sank to my knees and began calling a running commentary to Colin, who by this time was immediately opposite on the other bank and taking as intense an interest in the whole drama as I was.

I repeatedly cast my Black Beetle ahead of the pair, just to see what would happen, not actually thinking that it had any real chance of success, but rather I suppose because I had no other ideas in mind. The result was complete disinterest, while yard by yard the two fish slipped backwards, the big fellow purposely maintaining a position near enough to the edge to avoid the full force of the current and thus keep the loss of both ground and his own strength to a minimum. Quickly I snipped off the beetle and tied on a Black Matuka, with which I now proposed to tease the monster, hoping he might be provoked into making a snap at it. I dropped it all round him, skittered it across his bows, twitched it beside him and dangled it before him. The two fish drifted down over a shallow bar of clay, so I allowed the fly to settle on the bottom near the bank, waiting until the great head was level with it before giving it a short jerk shorewards. At least this brought some response. I was now close enough to detect a decided movement of the big fellow's eye as he looked over and down at the fly. He edged towards it a little, then turned off when only 6 inches away, while my commentary relayed the activity to Colin. Having by this time become somewhat exasperated, I changed my tactics completely, doing all in my power to cast the matuka so that it sank beyond the two fish in such a way that it dragged the cast into the angle between the tail of the small fish and the captor's head, my intention being then to give a mighty heave and foul hook one or the other, or at least bring about a separation. This proved a difficult task, however, and Colin suggested I try the landing net. Such was my sympathy for the unfortunate little fish which, during my most recent attempts with the matuka, had feebly wagged its tail, thus disclosing it was still alive, that I was probably willing to try anything to save it – even a blunderbuss, had I possessed one!

Accordingly I scrambled down the bank several yards downstream, hid myself behind a large protruding boulder, held the net out under the water, and waited. Slowly the fish approached me, still drifting with the current. The gap closed to about 10 feet and I could see everything very clearly – 8 feet, 5, 3. It appeared certain the scheme would work. Then, at the very last tense moment, just as I was about to raise the net, the big fish sensed the danger and eased away to the left into deeper and swifter water. Disappointed, I followed his travel, but suddenly, to my delight, the issue turned in favour of the smaller fish. It appeared that the force of the current was such that the victim was swept from the attacker's grasp. At all events they parted company and I watched them disappear in opposite directions.

Definitely heartened by this escape, I clambered back up the steep bank, but had only just reached the top when the noise of splashing drew my attention back to the water's edge a little downstream. What happened next can only be described as pitiful to look upon. The small trout lay half beached on the shore, partly behind a piece of rock, while, standing off in deeper water, the marauder eyed the lost prey eagerly. Then, without warning, in a reckless attempt at recapture, he rushed at the bank, desperately trying to seize the quarry. But, although almost stranding himself, this and further such efforts failed. Thwarted, be began patrolling to and fro, and it seemed that the game had been lost. Unfortunately the little fish, which had remained almost stationary during these ferocious attacks, stupidly made the dreadful mistake of forsaking his place of shelter – no doubt with the idea of finding a better one – and wriggling along through the shallows like an eel, finally coming to rest with his foreparts poked into an inlet but, alas, his tail end protruding. With one terrible charge the huge assailant swept in, closing his jaws on the projecting tail. Several heaves succeeded in dislodging the smaller adversary, which was towed backwards for almost a yard before, with lightning swiftness, it was first released then taken into the mouth crossways just as before, the dorsal fin hidden from view. A look of proud achievement surrounded the huge killer as he slowly disappeared with the prize, sinking from sight into the deepest part of the canal, probably to take up station behind a large stone on the bottom where I could no longer upset his gruesome plans, the final outcome of which remains unknown.

However, the matter did not entirely end there, for as I swore and declared to Colin that day, I went back looking for this outlaw, hoping to meet on even terms when his mind was not engrossed in such abnormal activity. I knew that my chances of at least seeing him were quite fair, since, in normal seasons, it is the policy of the Hydro-Electric Commission to reduce by degrees the outflow from Pine Tier Dam as the summer approaches, so that by January, if not before, there is an average depth of only a few feet of water in the canal.

On 8 January 1962, I made a quick search of the area, and in spite of a gusty wind, I was pleased to observe a huge green shape moving away downstream as I polaroided along, the fish obviously having seen me first. Apart from a few other large trout in the 5 to 6-pound class, the run in the canal has always, to my knowledge, been dominated by round about 2-pounders. This outsized specimen, and one other similar, possibly even the same, which Reg Clayton and I discovered the year before, were quite outstanding and unmistakable amongst the others. For this reason, coupled with the fact that the monster I had just scared was in the same vicinity as that where the incident I have just described took place, I concluded that I was face to face with the same person. I therefore departed, completely satisfied and determined to return under more suitable conditions to do battle.

The very next day turned out admirably. Hence, accompanied appropriately enough by Colin Gibson, who had met me the previous afternoon for a little fishing together before we moved on to Tarraleah for a few days to act as guides and ghillies to the then Governor of Tasmania, Lord Rowallan, and Lady Rowallan, I once more went seeking this special fish. It was a beautiful morning as we drove back to Bronte from our dawn patrol at the Dee Lagoon. The sun shone brightly. The air was still and warm. I took the right bank and Colin the left, just as we had on the day of the original meeting.

On the walk up we caught two rainbows and a brown on the dry, all three of which we polaroided with great ease. About 100 yards short of where I had seen the big trout the day before, I began to scan the water particularly carefully, determined if possible not to be seen first this time. Even so I was unable to resist the temptation of casting to yet another rainbow that I came upon swaggering downstream just bursting to rise at anything. Duly landed and bagged, I went cautiously on, everything at the ready, but feeling half certain I had already muddled my chances by fishing to this irresistible cruiser.

Then, hardly more than a chain and a half upstream, I saw him. Instantly, I dropped to the ground, warning Colin as I did so. Carefully raising myself I peeped over the bank and watched him coming downstream towards me close to the edge. Like all the others we had seen, he was clearly on the prowl for surface food, eyes cocked upwards and swimming quite near to the surface. Have you never had a feeling of absolute confidence as you cast to a trout, knowing while the fly is still airborne that he is yours? I have, and I know of others like me. Anyway, that is how I felt just then, as I lengthened line over the land, preparatory to delivering the fly in his path. But, with fiendish timing, as if conjured up from nowhere especially for the occasion, a willie-willie drove down upon me from the nearby hill, raising the dust and leaves and ruffling the water viciously. No longer could I control the line in the air. No longer could I see the fish or go on with the job at all. I let the fly fall aimlessly on dry land and sank to the ground disgusted and silent, while Colin cursed long and lustily. Almost at the same time as the wind arrived the sun went behind the only cloud in the sky. I was never meant to catch that trout, for when the wind subsided and the sun reappeared, search as I might, I found no trace of him. And although I have returned twice more, the visits have been fruitless. The last time I went the water was so low and clear that I have no doubt whatever that he was absent – either caught, shot, died naturally, or shifted camp down into Bronte Lagoon.

So ended an extraordinary experience, but I am not so sure that such unsavoury behaviour as that which I beheld is as unique between large ill-tempered trout and their smaller brethren as one might imagine. Although until this time I had never so much as heard of this kind of thing, I have since had discussions with two other anglers who have witnessed similar occurrences, and it is logical to suppose there are others also who are unknown to me. Against this it is just as reasonable to assume that attacks of this sort by large fish are not that frequent either, otherwise they would be common observations amongst fishermen. What I thought was probably a completely singular instance has turned out instead to be only something rare. Even so, an angler who views such a thing must count himself lucky. The majority, no matter how often they fish, will never see it.

Oddly enough, the first of those to hear my story and then come up with another like it was Bre Lutwyche.

In the summer of 1948 he was staying at Miena, Great Lake, and was fishing a wet on the rocky point opposite the hotel when he noticed something unusual drifting in the waves. This, of course, turned out to be a large trout with another held crosswise in its mouth. Bre was successful in foul-hooking the big one in the dorsal fin. Showing great presence of mind, he applied only just sufficient strain to guide the pair towards him, assisted by the wind, until eventually he netted them both! The assailant was a brown of some 5 pounds, only in moderate condition and with a large head, while the victim, already dead and considerably lacerated about the back and shoulders, was another brown of a little more than a pound. Returning to the hotel Bre told his tale, which caused much conjecture and speculation.

The other account was given to me by Martin Wallace, a Launceston angler who, in the early 1950s, was fishing the North Esk at 'Whisloca' when he came upon a big trout in the shallows holding a smaller one captive, once again crossways like a dog with a stick. Martin estimates that the weights of the fish were about 5 pounds and $^3/_4$ pound respectively and, as in the case of my own observation, the large fish had difficulty swimming against the current with the awkward burden. Martin likewise attempted to use his landing net, but was unsuccessful, the big fish cunningly manoeuvring into deep water and thus escaping.

By no means the least remarkable part of all these reports is the fact that in no instance did it seem possible for the larger trout ever to swallow the smaller one, no matter how attempted. It was just a physical impossibility. In Bre Lutwyche's case the captive appeared to have been dead for some time, and it does not seem likely, therefore, that having had both the time and opportunity, there was any intention on the part of the large one to swallow the other. I also find it difficult to believe that the assailant would finish up trying to bite or chew the prey into pieces to eat it. My conclusion is that the whole act is simply one of sheer brutality on the part of an old, senile, bullying type of fish, some kind of cruel satisfaction and pleasure being derived from holding the victim prisoner in this way until it dies through fear and exhaustion.

CARL MASSY

CARL MASSY was born in Yass, New South Wales, in 1906. After studying wool classing at technical college and doing some jackarooing, he moved to the Cooma district.

He began trout fishing in 1915, and spent the remainder of his lifetime fishing the waters of New South Wales and far northeastern Victoria, acquiring an unequalled knowledge of fly-fishing in the streams and lakes of those regions along the way. To him, fly-fishing was the ultimate challenge, requiring careful thought, observation and skill. He also fished extensively in Tasmania and New Zealand.

Carl's book, *Fly Fishing for Trout*, was first published in 1976 by A H and A W Reed Pty Ltd and quickly became recommended reading for anyone interested in learning the art of fly-fishing. A recent search on the internet listed 11 available at reasonable prices; it is well worth adding to any angler's library.

Permission for this article was given by Carl's son, Charles Massy.

CHAPTER 29

Fly-fishing for Trout

There is a bit of child in every fisherman, and with most of us there is a bit of a thrill linked up with opening day, especially after the long layoff from fishing in the winter months. During this time the only way the angler can participate in his sport is by reading about it, tinkering with his tackle, or fishing the lakes which are not closed, provided one does not mind nearly freezing to death and fishing a longtail blind. The preparation for the day and the dawning of the day are the high points.

Opening Day 1956 saw a party organised to fish George Taylor's Dam at Shirley. The party assembled at the dam the evening before the opening. Pack and John Sautelle had organised the tent flies and the bales of straw for our bunks, while we had each made arrangements for our own provisions. The party consisted of Frank Greene, Frank Timson, Pack and John Sautelle, Dick Carter, Allen Caldwell, George Sautelle and myself.

After we had set up our camp, we began to get to know each other better, as three members were new to the locals. Accordingly, quite a few fishermen's truths were told and lemonade was drunk. Later on in the evening George distinguished himself by quoting the whole of 'The Man from Snowy River' without a slur.

Time passed quickly, then Pack looked at his watch and announced it was 2 minutes past 12 and the season was now open. As our rods were assembled, we adjourned to the nearby dam and commenced wet fly-fishing. Almost immediately Pack caught a nice rainbow, and in half an hour we had eight or nine very nice fish – rainbows of from 1.5 to 2 or more kilograms – on the bank. The dam contained only rainbows, and mostly big ones. Retiring to our bunks, we arose early next morning and continued fishing. More fish were caught, but later on the sport tapered off.

Still the pleasant day continued and a little more grog was drunk. One of the party – no names, no pack drill – fell over head first in the dam while wading in less than a metre of water and maintained he had tripped over a stone.

It was my great friend and angling companion Dick Carter's inauguration to trout fishing; he is now a very dedicated and most capable angler, but as he often said to me in later years, 'By gee, I was raw in every way.'

Some years later the water and irrigation people compelled George Taylor to empty the dam for repair work. When George had had the dam constructed, he had a large pipe installed through the wall near its bottom with a gate valve attached. Some seepage occurred along the sides of the pipe, and for the safety of properties further down the creek the dam had to be drained.

Allan Caldwell, Pack and John Sautelle and I carried out the job of emptying the dam. We drove iron posts across the creek 50 or 60 metres below the dam, tied netting to them and stoned the bottom of the netting. Then the gate valve was opened full on. It took two and a half days to empty the dam, but few fish came through the pipe, as there were very few in the dam at that time.

The dam, when emptied, revealed countless thousands of mud-eyes in, under and on every log, stone or other cover below the water, hence the big fish. Some extremely big eels came through the pipe and these were killed. The fish were transported in a tank on a lorry up to the smaller dam in front of Shirley House.

However, the following morning it was found that they had all died – glorious fish up to 4.5 kilograms. Apparently they were too fat and not tough enough to stand the shift.

Rainbows are extremely suitable for stocking dams: they grow quickly, are more easily caught and are great fighters, but they are shorter lived than the browns and become spawnbound at an early age unless they have access to a suitable spawning area.

Back in 1932 I secured a copy of J.M. Gillies' catalogue from Melbourne. Malcolm Gillies was an excellent fly tier and his shop carried high-class rods and tackle. From this catalogue I ordered about six patterns of longtails, including red and black matuka, yellow and black matuka, and green matuka. I found the red and black matuka to be absolutely deadly on the McLaughlin, but (selfishly) I kept this pattern quiet, and told only one person of its success. This friend (for the sake of a name we will call him Jim) was sworn to secrecy. However, he gave a copy to a friend who tied flies and this was the end of the hush-hush.

Years later I wanted to try a very successful American fly and needed feathers so that Dick Wigram could tie me a batch of flies. The fly was the marabou, and the original wing feather was from a stork. The nearest available local feather was from a goose.

The next time I was in Cooma I told Jim that I had another deadly fly, but could not afford to let him know what it was after his previous effort at secrecy. However, I said the feathers are not terribly difficult to secure and we were having the bird they come from for lunch on Sunday. At the time my son Charles, aged about eight or nine, was home for a couple of weeks of school holidays. The following week we were going to Cooma and I realised Jim would try and pump Charlie. We persuaded Charlie that if Jim asked what he had for lunch on Sunday, he should tell him it was a humming bird – it was not really a terrible lie, only a joke. At that time Jim was secretary in a Cooma store. Placing ourselves strategically in the store, my wife and I saw Jim bearing down on Charlie. After the opening gambit, he said: 'Gee, you look well Charlie, they must feed you splendidly at school. But I suppose you get extra goodie on Sunday at home. What special dish did you have on Sunday?'

Charlie replied, 'Humming bird, Mr Blank', and parental laughter caused Jim to turn scarlet. Poor Jim never did discover the name of the great fly. Jim had a great knowledge of fishing spots on the Monaro and dearly loved a joke, even at his own expense.

Father was a very punctual man, and to a certain extent intolerant of anyone who did not come properly prepared for the day's fishing or who forgot some of his equipment.

On one occasion five of us journeyed to Burrinjuck to fish below the wall. Access was allowed in those days, and there was a great number of very big fish … On this day it turned out my father had forgotten his reel. He had taken it out of his creel the night before to oil it and left it on the dressing table. The upshot was that no one said he had a spare reel to lend. Father became grumpy under the ribbing he received, until finally Alan Smith produced a spare reel which the rest of the party knew was available.

On a Saturday afternoon these friends generally used to gather for a few drinks in the lounge of the Club House Hotel in Yass. The Saturday following the visit to Burrinjuck, while they were in the lounge, a knock came on the door. The proprietress, Mrs Duddlestone, answered it to find the Sergeant of Police, who asked which was Mr Massy and would she please send him over to the door. The Sergeant had been freshly posted to Yass and my father did not know him. When Dad went to the door the Sergeant presented him with a summons. Dad retired with a worried look to the corner of the lounge, with all the boys nudging each other and immensely enjoying the proceedings. The summons charged Dad with committing mutiny on the trip, being unbearable, and so forth. The judgement was attached and it directed that he had to shout two drinks for everyone who fronted the lounge bar that afternoon. I still have the summons, drawn for the High Court of Burrinjuck, and it was drawn up in correct legal style by one of the local solicitors, with seal and ribbons attached.

GREG
FRENCH

GREG FRENCH is a freelance photo journalist who writes regularly for major fishing magazines such as *FlyLife* and *Freshwater Fishing*.

His first book was *Tasmanian Trouting – Where and How*, self-published in 1984. This guidebook has been updated several times. The latest edition, retitled *Tasmanian Trout Waters*, was produced by the Australian Fishing Network in 2002.

Also in 2002, New Holland published *Frog Call*, a novel-length work of literary non-fiction based around fly-fishing.

Other publications include: *Trout Guide* (co-written with Rob Sloane) (Tas-Trout Publications, 1991) and *Western Lakes Trout Fishery Management Plan* (co-written with Rob Sloane) (Government of Tasmania, 1991).

This article is reproduced from *Frog Call*, with permission from New Holland Publishers and Greg French.

CHAPTER 30

Ephemeral Thoughts

My library includes a number of volumes written by anglers about mayflies, some of which are devoted to just one of the world's fifteen hundred or so species.

The word 'mayfly' is an old English term, reflecting the modest but welcome warmth of northern springtimes in which the local danicas are inclined to burst forth. Doubtless it was coined and promoted by gentleman naturalists, many of whom would have been complicit in the birth and development of modern fly-fishing.

When you think about it, the names of many insects are unflattering – dragonflies, mud-eyes, stoneflies. Robust and possibly apt, but hardly romantic. Mayflies, on the other hand, inspire gentle baptisms. America has its green drakes and light Cahills, mainland Australia has its Kosciuszko duns, and in New Zealand most species appear to have regal entitlement to their full and glorious taxonomic names. In Tasmania, we have Macquarie reds, highland duns and Penstock browns. I'll admit that we call the smaller versions smut, but I'll put this apparent anomaly down to the insect's ability to bring out in the man something of the little boy.

For several months since my daughter's birth she has remained seriously ill. Finally (against what I think is my better judgment) Lester convinces me to leave her bedside and accompany him on a day trip to Arthurs Lake where the mayflies are in full swing. The weather is perfect: warm and still with the full blast of the sun tempered somewhat by a thin skin of high-level cloud. Countless fish are rising, their rhythmic slurps, sucks and clops clearly audible 100 metres from the water's edge. These are days that fly fishers dream about, the sort that even junkies might encounter just once or twice in a season. But I simply don't have the energy to fish. Nor am I especially good company. I sit alone on the lakeshore, watching mayflies.

Staring into the weedy shallows I see a scurry of tiny green nymphs and watch transfixed as one after another they ascend to the surface film. How vulnerable they seem and, indeed, trout are ruthless and relentless in their pursuit of such easy tucker. Once an insect feels the resistance of the meniscus, the transformation to the next phase is instantaneous. Only if the animal is especially weak or deformed can I observe the actual splitting of the nymph shuck and the emergence of the sub imago, the revered dun. Mostly it is quite an illusion, akin to magicians pulling rabbits from hats. And, like rabbits, they are prolific.

Duns are anything but confident, sharing an awkwardness common amongst pimply adolescents. They are dull in colour, with damp opaque wings, and have difficulty flying. Today they sit moodily on the water for long periods, holding their wings erect and together, drifting aimlessly.

Trout are unhurried in these conditions, clomping down the hatchlings one after the other, their rises being rhythmic and entirely predictable. I am sure that Lester is having a ball.

Duns that do not succumb ultimately fly away or drift onto the shore, where they split again and emerge as adult spinners. On perfect days such as this one, the dun phase can last for less than an hour.

The adults, shiny and vibrant, come swarming back over the lake in big spiralling clouds, dancing a pagan ritual that causes light to refract in rainbow colours from their transparent wings. The trout, quickly seduced, begin leaping high into the air, desperate in their attempts to get early samples of the feast to come. Their impatience and recklessness are breathtaking.

Finally the spinners exhaust themselves and, in the closing scene, they fall spent to the surface, where the trout are able to eat them at their leisure. And, of course, they do so with gusto.

Many non-anglers know mayflies as dayflies, and many poets have remarked on the tragedy of their brief existence. Even in science we allude to this, lumping them in the insect order Ephemeroptera. But strangely enough, as I watch the swimming, the popping, the hatching, the swarming, the mating, the dying and the being eaten, it doesn't seem in the slightest bit absurd. Melancholy, yes, but beautiful too, as intimate as a symphony.

Suddenly I need more than life itself to hold my daughter. I do the unthinkable, the unforgivable – I call Lester off the water mid-rise and force him to drive me back to my family.

• • •

Jane is older now, and as healthy as can be. She shares her father's love of animals and yesterday she pointed out that if you look really closely at a mayfly's thorax it looks almost prehistoric, bearing an uncanny resemblance to the bodies of dragonflies and damsels. She is right, of course. Ephemeroptera has a primitive ancestry, a genesis in the Permian. Mayflies have survived the global catastrophe that obliterated dinosaurs and, no doubt, many other disasters besides. They are not so ephemeral after all.

I gaze into my daughter's eyes. Life, it seems, is at once far more fragile and far more robust than I ever suspected.

ROB
SLOANE

ROB WAS born in Manchester, England, in 1955. His family emigrated to Australia in 1961 and settled in Devonport, Tasmania, later moving to Hobart. Introduced to fly-fishing by his father Tony, he wrote his first article for *Australian Outdoors* while still a student, at age 15.

Now married with three sons, he lives on the banks of the Coal River in Richmond, Tasmania, where he edits and publishes the quarterly fly-fishing journal *FlyLife*.

He gained a First Class Honours degree and later Doctor of Philosophy at the University of Tasmania, and worked as a trout biologist with the Tasmanian Inland Fisheries Commission before being appointed as Commissioner of Inland Fisheries in 1984 (–1990).

As well as numerous scientific and technical publications, he has contributed hundreds of popular fishing articles to magazines including *Australian Outdoors, Freshwater Fishing, Flyfishers Annual, Modern Fishing, Fly-fishing, Better Fishing, Fishing World, Flyfisher* (New Zealand), *The Complete Fly Fisherman* (South Africa) and *FlyLife*.

He has also written a number of books, including *The Truth About Trout* (1983), *More About Trout* (1987), *Trout Guide* (1992), *Fly-fishing Fundamentals* (1993) *Australia's Best Trout Flies* (1997), *The Truth About Trout Revisited* (2002) and *Short Casts* (2004).

Rob secured and organised the VIIIth World Fly-fishing Championships, which were held in Tasmania in 1988.

In this chapter from *FlyLife* issue 24 winter 2001 Rob explains the fly-fishing fascination of lakes, particularly his home waters in the highlands of Tasmania. This and the following chapter from *FlyLife* issue 4 winter 1996 are included with his permission.

CHAPTER 31

In Praise of Still Waters

One of the great attractions of stream fishing is the sense of intimacy that develops between river and angler: knowing each stretch with all its features and intricacies, its do's and don'ts; knowing where to cross and knowing which bank gives the tactical advantage; knowing the prime trout lies and even getting to know the haunts of individual fish. Surprisingly, lakes, even the larger ones, offer the same intimacy, although it may take far longer to establish. Only after many years, fishing week in and week out, does a vast stillwater reveal its true character.

If one were to equate the challenge of fishing a river to solving a crossword puzzle, then the cryptic clues to the same puzzle might well equate to fishing a lake. The clues are there all right, but they are not immediately apparent; they are jumbled and a little confused.

The skilled stream exponent knows where the fish are in a river – there is always a sense of fish being close by and within range. See them or not, you know that a good pool holds a fish or two, be it an educated guess or a recollection based on past experience. By following the thread of current through a pool you can reasonably predict where a fish might intercept the fly – where the water deepens or the bubble line runs close to an undercut bank or sunken log.

Even on unfamiliar water a basic knowledge of streamcraft will stand you in good stead. But lakes rarely concede such predictability. To stand on a windswept lake shore and be confident of finding fish is not a task for the fainthearted. To know a lake intimately and to stalk its trout with reliable success requires great dedication, a lot of thought, careful observation and very keen eyes.

One-eyed

The best thing about Tasmanian lakes is that for the most part they are relatively shallow, which facilitates sight fishing from both bank and boat. A floating line is all you need on most occasions. At elevations around 1,000 metres and latitudes close to 40°S, water rarely becomes too hot for surface and shallows feeding even at the height of summer. Essentially it is 'flats fishing', which combines drifting or wading with stalking individual fish. This inevitably means keeping on the move and covering lots of water. For me the pleasure is in hunting down the fish, not waiting for the fish to find the fly.

Though I once wandered along shores with enthusiasm to search blind with the fly, I now find this less rewarding in terms of both catch and satisfaction. Doing the 'hard work' is, however, a very important foundation in one's later understanding, and unless you are prepared to rely on a guide, you must invest time and effort to make sense of lakes and in so doing achieve consistent results.

For me, seeing and stalking fish is the real challenge in any environment and the best trout lakes offer this sort of fishing in abundance. Whether it be rising fish, polaroiding, or tailers in the shallows, lakes still provide that one to one encounter which lies at the heart of the best forms of fly-fishing.

One Chance

One of the most stimulating aspects of lake fishing is that so often it is 'one chance' fishing. Whereas a river fish on station may hang about and pass judgment on several of your flies, rarely does this luxury extend to lakes, where fish come and go as they please and rarely stay in range for long. If you mess up a trout in a stream and return an hour or so later, or perhaps the next day, or even a week later, there is still a chance you might correct that initial mistake.

But lakes are less forgiving in terms of time and place, although sheer numbers of fish can be adequate compensation. There is rarely much cover to conceal your approach and the fish are constantly on the move. Once committed to a cast there is no going back, and the fish are as flighty as any in a stream.

In lakes the fishing is spiced by a sense of urgency which demands fast, decisive action and first-time precision. This puts a very keen edge on the whole lake performance, and leaves you pleading for a second chance.

One Fly

I know several leading guides and competition anglers who use multiple flies to great effect on our local lakes and I've fished with some of the world's best 'hangers and dribblers', but I still find that more than one fly can be a real nuisance in a sight-fishing situation when it matters most. When fishing downwind in front of a drifting boat it is easy to turn over and lay out a team of flies, but when turning instinctively to cover a fish upwind, my leader invariably ends up in a mess.

Inevitably, unless you opt to keep two rods made up at the ready, one with a single dry and the other a loch-style or dry fly team, you have to decide whether to cover the water or actively seek out and target individual fish. I'm clearly in the latter camp, so I'm normally a one fly man.

I have said previously that fly is often a functional nondescript, and between November and March it is invariably a dry. Lake fishing, with its sense of urgency, favours reliability and versatility in a fly – perhaps a Red Tag, beetle pattern, or mayfly dun or spinner, depending on the mood. Often it makes no difference, but if somebody tries to tell you that lake fish are not as discerning as their relatives in the rivers, then offer them soap to wash out their mouth. The most difficult trout I have encountered have been lake fish sipping tiny mayflies, taking midge emergers or grubbing amphipods out of the weed. And around lake shores in the late afternoon, trout leaping at adult mayfly spinners can be just as hard to fool as those in any meadow stream.

One Theory

Streamcraft can and has been explained worldwide in considerable detail, but similar analysis of lake fishing skills, particularly those that are sight dependent, is comparatively futile, because firstly you need to find the fish. Techniques and flies can certainly be described, but when it comes to facing up to a vast expanse of seemingly featureless water, it's a question of where to start applying that theory.

Doubtless, local knowledge is more important on lakes. Whereas most streams are predictable enough to instil some confidence from the start, lakes suffer many more variables related to weather, wind, season and water level changes (especially on hydro impoundments).

In the faster rivers, trout tend to favour places where a supply of food is carried to them. A trade-off between a safe hiding place and a good food supply, in competition with other fish, will generally establish a stream trout's territory. Insects drifting directly overhead create a hatch and the fish's response establishes the rise. In a lake these clues are far more cryptic, because the food supply can be scattered far and wide and the fish will move considerable distances to take advantage of it. Even if you are in the right area, on windy days their rises will often go unnoticed by all but the most highly trained eyes.

'Find the food and find the fish' is one of the basic rules that drive sight fishing on lakes, whether boat or shore based. Always be on the lookout for signs of a likely food source in or on the water – lake trout will invariably gather and be most catchable wherever there's an easy meal. When food is really concentrated, in a narrow windlane for example, they will abandon territorial instincts and feed happily together, a sight for sore eyes.

Evidence of trout food may take the form of a conspicuous hatch, nymph shucks in the water or clinging to rocks or tree stumps, drowned worms and grubs along flooded edges, or windfall litter rafted up on a warm and windy day. And don't just head for quiet corners; wind-generated currents will carry food along exposed shores as well.

Just as the knowing stream-angler understands the relationship between cover, flow, drift and depth, those familiar with lakes can identify physical features which reliably attract fish. Shallow weedy bays and flooded margins, deeper points and drop-offs, windlanes and surface slicks, wadeable flats near inflows and outflows – these are all good places to start looking. These aspects are well summarised in *Fly-fishing Fundamentals* and I won't repeat myself here, but bear in mind that persistence, confidence and keen eyesight are factors which deserve greater emphasis in all honesty.

In time the true personality of a lake will be revealed and a relationship develops that can be as rewarding as any in fly-fishing. Some lakes, I admit, don't offer much challenge – they may be relatively featureless or the trout too small and predictable – but others can present a lifelong challenge and well and truly earn your respect.

As with stream fishing, you will eventually find that the principles learned on one lake will help you get started on others, and when you travel interstate or overseas you will find that foreign lakes that support wild fish share much in common with local waters. In the Snowy Mountains, Chile and New Zealand I have found that a 'Tasmanian' approach to lake fishing pays dividends with trout inhabiting the same familiar places with a surprising degree of predictability.

Eventually, as you drive over a hill and first sight a lake you'll be saying 'Look at that windlane', or 'That bay looks great', or 'Let's wade that sand flat', with the same enthusiasm that has always rendered bridge crossings so dangerous when fly fishers are at the wheel.

CHAPTER 32

Doing It Tough in the Western Lakes

Without doubt, Tasmania's remote Western Lakes region offers a unique experience in the world of fly-fishing. Stories of backpacking in to unfished waters and stalking trophy brown trout across clear water shallows paint a glamorous picture for the uninitiated. But this exposed plateau of countless natural lakes is hardly glamorous country. Much of it is rocky, barren and relatively featureless, and it can be bitterly inhospitable, even in midsummer. Good days in this region are like rare gems, to be collected, treasured, talked about and revisited time and time again.

Don't get me wrong, I love this country, and in all my travels I have not found fishing that is more challenging or offers greater reward. But for most visitors, unrealistic expectations are the biggest problem – words like 'remote', 'unfished', 'untouched', 'unexploited' and even 'virgin', conjure images of trout swimming between the legs and fighting each other to get to the fly. This couldn't be further from reality.

I am reminded of a trout guide who was booked by a well-to-do client with a special request to camp out and fish in the wilds of the Western Lakes. On the way up from the airport they stopped at Arthurs Lake and the client took half a dozen nice browns on the dry. After enduring the initial bone-jarring four-wheel-drive trip, and walking their legs off in search of fish the following day, the next three days were spent playing cards in the tent as the wind howled and threatened to blow them away. With time running out, the client had little hesitation in opting to pack up and return to Arthurs for the last couple of days, with the romance of the Western Lakes well and truly blown out of his system, probably for life!

In reality this is very tough country, dangerously severe at times, and the trout are rarely bigger, and certainly no more plentiful, than in any number of other lakes that can be reached in the family car. Even in the furthest corners of this region, in those so-called unfished waters, I can introduce you to trout that have degrees in cunning from no lesser institute than Cunning University.

So what is the attraction? Western Lakes adventures are exactly that – adventures. Good trout and red-letter days spring to mind, but so too do disastrous trips, snow storms, tearing gales, flattened tents, unintended detours, unusual meals, secret places, devils chewing cork rod grips and stealing fuel bottles, snake stories … and, most of all, good company. If ever the saying 'there's more to fly-fishing than simply catching fish' has a place, it would have to be in the Western Lakes, where if numbers of fish caught were to be divided by hours expended in catching them, there would be some very, very red faces!

Yes, the attraction is measured in the tiniest nips of the sweetest water on the planet, clear-sky days of cobalt blue, sunsets of fire-engine red, brilliant star-filled nights, vibrant aurora displays and occasionally, just occasionally, some modest success with the fly rod.

Sage Advice

Firstly, the sage advice I'm about to offer is not related to any particular brand of rod … if only catching fish in the Western Lakes were that easy! No, the rod you carry is basically irrelevant, though I might suggest something in at least four pieces for convenience, protected in an aluminium or sturdy PVC tube for insurance, and perhaps something in the vicinity of a 5, 6 or 7 weight, depending on your preference – I use a 5.

No, the important thing is that you must be prepared to fish in the wind, and, even more importantly, be able to cast into the wind! If you can't, then stay at home. There are no willow trees to hide behind out here; in fact, on the more elevated parts of the plateau, there are very few trees at all. Should you be lucky enough to actually see a trout (don't laugh, some people spend a week in this country and never see one) – perhaps a rise or a slash in the waves, or a hesitant tail along some sheltered edge – then you must be able to present a fly post-haste, right on the spot, or the opportunity will be lost.

You don't have to be able to unload the whole fly line, or cast with two rods at once, but you do need to be able to punch out a short line accurately with the wind right into your teeth. A stiff, tapered leader with heavy butt and a shooting taper line with a short belly and steep front taper will help in this regard, but, most of all, you must practise your casting before venturing into this domain.

Doing It Tough

If your back is against the wall, the weather is foul, and the fish aren't showing, then you're going to have to pull down your balaclava and start flogging the water. This sounds pretty grim, and it probably will be … but if you've come to fish the Western Lakes, then so be it.

Put on a big wet – a Fur Fly, Yeti, Robin, Mrs Simpson, Matuka, Fuzzy Wuzzy, Woolly Worm or whatever – and start fishing along the edges. Get into the water if possible – the ruffled surface will help disguise your presence. If you stand on an open bank waving a fly rod around you will stick out like a sore thumb.

One peculiarity about many of these waters is that they are relatively shallow all over. This makes the banks with their undercut edges an attractive proposition for the trout. Here they can stay close to cover and take advantage of all sorts of interesting food. Just standing on the bank and casting straight out will mean you've missed the most productive water, between the rod tip and where you lift off the fly to recast.

Undoubtedly, the way to search this water is by wading quietly along and poking the fly into every likely edge cavity, drain, ditch and runnel. Large rocks protruding out of the silt bed are also worth a cast. These generally harbour undercut depressions caused by wave action, and in many of the shallower lagoons the trout have nowhere else to hide.

In a past life I thrashed the more accessible waters in the early months of the season – snow storms and all – and the wet fly-fishing is generally best from late September through October and November. It is especially good (there I go again!) after rain, when the fish move confidently into shallow drains and backwaters to ambush spawning frogs and, later, tadpoles.

Tailers

Now that I'm sounding more confident, and talking about springtime fishing, then I had better warn you about another Western Lakes wet dream – the tailing trout. It is true that in the shallower lakes with grassy shorelines, or gravelly edges, tailing fish are a likely prospect.

Whether it should be listed as a positive or a negative I'm not sure, but in this part of Tasmania the fish will tail all day … in miserable conditions. When it's cold they tend to become active in the shallows during the warmest part of the day – this reduces the need for really early starts and late finishes.

Again, the wind can make finding them quite difficult, because those subtle dimples, bumps and faint stirrings which give tailing fish away in calm water are that much harder to identify in blustery conditions. And then you've got to be capable of delivering the fly …

As many readers will already know, I'm in favour of inert presentations where tailing fish are concerned, and my favourite fly is a wet beetle – the Fiery Brown. If the fish are on frogs or tadpoles, a variety of big wet flies will work; otherwise you might try your favourite beetle, nymph, scud or snail pattern.

Polaroiding

These days I only fish in the Western Lakes between 9.00 and 5.00 (I don't like to work outside normal hours if I can help it!), and I rely entirely on sight fishing, which generally means polaroiding.

I've written volumes about polaroiding, and mostly this is how we fish from the beginning to the end of the season. But again, I've been accused of making it sound too easy, and without some practical polaroiding skills or someone to show you how, and where, you're going to be doing it tough. My advice is to go out there with someone who already knows the ropes, either a friend or a professional guide.

Provided you can cast into it, the wind can be used to advantage –

to get close to the fish and to disguise your movements. Get in the water and wade where possible, and let the waves open up the water to give you a better view through your polaroids – quality polaroid sunglasses are a must.

While the sun is out, wade quickly but smoothly and scan the water at the very limit of good visibility. If the sun is hidden behind cloud, or the water is discoloured, wade much more slowly and look for any hint of a fish at close range.

I'm yet to find a suitable light-weight boot and wading system for fly-fishing in this country, where chest waders are a must but backpack weight has to be kept to a minimum. I am, however, more than happy to try anything that arrives in the mail – size 11 boot, with a long leg. (You need long legs for polaroiding, though some short people do manage to catch fish!)

Around the deeper rocky-shored lakes where wading isn't an option, we tend to polaroid the water pretty quickly by rock hopping and scanning from high ground. Veterans like Greg French have turned this into a sort of 'freestyle' combined endurance and speed event!

The trick here is to be alert for trout cruising right at your feet – right in under and around the boulders and overhanging dwarf pines – whilst at the same time scanning the open water beyond to the limit of visibility. In the summer months trout cruise these rocky edges in the middle of the day in search of pale-coloured mayfly nymphs which actually crawl out onto the rocks to hatch.

Whether wading or rock-hopping, it always pays to hold the fly at the ready, with a measure of fly-line pulled through the rod for an instant cast. The emphasis really is on seeing the fish in good time to land the fly right in front, where it can't possibly go unnoticed. Consequently, the actual fly used is not a major drama.

For the most part, these elusive Western Lakes trout are fairly keen to find something to eat, and if they're going to be choosy, you'll probably do it tough no matter what I recommend. First choice has to be a good floater that's easy to see, bearing in mind that these fish will often take a well-presented dry fly when there isn't a rise to be seen.

If you're like me, you will be well stocked with about half a dozen ever-reliable patterns in one pocket, and the rest of your fly vest will be loaded with a plethora of your own one-day-wonders and everybody else's as well. For polaroiding I tend to stick to just three main patterns: a Red Tag, Black Spinner or a floating nymph. Sometimes you'll need to use a sinking nymph or scud pattern, and it pays to have a few duns and sedges on hand.

Relatively 'good' fishing is to be found within range of short day trips throughout the Nineteen Lagoons region, accessed via Liawenee Canal and Lake Augusta. But for the true Western Lakes adventurer it's a matter of putting on a pack, grabbing a compass and heading off for waters unknown.

For details of literally hundreds of individual waters, get hold of one of Greg French's books, or our collaborative effort, *Trout Guide*.

Walking in this country requires only a moderate level of fitness because it's fairly flat and featureless, but in the interests of personal safety a professional guide is recommended, unless you have the necessary skills and equipment – even then it pays to be conservative.

If I still haven't managed to put you off, then it could be that you've got just the right temperament to join the growing band of Western Lakes disciples. But don't say I didn't warn you!

JOHN HARRISON

JOHN WAS National Executive Director of Recfish Australia from March 1995 to April 1998 and then Executive Officer of the Amateur Fishermen's Association of the Northern Territory (AFANT) from June 1998–April 2005. John is Chief Executive Officer of Recfish Australia from April 2005.

He also served as President of Recfish Australia from November 2001 – July 2003.

Heavily involved in many government committees connected with angling, he still finds time to 'Wet a Line'.

CHAPTER 33

Recfish

It has been over 10 years since I took my first step into the politics of recreational and sport fishing. Having been in middle management of Telstra for too long, it was time for a change. In late 1994 I was reading *The Weekend Australian* job vacancies and this job jumped off the page and had my name written all over it. So I went through the process, got an interview, and then, finally, after a couple of months, got the call offering me the job.

As a passionate angler, I thought I had just cracked the best job in Australia – National Executive Director of the Australian Recreational and Sport Fishing Industry Confederation Inc. (what a mouthful), or as it is more commonly known, Recfish Australia.

I could see it all before me: fishing trips to exotic locations, fishing for fish I had only ever dreamed about catching and rubbing shoulders with all these great fishers that you read about. How wrong was that?

Down to earth with a deafening and bone-crunching thud. The organisation was essentially running on the smell of an oily rag and the trips to faraway places teeming with so many fish that you had to bait your hook behind a tree would remain a dream.

Before I read the job vacancy in 1994 I had never heard of Recfish Australia – just like the majority of anglers in Australia. But I quickly learnt that there was, and today more than ever there remains, a need for a voice for recreational fishing at the national level. The range of things that the Australian Government and its bureaucratic arms and legs are mixed up with that can and do impact on fishing is astonishing.

My eyes (and head, for that matter) were like a sponge in the middle of a tropical downpour, absolutely chockers – things are not much different today, except the whisky in the ensuing 10 years has probably decreased the size of the sponge.

When Les asked me to write this chapter he said he didn't want any boring bits about the political processes, so that narrows down what I can say about the people in the 'House on the Hill'. But to give you one example of the challenge facing an advocacy or lobby group, in the 10 years that I have been around there have been 10 or 11 fisheries ministers in the Australian Government. It's really hard to build a relationship with a moving target.

I had had a bit over 3 years with Recfish Australia when Howard won government in 1996. He inherited what all new governments seem to inherit these days: a big black hole and too many advocacy groups. The umbilical cord was severed in late 1996. Recfish Australia almost bled to death, and for the next 6 or 7 years was basically forced to pare itself back to absolute core business, and even then some of this couldn't be achieved.

Some might say, Why rely on government for funding? and How can you bite the hand that feeds you? But getting a secure source of revenue for Recfish Australia has always been extremely difficult; you could write an entire book about it. And a revenue stream free of government dollars is even harder. You would think it would be easy with 3.5 million anglers in Australia, because at just one dollar per year from each angler I could be head of one of the most powerful groups knocking on the doors of the pollies.

Now by this stage you are probably wondering what all this tripe is about, and asking why hasn't he said something about what the organisation actually does? But before I do that I thought I would fill in the missing 7 years.

I resigned from Recfish Australia in 1998 after securing what could be argued is the best job in Australia. I moved from the chilly confines of Canberra to the tropical bliss of Darwin to work for the

Amateur Fishermen's Association of the Northern Territory (AFANT). How good was this – the barra capital of the world! My thirst for saltwater fly-fishing was quenched. I also happened to learn a few odd bits and pieces about the machinations of politics at the State (or in this case the Territory) level.

But if Les will let me waffle on a little longer about the Northern Territory, I will tell you that it is the crown for saltwater fly-fishing. And the jewel in the crown is Bynoe Harbour, to the west of Darwin. What a place!! When you can catch 10 or 12 species off one rock bar and sight fish to barra, queenies, threadfin salmon, just to name a few, on the flats, all with the long wand, that is heaven. On the odd occasion it can be a little hard on the pocket. Especially when you put a brand new fly line on and toss a white deceiver in amongst a very nervous school of baitfish, only to see the backing rapidly approaching and the fish on the end of the line disappearing around a rather jagged rock bar and – well I think you know what happens after that. Serious fish, GTs looking like Volkswagens rather than fish.

Or another occasion when I was fishing with a well-known fly-fishing guide in Darwin Harbour chasing queenies, we moved from one spot to another and he left his fly in the water while cruising slowly over to a new spot, only to have the line lock tight on the reel and the rod flip over the transom of the boat into 60 feet of water. No big deal, I suppose – happens all the time – but it was a brand new RPLXi 9 weight Sage, new Shakespeare reel and a new fly line; it hurt, because it was around two grand.

Well, enough of my exploits in the Territory. Suffice it to say that I had the privilege of visiting some unbelievable fly-fishing locations: wolf herring in Port Bradshaw, five species off the beach at Cape Scott, and the list goes on.

Prior to the 2004 federal election, the Howard Government, as part of its platform for the upcoming election, offered to reinstate the funding support for Recfish Australia for 4 years. I was the successful applicant for the Chief Executive Officer position, and commenced my second stint as a paid employee in April 2005.

I suppose I'd better get to the point now, otherwise Les will be less than impressed. The list of issues is so extensive that the headings alone would fill a couple of pages, but I will tackle some of the more important ones on the go at the time of writing.

Recfish Australia's mission is to represent the interests of recreational and sport fishing at a national level to ensure high-quality, enjoyable and ecologically sustainable fishing. So what does that mean and what have we done to achieve this?

Probably the first thing to try to explain is the fact that almost 100 per cent of the fisheries that we chase are managed by the states and territories, so our role does not include direct involvement with this. Rather, we leave this to the State peak bodies, who are our members. If you want to see who they are, check our website, www.recfish.com.au.

Well where do I start? Most of you would have heard of the recent changes to access to the fishing grounds adjacent to the Queensland coast in the Great Barrier Reef (GBR) Marine Park. While Recfish Australia was not directly involved, it has had a profound impact on access in some particular areas. I do not wish to dwell on this specifically, but more the overall issue of MPAs – marine protected areas. They are the bane of many anglers, but they are here to stay.

Our role will be addressing the grass roots needs when it comes to MPAs in the Commonwealth-managed waters, which is ostensibly beyond the 3 nautical mile line, and out to the 200 mile limit. While the vast majority of this expansive area is not in the sights of the every-day angler, there will be areas close to inshore in which we do fish. We intend to hold a series of meetings with the anglers in the region where an MPA is proposed with the goal of getting their input and hopefully influencing or minimising the impact. The Department of Environment and Heritage will be contracting our services to do this.

It is a type of liaison between the government and the anglers – let's hope it works better than the GBR process.

Recently the Federal Fisheries Minister announced that longtail tuna would be declared a recreational only species right around Australia. This has taken some time to achieve, and came as a bit of a surprise to most players. This species can be caught from about the NSW–Victoria border north around the top of Cape York and the Northern Territory and down the west coast of Western Australia to about Geraldton. It has a wide range, and is a highly prized sportfish. I had been working on getting this fish for the recreational sector in my role in the Northern Territory, specifically because it was one species of fish that the commercial sector had not really targeted and I wanted to see it stay that way.

An election can bring a lot of results for advocates, and the last federal one was no exception. With the seat of Solomon (NT) being the most marginal in the country from the last election in 2001 (held by a mere 0.8 per cent), the Fisheries Minister arrived unexpectedly in Darwin, prior to the election, and announced that there would be a $15 million Recreational Fishing Community Grant Program over 3 years and (and what a big 'and' it was), that longtail tuna would be declared a recreational species only – the commercial sector were caught with their pants down.

They went into a spin. Today we are walking through the bureaucratic maze to get this in train. The longtail tuna is a superb sportfish, unbelievable on fly and basically worthless to the commercial sector – at least for the time being, until they plunder the other tuna stocks. And unfortunately for yellow fin, southern bluefin, big eye and other tunas, this is already a sad reality.

Releasing fish today is almost like sending text on a mobile phone: everyone is doing it. However, we need to know what the consequences of this are. We think we know, but for some species there are many gaps in our understanding. To help with that, the Fisheries Research and Development Corporation has invested heavily in the Released Fish Survival program, which has initiated a number of important projects that are aimed at finding out the answer to the survivability of released fish.

Projects on bream, flathead, whiting, barramundi and Samson fish, to name a few, are either underway or completed. But it is more than that: circle hooks, knotless landing nets, and release techniques are all part of the 'Gently Does It' campaign, something that Recfish Australia has been closely involved in. This is all helping us be able to enjoy a sustainable fishing future. For more on the best practices, visit our website.

I was in Norway recently for the 4th World Recreational Fishing Conference, and some rather telling issues that all countries are facing were discussed: catch and release (CR) was on top of the agenda.

As we begin to overhaul and refine recreational fisheries management, including CR, we will need to know the effect of releasing fish so that we can understand the impact of 'high grading', the impact of pure CR and the impact of CR post anglers reaching the bag limit (for example). We also need to adopt some common terms so we all know exactly what we are referring to; we need to agree on what CR is or means.

One paper of interest dealt with overcoming indigenous people's concern that CR only leads to the death of the fish, or that a released fish will communicate with his 'colleagues' and all the fish will leave.

A paper on the experience of growing sportfishing in rural Alaska, and the gradual acceptance by some villages of the benefits of correct CR and the opportunities this has delivered, was presented. This could be useful in the development of recreational and sport fishing in Aboriginal lands of northern Australia.

It is clear that we in Australia must further improve our knowledge and understanding of CR, and then extend our knowledge to anglers to maximise the survivability of all released fish. To not do this could leave us exposed to the animal welfare critics, and they have had profound impacts in some countries – Germany, for instance, has legislation that prohibits CR and bans any form of competitive or tournament fishing.

We are embarking on a tournament accreditation process where fishing competitions can voluntarily go through an assessment to gauge their environmental management systems. Sound strange? If we don't get on the front foot and prove that our competitions are in fact ecologically sustainable, we could face the German scenario! More on this from our website.

There are many issues that we are dealing with, but the reality is that in the local economies things are changing continually. Travel, more leisure time (for some) and the increasing number of grey nomads in Australia means that people are looking for the opportunity to catch a fish wherever they go. I love the idea that I used in the Northern Territory to great effect, and which is relevant right around this great country: once the money came from taking the fish to the people, but today the money comes from taking the people to the fish.

I guess to finish I want to use a wise and clever statement: United we stand, divided we fall. If you think that your own little patch is fine, take off the blinkers and look around. We must stand tall and make sure that our needs are being dealt with at the national level, otherwise we will sink like the proverbial sinker. The answer is a powerful national body, and we need your support.

Good fishing to you all.

RAY
BROWN

RAY BROWN is a well-known commercial fly tier who lives at Port Noarlunga on South Australia's Fleurieu Peninsula. His privately published book, *Dry Flies of the Fleurieu Peninsula*, is one of fly-fishing's most sought-after books.

Over the years he has contributed hundreds of stories on fly-tying, entomology and conservation to bulletins and newsletters of fly-fishing clubs. He has also given many talks and fly-tying demonstrations to fishing clubs Australia-wide. His fly patterns have appeared in many books and magazines for a couple of decades.

He has been an active member of the South Australian Fly Fisher's Association (SAFFA) for 30 years; he was awarded an honorary life membership some years ago. Ray also served as a councillor, secretary and president of SAFFA.

He has been active in many other organisations as well: he's been a delegate to Recfish Australia, President of the Fresh Water Fisherman's Assembly, a member of the South Australian Inland Fisheries Management committee, chairperson of the South Australian Inland Recreational Fishing Committee, and a member of the South Australian Recreational Fishing Advisory Committee Board, as well as being a member of other fly-fishing organisations.

A move to Tasmania is currently under consideration: this would allow him to finish writing his second book, something that he has been working on for 15 years.

However, it seems fishing continues to get in the way.

CHAPTER 34

Some Thoughts on Trout Flies

I never wander where the bord'ring reeds
o'erlook the muddy stream, where tangling weeds
perplex the fisher; I nor choose to bear
the thievish nightly wet, nor barbed spear.
Nor drain I ponds the golden carp to take,
nor trawl for pikes, dispeoplers of the lake.
Around the steel no tortured worm shall twine,
no blood of living insect stain my line.
Let me, less cruel, cast the feathered hook,
with pliant rod athwart the pebbled brook.
Silent along the mazy margin stray,
and with the fur-wrought fly delude the prey.

The Blue Dun

The above passage is a poem from the book *Poems on Several Occasions*, written by John Gay and published in 1720. Many of the old authors still have the ability to influence our modern-day thinking. Fly-fishing is an old traditional sport whose heritage goes back beyond the fifteenth century, when the *Treatyse of Fysshynge Wyth an Angle* was written, the best published book on angling. You would be aware that twelve flies were mentioned in the *Treatyse*; eleven of the original ones are in use today. The Blue Dun was one of the twelve *Treatyse* flies.

I thought that we could look at one of the older fly patterns and the instruction given back in 1747:

> *The Blue Dun fly comes down in the beginning of March and will kill fish in the forenoon till the middle of April. He is made of a blue dude's feather or starling wing with a blue cock's hackle, the dubbing yellow mohair mixed with the blue fur of a fox:*
>
> *As it swims down the water, his wings stand upright on his back: His tail is forked, and of the colour of his wing. He is always thick on the water in cloudy, gloomy days.*

> *Those instructions are from Richard Bowlker's Art of Angling Improved; this volume was especially notable for its histories of flies and their imitation as well as knowledge of the naturals.*
>
> *Modern fly dressing books, especially American ones, stress the importance of lightly dressed well-proportioned flies. The following paragraph is from W.C. Stewart's Practical Angler, published in 1857:*
>
> *The great point, then, in fly dressing, is to make the artificial fly resemble the natural insect and neatness of form. Our great objection to the flies in common use is that they are much too bushy: so much so, that there are few flies to be got in the tackle shops which we could use with any degree of confidence in clear water. Every possible advantage is in our favour with a lightly dressed fly: it is more like the natural insect; it falls lighter on the water, and every angler knows the importance of making his fly fall gently, and there being less material about it, the artificial nature of that material is not so easily detached: And also, as the hook is not so much covered with feathers, there is a much better chance of hooking a trout when it rises. We wish to impress very strongly upon the reader the necessity of avoiding bulky flies.*

The modern version of the Blue Dun I have taken from Eric Leiser's *Book of Fly Patterns* (1987):

Hook	Partridge L3A
Thread	6/0 Grey pre-waxed
Wing	Mallard wing quill sections

Tail	Medium blue dun hackle fibres
Body	Muskrat dubbing fur
Hackle	Medium blue dun

This gives a creamy blue body, very similar to the Bowlker recipe that precedes it by 240 years. The pattern remains popular today. Here in Australia it is a good imitation of the various mid-size Leptophlebiidae Duns that are predominant mayfly genres found in Australia.

The Evolution of the Trout Fly

How many of us have asked the question: where did it all start? We all know that fly-fishing is an ancient sport, but how old is it really? The trout fly is the main focus of our sport, and it is with the fly that we can trace our sport to its very roots. The first mention of 'Fly-fishing', that is fishing with a 'Fly' is quoted as follows:

I have heard of a Macedonian way of catching fish and it is this; between Bercea and Thessalonica runs a river called the Aestraeus and in it there are fish with speckled skins; what the natives of the country call them you had better ask the Macedonians. These fish feed on a fly peculiar to the country which hovers on the river. It is not like flies found elsewhere, nor does it resemble a wasp in appearance, nor in shape would one justly describe it as a midge or a bee; yet it has something of each of these, it imitates the colour of a wasp and it hums like a bee. The natives generally call it the Hippourus. The fisherman cannot use the natural fly, for a touch of the hand rubs off its delicate blooms and destroys its wings. They have planned a snare for the fish and get the better of them by their fishermen's craft. They fasten red wool round a hook and fix onto the wool two feathers which grow under a cock's wattle sand, which in colour are like wax. Their rod is six feet long and their line of the same length. Then they throw their snare, and the fish, maddened and excited by the colour, come straight at it, thinking by the sight to get a dainty mouthful. When, however, it opens its jaws, it is caught by the hook and enjoys a bitter repast, a captive.

The above is a versioln from *De Natura Animalium* by Aelian, a Roman-born writer. The sport of fly-fishing has its roots in that passage. The plot could not have been clearer. The fly, tying instruction and the artificial created, then the hooking of the trout.

The trout was played on rod and line, and captured. The deception by means of the artificial fly was complete.

From here there is a huge gap. Centuries passed, until the age of William Caxton, who in 1474 introduced printing in *The Book of St. Albans.* In 1496 *The Treatyse of Fysshynge Wyth an Angle* was published. The author was supposed to be Dame Juliana Berners, the prioress of Sopwell Priory, but this has never been firmly established. Most angling historians credit the Dame with its authorship. The treatise is a book about all disciplines: all the popular fish are mentioned, along with the best methods of angling for them. Rods, lines, hooks and baits are discussed in detail.

But the real value of the treatise is the list of twelve flies – eleven of which survive today. They are all imitative of the insects found on the streams of the day. The list is complete – where did they come from? Certainly Dame Juliana just didn't devise them for the book. Obviously there were scripts held in the monasteries that detailed fly-fishing was practised in the fifteenth century or before. We can only assume that other volumes on our sport existed before this time. Of the twelve flies, the most prominent is the Ruddy Fly:

In the beginning of May a good flye to body of Roddyd wull and lappid abowte with blacke sylke; the wynges of the drake and of the redde capons hakyll.

The twelve flies of Dame Juliana Berners were listed according to the month of the year when they were used. This corresponded with the approximate hatching dates of the insects. The Ruddy Fly was the fly for May. Bowlker later in 1747 named it the Red Spinner and added the starling wings; other than that the fly is essentially the same today. This fly forms the foundation of dry fly-fishing. Its origins are over 500 years old. One interesting aspect of the treatise is the Dame doesn't give any fly tying instructions at all: she explains how to make rods, lines and even hooks, but no mention is made of the manufacture of the flies, even though fly recipes are given.
The Treatyse concludes thus:

The Treatyse concludes with a high appeal to all anglers to use the sport only for pleasure, health of body and mind, and not for profit, to respect the rights of other men, to eschew idleness and to serve God, devoutly.

Well, well. Ethics. Haven't changed much, have they!

Not much happened for over a century other than one volume called *The Art of Angling*, published in 1653. It's interesting that G.E.M. Skues wrote, in a letter to a friend, that Izaak Walton was 'a miserable old plagiarist who owed what he knew about fishing to a Lady Dame Juliana, in fact of the first part and of the second, to that good young gentleman Charles Cotton'. Obviously Skues knew nothing of *The Art of Angling* – but he knew something of old Izaak.

Both Markham (1614) and Barker (1651) mention flies. Markham states, 'Live flies, and copy their shape and colours as closely as you can'. But he doesn't go any further. Barker (1651) is the first to give tying instructions – they are sound and very clear:

Cut off your wing material, lie feather on top of the hook, pointing away from the bend, strip one side of your hackle and tie it and the body and ribbing in at the bend; make your body, run on your tinsel and make fast under the wings, turn your hackle and make fast. Divide your wing in two, whip between with a figure of eight, then with your thumb press the wings towards the bend of the hook and take two or three turns of silk to keep them in place.

This is very sound advice – the instructions are very clear and precise. The author obviously knows what he is doing. I believe that this is fair advancement from the treatise. The fly itself is starting to evolve into the modern-day fly. Remember, we are still talking about wet flies. Venables (1662) in *Experienced Angler* and Charles Cotton (1676) in *The Compleat Angler* were more detailed but not much different, although Cotton did give a list of no fewer than 65 flies, all of them attempted imitations of naturals.

Cotton penned that famous phrase, 'Fish fine and far off is the first principal rule of trout angling.' Both Venables and Cotton wrote of matching the colour of the natural and the fly, how to dress hackled flies and also a little about the proportions of a trout fly. Cotton believed that the flies found in London tackle shops were fat and cumbersome – really useless for trout fishing. His were slender and short in the bodies, much more life-like. Venables makes a brief mention of fishing upstream.

As we can see, the imitative school of thought has prevailed down through the last 200 years. In Chetham's *Anglers Vade Mecum* (1681) we find the first modern tying of the famous March Brown: 'Hares fur ribbed with yellow silk, partridge hackle and a wing of hen pheasant'. His 20 patterns, with modern names and dressing, survived to this day from their 1682 recipes.

Modern fly dressing starts with Bowlker's *Art of Angling* (1747). He didn't engage in the plagiarism that the authors before him had engaged in. (This was with the exception of Chetham, whose work was highly original.) Bowlker lists 29 flies, and his list too survives with little change today (there were two Bowlkers, Richard and Charles, father and son, from Ludlow in Shropshire).

The next major step in the evolution of the trout fly happened in 1836. Alfred Ronalds published the book *The Fly Fisher's Entomology*. The *Entomology* gave us coloured plates of natural and artificial flies; the naturals were all classified and named. It took another 85 years for another book like it (Mosely's *The Dry Fly Fisherman's Entomology* in 1921). Up to this stage, bodies were made of fur and wools, and wings were composed as a single strip, tied on as a bunch and then divided. (This developed into the rolled wing made famous by Stewart in the 1857 book *The Practical Angler*.)

The age of the double split wing and floss silk bodies was about to begin. Up to then these flies had been wet flies, although they had been mentioned in Scotcher's *Fly Fisher's Legacy* (1800): 'The fly that floats and kills fish because it floats.'

The first mention of the dry fly was by Stewart (1857), who pioneered upstream fishing, but it is in Pulman's book *Vade Mecum of Fly-fishing for Trout*, 6 years earlier, that the dry fly appears full-blown, totally developed:

> *Let a dry fly be substituted for the wet one, the line switched a few times through the air to throw off its super abundant moisture, a judicious cast made just above the rising fish, and the fly allowed to float towards, and over them, and chances are ten to one that it will be seized as readily as the living insect.*

All attributes of the dry fly are present: (a) a fish taking naturals, (b) artificial must be a good imitation in colour and size, (c) it must be floating naturally on the surface, and (d) the fisherman must imitate action.

Who first dressed a fly to float is uncertain, but both Ogden of Cheltenham and Fosters of Ashbourn were selling trout flies in the 1850s, if not earlier. The first directions for tying a dry fly are in Odgen's *Fly Tying*, published in 1897. It must be remembered also that many of the popular wet flies of the day were just converted to dry flies: the Greenwells Glory (1854) and the Welsh fly invented by Mr Flynn in 1850 called the Worchester Gem (renamed the Red Tag in 1878).

By the time Frederick Halford wrote *Floating Flies and How to Dress Them* in 1886, the dry fly was in full swing on the Hampshire chalk streams. Halford's next book (published in 1880) was his best. *Dry Fly-fishing in Theory and Practice* established the dry fly in England. Since then the changes in fly dressings have been few; tackle is what has changed.

Halford systematically matched artificials to the natural insects. Strict imitation was the code. He matched exact colours of imitations to the naturals. A large inventory was developed; some believe there were too many. Halford was very dogmatic: he believed that his was the only line of thought. He considered that the dry fly had superseded all other forms of fly-fishing, and those who thought otherwise were either ignorant or incompetent.

We had four centuries of hardly any change, then in the space of 50 years there was a complete reversal. Two streams of thought had developed:

b *Wet fly – Downstream and across*
c *Dry fly – Upstream and across*

Halford was the instigator, the prime mover for this change. But not all believed he was right. Halford was a dry fly purist, but he may have put us back 40 years. It must be noted that tackle technology advanced greatly in the Halford years due to the new style of fishing: leaders, fly lines and rods developed rapidly. It was a period of great change. Fly-tying was starting to develop into an art form. The precise matching of colour, shape and size, as well as the double and single split wings, and the much stiffer cock hackles, all had a profound effect on the turn of the century fly tiers. Halford died in 1913, but the battle he created between the modern wet fly fisherman and the dry fly purist waged well into the 1930s.

Halford's mentor was George Selwyn Marryat, who had earlier visited Australia and taken Possum fur back with him to England. His famous fly was the Little Marryat, tied with a body of Possum fur.

Now before we get into the twentieth century, let's look back on the progress that has been made. We have had 400 years of trout fly development. Three conclusions can be drawn:

1 From the beginning, flies were imitations of living insects.

2 Imitation was good in respect to the materials at hand (farm, field and forest). Now materials are drawn from everywhere – early fly fishers didn't have this advantage. Dame Juliana Berner's flies had stood the test of nearly five centuries. Many of the earlier writers, including Walton, plagiarised her twelve patterns.

3 Lastly – it is impossible to believe that the Dame originated all the dressings described in the *Treatyse*. The *Treatyse* embodies a long previous history, a traditional history passed down through the ages before the Dame by word of mouth of generations of anglers.

Up till 1800 it had been all wet fly. After this date mention is made of the floating fly – still fished downstream. Pulman (1851) is its true beginning. He describes the method. The great advance occurs in Scotland in 1857. Stewart recommends fishing upstream. Halford and Marryat take up the cause and spread the gospel through Halford's six books. The use of the wet fly ceased on the chalk streams of southern England.

G.E.M. Skues was nominated for membership to the Fly Fishers Club of London by Frederick Halford. I doubt if Halford realised what was about to follow. Skues became the champion of the sunken fly, but in a new form: nymphs. These were true imitative patterns, revised and updated methods that had been practised for centuries. Skues developed the new art of upstream wet fly-fishing with the imitative fly. This was called nymph fishing. His tying techniques created flies that closely resembled the naturals. *Minor Tactics of the Chalk Stream* appeared in 1910. Skues was a brilliant writer, easy to read; as well as having an enquiring mind, he had the prose to put it down on paper, helped no doubt by his work in the legal profession.

He believed that all forms of imitative angling had their place. Wet, dry or nymph. He popularised many patterns in use today, both nymph and dry fly. Two of the most widely used are the Orange Quill and the Blue-winged Olive (both dry flies). I have been convinced that he was also England's finest dry fly fisherman. Skues wrote four books, and to this day is the champion of reason in our sport. Skues wrote the following passage in *Minor Tactics* in 1910:

> But one result of the triumph of the dry fly of which that work [Halford's Dry Fly-fishing in Theory and Practice] was the crown and consummation was the obliteration from the minds of men, in much less than one generation, of all the wet fly lore which had served many generations of chalk stream angler well.

By the late 1930s the tide was again turning. Both wet and dry were accepted. In the North the wet fly was never really evicted; that had happened only in the hallowed water of the South. Since that time a lot of progress in flies has come from the United States. When brown trout were introduced into New York State before the turn of the century, brook trout and the wet fly predominated. But with the brown trout came the dry fly as pioneered by Theodore Gordon. Halford flies crossed the Atlantic in about 1890. Gordon was the destination. The Catskills School of fly dressers evolved. The famous Quill Gordon was born. The dry fly had progressed again, from the heavy softer hackled (over hackled) English split wing dry fly to the sparser, stiffer hackled, wood duck feather wings of the American dry fly.

Most of the advancement had occurred because of the imitative school. Dame Juliana Berners, Ronalds, Halford, Gordon and Skues were all members of this school, but it should be noted that Stewart (*Practical Angler*, 1857) was a professional angler who only used a few palmered flies: a red palmer and a black palmer and one other that I could recall. He was a very successful angler, and was very well read and well liked by a generation of anglers to follow.

So three separate schools developed: (a) Imitators, (b) Deceivers, and (c) Attractors. Most can name different flies in each group.

Fly-fishing has three essential elements:
1 Equipment – centres on the artificial fly.
2 Knowledge of stream life – knowledge of the habitat of aquatic insects and fish.
3 Presentation – skills both acquired and magical in presenting the fly to the trout.

Presentation is what created the overlap between the imitators and the deceivers. Having a perfect copy is not enough if the fly is not made to behave as the insect does. The fly fisherman must be able to make the fly swim properly (or float properly). The idea is to deceive the trout into taking the artificial as the natural.

Skues once said that if he thought that the trout didn't accept his fly as an imitation of what they were feeding on, then all the interest in fly-fishing would be lost. Imitation is 20 per cent of the picture; presentation is the other 80 per cent, but it too is part of the imitative process. Some of our flies are hundreds of years old; others were invented last night at our own tying bench.

They have developed over the years. I hope that I have explained a little of how the whole picture evolved.

RICK
KEAM

RICK KEAM is a freelance writer and editor. He has contributed to a range of Australian and international angling publications, edited *The Australian and New Zealand Flyfishers Annual,* and achieved acclaim for his innovative and effective fly designs.

He was also an early recipient of Port Fairy Folk Festival's Lawson–Paterson Award for Australian Songwriting – 'Wife to a Cocky Farmer' has become a classic of the folk repertoire – and a winner of the Traditional Bush Recitation competition at Tamworth Country Music Festival.

CHAPTER 35

The Desperation of Doc Bell

As a fellow-patient of Doc Bell once lamented, 'You'd reckon a bloke that takes horses over the jumps'd have a better pair of hands on him, wouldn't ya? By God he's hard on the reins.'

Doc did have a kind of perverse cranky charm once you were used to him, but few people ever stayed 'under his care' for long enough to find out. He would keep up the pleasantries for as long as it took to ask 'How are you today?' and you would reciprocally enquire after his own health on such a bright Monday morning, and he would say something like 'Right now I feel like a bear rolled in fish-hooks, but let's get that wisdom tooth out.'

Once seated in his chair, you gazed at a relaxing print of a mediaeval woodcut in which a psychoanalyst might have taken interest. It showed a village square and a fellow on horseback, wielding an immense pair of tongs. The far end of the tongs was inserted in the mouth of the patient, who was kneeling on the cobblestones and surrounded by interested bystanders.

'It's all about leverage,' Doc used to quip. He pronounced 'out' and 'about' like 'oat' and 'aboat', having come from Ontario in Canada 'to make up for all those Aussies doin' dental postgrad at Toronto', as was common at that time.

After Doc's professional attentions, the soft tissues of your mouth took a day to settle down from the knuckling. Whilst being worked over, and hoping that his cigarette ash wouldn't drop on your face, you were expected to respond with glottal mmnms and aorhnns to his commentary about the ever-present talkback radio, the Randwick horse races, climatic trends, taxation and politicians. His nurse – daily confronted with such subtleties as 'Where the goddamn hell's the amalgam?' – was widely known as Saint Shirley of The Bells.

There was a good reason why at least some of his patients were prepared to put up with this. On his property just a quarter of an hour out of town, where he and his wife ran their horses and lived the good life, was a large dam. A previous owner had constructed it across an intermittent watercourse that joined Ten Mile Creek a couple of hundred metres downstream. The Ten Mile was essentially a chain of deep still pools punctuated by reeds and a trickle of water, which in successive years of good rainfall supported occasional stocking with trout. Once, its flows had been more dependable. But as subdivisions grew and farm dams multiplied, it was little by little being starved of its lifeblood.

To this degree the public loss had been Doc Bell's gain. His dam had weedy shallows at the top end, sloping into deep water, and was sheltered by timber on the west. For patriotic and pragmatic reasons, he had wanted to stock it with brook trout ('real pretty and they pull out real easy'), but the regional hatchery was uncooperative and he settled for rainbows. These were rumoured to have grown to an impressive size. Stillwater fishing was virtually non-existent in the area at that time, and every summer, when the trout in the streams were lethargic from the heat, a few anglers endured Doc's dental attentions in the hope of securing an invitation to fish his lake. None were ever successful.

Then came his summer of desperation.

It began at Rotary as he savoured a vol au vent. A voice close to his left ear hissed, as if in italics, 'Is it safe?' Then came a slap on the back that nearly spilt his Ben Ean moselle. 'No worries Gord, you'll survive, eh? Hah hah hahhh!'

Doc Bell was mystified. He took it to be some kind of reflection on the catering. But before he could respond, the back-slapper had circulated elsewhere.

The next day Pete McDonald, passing him in the arcade, also demanded to know 'Is it safe?' before dissolving in laughter.

'What the goddamn hell is going on?' he asked Shirley.

Marathon Man, the suspense classic that did for dentistry what *Jaws* would later do for beach swimming, had opened at the local cinema. *Marathon Man*, with Laurence Olivier as the nightmarish dentist Szell bent on extracting – as it were – the whereabouts of his wartime loot from Dustin Hoffman's bone-terrified, unanaesthetised, mistaken-identity innocent: 'Is it safe?' By week's end the brass plate outside Doc's surgery had been amended, in some illiterate schoolboy's black Texta-colour, to 'Dr Gordon A. Zell'. And Saint Shirley was reporting an unusual number of cancelled appointments.

To make matters worse, Doc discovered that he was about to have competition. *Marathon Man* notwithstanding, two newly arrived young dental graduates had begun renovating a run-down building with a view to establishing a clinic. There would be cool seventies décor and relaxing music and tropical fish in a big aquarium, and the latest in minimal-discomfort dental technology.

Doc was in trouble, and he knew it. Desperate situations call for desperate measures, and so it was that he arrived at his Big Idea.

'Dave,' he confided to his Rotary Vice-President, 'this town's been good to me and it's time to give something back. I've been thinking of making our place available as a charity weekend fund-raiser. Horse rides for the kids, service clubs barbecue, Carol putting on a field day for gardeners. Oh, and if anyone might want to wet a line there's the dam, too.'

The V-P swallowed hard. How much Canadian Club had Doc been putting away? Affecting the greatest nonchalance, he declared that it sounded like a good idea and he'd present it to his committee. Apex might want to get on board too.

'Catch-and-release fishing, of course,' added Doc.

'Oh ... yeah, of course,' affirmed the V-P, pretending to an awareness of something he knew only from astonished hearsay.

At that stage catch-and-release was a novel idea known only from imported American magazines such as *Field and Stream and Outdoor Life*. True, Harry Persson claimed to catch and then release local trout to three pounds, on a skinny rough thing he made with hair from a deer's tail and claimed to represent a yabby. Harry was not a boastful man: he was understated to the point of being taciturn. The trouble was that in the absence of any 3-pounders in his freezer, there was never any corroborative evidence.

At any rate, you didn't kick a gift-horse in the mouth, especially if it was Doc Bell. Catch-and-release it had to be, and the date was fixed for early February. Posters advertised the event, and the local newspaper and radio stations ran interviews with the on-the-ground organisers and with Doc, newly emerging as a community benefactor.

What nobody really reckoned on was the weather.

The spring of 1976 had seemed to promise a good trout season, but by November the streams were worryingly low. The usual January afternoon thunderstorms were brief affairs that failed to deliver much respite. By February, things were desperate. The attractions of Doc's dam increased proportionately.

A week before the big event, a rain system that had been drenching Queensland spread further south. Low clouds brought gentle drizzle, setting in at noon and intensifying through the night and the next two days. The land soaked up each droplet in delight.

Then, instead of lifting, the cloud thickened and the rain became heavier. The saturated topsoil could handle no more. Water lay in sheets across every slight depression, flooding into drains and gutters and stormwater courses and spilling over roads. Dry gullies became foamy torrents.

By dawn on the day of the Charity Gala – most people said it as 'Galah' – the rain had eased off to a drizzle. The roped-off car area filled early. Men and women in mud-splattered white moleskin trousers, Gloster shirts and oilskins emerged from mud-splattered white Holdens and Falcons. Cars and utilities lined the edges of the driveway and the soft road verges outside the gates, where a couple of late arrivals bogged their vehicles. Despite the mud, the refreshment marquees buzzed with celebration of rain.

In the corner of one marquee stood Wally Jacobs and Jim Meszaros, 'refreshing' themselves with a couple of early snifters while keeping a close eye on the dam. At its top end, what was normally pasture had become a bay. The consensus was that fish would work these shallows at low light, feasting on worms and drowned insects, and the dull day might encourage a few of them to stay there. A few hopefuls were already casting flies and spinners.

At the other end, water was pouring around the far corner of the retaining wall, then running ankle-deep down a grassy depression to the gully below, which had become a sizeable creek.

It was Jim who first spotted the unusual movement where the floodwaters exited. In the blink of an eye, two glasses stood abandoned in the marquee and two middle-aged men toting fly rods challenged the world veterans' sprint record.

From their subsequent body language, it was clear they were in a state of high excitement. But they were not engaged in anything that might reasonably be called angling. In fact, they had thrown their rods on the grass and were splashing about in the outflow, bending over as if trying to get their hands on something.

What they held aloft in due course was not a piece of flood debris, but a rainbow trout bigger than anyone in the district had ever seen. In the marquee area, someone exclaimed 'God, what a fish!' Conversations stopped as people turned to look. Small boys began to run down to the dam, followed by a photographer from *The Northern Sentinel.*

Just as the cameraman arrived, however, the hefty trout kicked and slipped from the two men's uncoordinated hands. Eluding Jim's desperate attempt to fling himself on it, the panicking fish headed straight through the outflow and down the slope, wriggling and flapping through water, grass and clover, into the creek.

'It's not the only one,' yelled Wal to the growing crowd of spectators. 'There were others round here too, in the running water right at the edge. Almost like they were trying to spawn. The flood's exposed a bit of gravel.'

'Look down there!' shouted an excited lad. At the lower end of the outflow, lying dead on the grass, was another equally big rainbow that had apparently become stranded. The crows had removed one eye.

Driven by unresolved spawning urges pent-up from spring, then by the ancestral Pacific salmon within, or perhaps by sheer boredom with stillwater life, an unknown number of fish had 'done a runner'. Instead of heading up into the inflowing waters like trout were supposed to do, they were heading down and out.

Doc Bell, who had by this stage arrived on the scene, was livid. 'You better not claim you caught that fish!' he thundered.

A flash of wicked inspiration struck Wal just when he most needed it. 'We don't, Doc. We just couldn't resist extracting it!'

'Yeah,' added Jim. 'A painless extraction. Then we put it back.'

The only person who wasn't laughing was Doc.

Whatever the man's private chagrin at the possible extent of his fish loss, by the end of the day he had recovered a degree of public composure. He even managed a forced smile when, in response to his announcement that the takings would contribute a substantial sum to local charities, some wit at the back interjected 'Is it safe?' And in due course, he consolidated his reputation as a public benefactor, though not quite in the way he had planned.

It was noted that Doc later placed a large order for fingerlings, and engaged contractors to build a highly expensive and sophisticated outlet barrier. But the Ten Mile Creek downstream produced some of the biggest trout anyone had caught in decades, or would ever catch again. The locals still talk about it.

DAVID
CAMPBELL

FORMERLY A champion all-round sportsman, Cambridge-educated David Campbell (1915–79) won a DFC and Bar as an RAAF pilot based at Port Moresby and Darwin. He returned to Australia after the war to farm a property near Canberra. His poetry gradually earned him recognition as one of the leading figures of Australian literature. He was a frequent fishing companion of Douglas Stewart.

This article is reproduced with permission from David's wife Judy and the National Library of Australia.

CHAPTER 36

Trout Fishing

There's a long reach of river bordered by tea tree and blending tussocks; and the mountains are behind you. You've fished the length of that reach and not a trout has risen. You've cast your fly here on an acre of sky, and there on a suiciding dogbush.

And you've got a bit exasperated and caught the white sally-tree over your shoulder.

At the head of the reach where the river runs through stones to stiller water, you drop a fly beyond the green weed. There's a deep swirl and your reel is singing. A 3-pound rainbow is standing on its tail down the reach and you're remembering your hair-thin cast and fighting to keep the fish away from that lazy brown log in the deep hole across the river there.

Or you're standing above your knees in the swift run-out from the pool. The sun's on the water, but you can see, not 10 feet from you, a big trout feeding in the current.

You've been there for three-quarters of an hour. Your friend has been scouting to either side, but returning each time to the same brown stone. How big he is, you wouldn't like to say. You can see the rainbow along his flank, the speckled brown above the long cruel jaw of a male trout. And you're feeling a kind of delayed excitement; for he is an old fish and has had a look at almost every fly you've got.

He rises, sipping, short of the dry flies; wet go past him down river. Cast in mouth, you study your case. Well, you've tried everything else. So you take out a silver-bodied affair with black and gold wings, a ballerina of a fly.

You cast upstream beyond the trout and lead her past those lean jaws. And the fish moves forward: his mouth is open, and he gently sucks her in.

Awestruck, you strike. He darts forward, swings back. And your elation is beyond bounds. The fish is yours. But he turns. In three leaps he's across the broad pool. Your line is around a fist of rock and he's still leaning in the air upstream to the right of you. Then your line goes slack; all is ash. You reel in and struggle to the bank. But a stranger is there, uncouth but wide-eyed. 'What a fish was that!' He'd never seen such a fish. And he is your best friend. You shake his hand; you wipe the mouth of your rum flask for him. And you lead him along upriver to where your fishing partner stands cynically by a waterfall, a 2-pound trout at his feet.

We went fishing this year up the Badja River in a spur of the main range of the Australian Alps. The year before, at Wee Jasper, we'd cooked for ourselves and starved; so when we heard of a farm house on the Badja where they'd cook for us, we booked in for ten days.

Willow Farm it was called; and the name of the farmer was Jack Snow – which had the right ring for the high country. But the phone number – Boggy Plains 2 – made us pause. Whoever fished in a bog? Still, we had a jeep, and we drove up through the great blond treeless uplands of the Monaro – nothing but earth and sky and the mountains dreaming in the distance; through some rough hills and a couple of backwood townships; and down, with the smell of the sea blown over from the coast, into a high half-cleared valley with a lonely farm house in it, a river and a willow tree. But what a house it was; we turned a tap – hot water; we pulled a card – light. For a fisherman, such things are as rare as 8-pounders. And in the hall, there was an 8-pounder – in a glass case.

It had been caught in the long curving reach of the river that ran slowly between open banks right past our front door.

We'd wake in the morning and below our windows see wild ducks feeding on the pasture. I counted ninety-one together at one time –

and through the yellow broom, the gleam of the river. And on still evenings when moths were hatching in the white flowers of the tea-tree, there'd be a staggered chain of rises down the length of the reach, each the deep sulky swirl of a big fish.

It was good water and Jack knew many of the fish; and some were named. Sally, for instance, had her own pool, the Sally Hole, and a log where she broke all casts. We kept this reach up our sleeve – if you can talk of two miles of river in that way – and when we lost fish or patience elsewhere, there was always Sally to court at our door, and others to catch.

Usually, though, we went further afield. Downstream where the river dropped 500 feet through a wild gorge and ran out into a string of small pools on Andy's Plain; more often we'd take our lunch and the jeep up into the mountains along the saw-mill road, clamber over giant tree-covered ridges, and come down steeply onto the river at the pockets, knowing that few fishermen had ever been there before us.

A wallaby would crash off over the stone between the slim trunks of the white sally-trees; a platypus would do a jack-knife dive in the centre of a rock-brown waterhole; and we'd wade to our waists up a green stretch of river with a road of sky above us, and – you can believe me or not – put back anything under 2½ pounds.

It was seldom we left the river before dark, but there was always a hot meal for us at the farm, and beer, and perhaps a game of darts before bed. Jack was a good hand at throwing double twenties.

Jack had been in England during the war with the air force, and sometimes over darts we'd talk of drinking cider in Devonshire, and occasionally we'd bomb Berlin, dropping easily into that night world of fronts and flak and pieces of cake; but mostly we talked of the locals: the dances in the bush hall, of Harcourt Read, the dingo trapper, and of a neighbour who had aroused suspicion by buying a bath. The suspicion was well founded, for not long after that he returned from a holiday with one of them foreigners – in fact, a city wife.

Then of course, there was Davie. Davie was the mailman, and the week before he'd been 'struck be lightning'. 'How's Davie getting on?' Jack had asked the father. 'Well, Jack, 'e's a bit stary, yer know. But they tell me lightnin's a wonderful thing fer the teeth. Don't get no more toothache once yer've been struck by lightning, they tell me.'

And Davie was a fisherman. When he wanted a fish dinner, he broke a branch from a tree, tied a length of cord to it, and baited his hook with one of those 'wicherby' grubs. When the fish struck, so did Davie. His strike brought the fish over his shoulder onto the bank. Then Davie broke his rod and went about his rounds. Fortunately he only wanted a fish dinner occasionally, and Jack, who was a fishing inspector, kept his love of the sport in check. Some remark – 'Funny flapping sound your motor's got today, Davie' – when the mail was being dropped, was usually enough.

We left him to his wicherby grubs, and fished dry fly. For the first few days, Hardy's Favourite was ours too, with March Browns and Hare's Ears. Douglas, who was with me, caught some good fish, but few of mine would cover a rule. Well, I was no fisherman.

And with loss of confidence, I caught, as the Scottish ghillie says, little but myself and other trash.

Then I changed flies. I'd noticed a big moth in the tea-tree similar to the Irish Grouse and Jay, a large fly with a red–brown hackle and a pheasant's tail. I tried it. I won't forget the next 24 hours quickly.

We'd lunched at the top of a waterfall looking down over the first long reach of the pockets. The waterfall dropped 200 feet in pools and rapids over stones rounded and flanked like elephants. Water for thousands of years had smoothed their sides unseen. And ah, I thought if I could catch a fish in that deep rock hole at the foot. I slithered down and in the black water dropped my Grouse and Jay in the flood, under a shelf of stone; and in a moment a rainbow was dancing on my line. It wasn't altogether a big fish, but it meant a lot to me in the tumult of that rushing water.

We climbed again, and in the dusk, fished the tree-lined stretch above. I cast over the tea-tree and away went my line with a wild 3-pounder on the end. I checked him as he came back leaping. And with half my line in my hand I was playing to keep him away from some iron-coloured rocks upriver. He went around the rocks and back again; and with both of us panting, he came into the net. My next cast landed a four and a half brown trout. And he fought well for a brown, leaping half up the bank in one rush, but tiring quickly. By moonlight we fished the final shallow hole. And wherever I cast, the track of the moon was broken and fish of a pound or pound and a half came to my net and I let them go.

We were back again next morning, and wading in the long reach below the waterfall. I got a 3½-pound rainbow among the reeds, and within half an hour, another the same size, and lost a big one.

Doug this time was catching them too, on the same fly. But his loss was greater than mine. It left him pale and tired, for when a big trout has taken out all your line, and you've managed to turn him, when he's leapt in the air to smack on his side and sent ripples coursing to the banks of a wide oval pool, when you've played him until he's turning belly-up in the weeds, and then he slips the fly and with a slow twitch of the tail is gone – well, it's time to sit down and draw thoughtfully on a cigarette.

'Must have been about the size of that one I lost in that strong run-out at Wee Jasper last year,' I said.

'Bigger,' said Doug.

'But you didn't see mine. Remember that fellow ...'

Doug sighed.

'They don't come that big very often,' Doug said.

When our 10 days were up, we said goodbye to Jack and Molly Snow, to Willow Farm and Sally in her Sally Hole, and we drove home with some good fish in the back. But the big ones are still behind us in the river. Maybe we'll catch them next year.

PHILIP
BAILEY

PHILIP WAS born in Mildura on the Murray River, and began fishing at the age of 3. He moved into fly-fishing nearly 30 years ago. An accomplished fly fisherman, Philip has been President of the Victorian Fly Fishers Association, President of the Council of Victorian Fly-fishing Clubs, a recipient of the Council's award for recreational fishing and the Norm trophy from Greenwells Fly Fishers.

Philip has worked in the financial services industry for over 35 years and now works all over the world. Currently he is working in the United Kingdom as a management consultant.

He spent a short period outside the financial services industry, as owner of a small fishing tackle shop and professional fishing guide, leading clients on wilderness excursions in Tasmania. During that period Philip acted as a lobbyist on behalf of recreational angling and was a key member of the task force that established the peak angling body for Victoria.

Philip served as an inaugural board member on this body, which represented nearly a million recreational fishermen. During this period, effective lobbying removed the devastating effect of scallop dredging in bays and inlets around Victoria.

He was also a founder (and the inaugural chairman) of high-profile lobby group The Australian Trout Foundation, which helped achieve the return of a closed season and bag limits for the Victorian Trout Fishery.

Editor's note: Although the following story is more of the 'how to do it' style, it is so interesting that I decided to include it anyway.

CHAPTER 37

Czech Nymph Fishing

In 1990 the Polish and Czech fly fishers cleaned up the World Fly-fishing Championship when the competition was held in Wales. They won both gold and silver in the team events and all were highly rated individually.

When the event was run in the Czech Republic in 1996, these two teams were again highly placed. So what was it that they were doing differently?

I first started reading about Czech nymphing when Oliver Edwards wrote a series of articles in the British *Fly Tying and Fly Fishing* magazine. Oliver is one of the best known fly tiers in the United Kingdom and represented England in the 1996 championships. I have kept up with his writings on this subject and have enthusiastically delved into his publications and DVDs. A lot of articles are now being published by other fishing writers who put themselves at the forefront of this technique. Not so: Oliver is without doubt the leader of this new tactic in the United Kingdom. He has a vast knowledge of the subject, having fished with the Polish and Czech experts.

As I am now residing in the United Kingdom I wanted to get an even better understanding and embellish my trout fishing techniques, because like a lot of Australians, I spend a good deal of time fishing still waters in New South Wales and Tasmania.

I am fortunate to be living close to the Wharfe River in Yorkshire, and have an annual licence to fish 5 miles (8km) of the river at Bolton Abbey.

Bolton Abbey was destroyed by Henry VIII in his attempt to impose the newly formed Church of England on all the Abbeys across England and extract the vast wealth that they had accumulated over centuries. The river is a typical freestone river, not too dissimilar to the Goulburn River in Victoria. At one spot the river enters a short gorge, and in this area it is very reminiscent of the upper Kiewa River in that same State.

What about the patterns? Given that most of what trout eat (and grayling in the northern hemisphere) is subsurface, then it goes without saying that I needed to make sure that I had the correct patterns. Oliver Edwards would advocate that you undertake a small insect survey to find out what food type is in the area that you were about to fish. I have to agree.

The methods used for this type of fishing mean that the fish will get a very close look at what you are offering to them. No general patterns here. You will catch fish, but not as many if you are fussier with your designs. Try it. If you take a small seine net and kick up gravel into it you will get a good idea of what is on the diet of trout in that area. I actually use a piece of mosquito netting sewn into a 'bag' which I simply slide over my net. Easy to use and it doesn't take up too much room in my vest.

When I did it, I got lots samples of caddis grubs, mayfly nymphs, damsel nymphs and small crustaceans, the caddis grub being the most prominent, followed closely by mayflies.

I have long believed that caddis is the staple diet of trout in our Australian streams.

When I was instructing people on fly-fishing a few years ago I classed trout food into five classes so that the students could quickly understand the food chain and group into fly patterns. They are: 'the shredders' – those that chew up things that are either growing in or fall into the water; 'the catchers' – those that catch the by-product of the 'shredders'; the 'scrapers' – those that keep the water clean by feeding on algaes; 'the terrestrials' – those that fall into the water; and 'the predators' – those that prey on everything else, including their own species. I found 'shredders', 'scrapers' and 'catchers' everywhere. This made it easy for me to begin the development of patterns.

Rivers and streams are funny places. Sometimes you get to the bank and you would swear that the water was barren of fish and food. Other times the opposite. My observation is this: if you count all the items of food that you found during your survey, then multiply it by the stream bed area in front of you and then extend that to the whole stream, you soon get a good idea of just how much food is available to the fish without even coming to the top to feed. I surmise that you only get to see 15–20 per cent of the fish even on the best of days.

Given that current speed is much slower at the bottom of streams and that river fish won't over-exercise themselves too much to feed, then it is logical that that the majority of fish will hold where the current is less. So where do you need to fish? On the bottom!

I am sure we have all read that nymphs and larvae are dislodged or lose their adherence to the rocks, stones, gravel and debris that lies on the bottom of rivers and streams. It is this knowledge that the Polish and Czech fly fishers have capitalised upon. The first part of the equation is, what flies to use?

Czech nymphing, as it is known (the Polish seem to have converged into this term), requires flies that are heavy and a fairly accurate match to the type of insect that is being imitated. Even Frank Sawyer knew this, as his flies matched the need to get down to the fish and represent the insects in his beloved Avon River. So it is not new.

Lead is added to the flies as an underbody – and a good deal of it. I fish with two patterns here in the United Kingdom and I am certain the same patterns would work just as well at home and even in the rivers on the south island of New Zealand. I have flies in various sizes and colour that match the various caddis and mayflies species (such as the 'shredders, 'scrapers' and 'predators' of these two species).

The caddis 'grub' is tied on 'Czech' nymph hooks (which I get direct from the supplier, chemically sharpened and hand made), but a 'grub' hook can work just as well. The mayflies are tied on either 2x or 3x long shank hooks, all in sizes 10 to 16. Notice how close they can match the natural.

By the way, in the United Kingdom there is a huge push for barbless hooks. In the Wharfe there is a £100 (AUD$250) fine for any hook that has a barb, and the largest legal hook size is a 12. I have to say that this has not affected my catch rate; nor have I lost any fish because of it. I believe all fly fishermen should become vocal advocates of barbless hooks, as they make it very easy to release fish. Normal barbed hooks can be made barbless by simply squeezing down the barb using pliers. A small 'pimple' remains, which might just appease those disbelievers in barbless hooks and encourage them to make the change.

While fishing is more expensive in the United Kingdom, the management is far superior to anything we have in Australia and the fishing is equal to anything we have. Each part of a river is managed by a river keeper (read ranger) and rules are enforced strictly according to the book. Some food for thought!

The patterns for these flies can appear difficult, but with a little practice they become easier.

Mayfly Nymph

The pattern I use is a hybrid of the pattern developed by Oliver Edwards.

Hook: Size 16 to 10, 2x long shank. (This could be made smaller by using a standard long shank hook.)

Thread: Light olive or yellow 8/0, very strong.

Underbody: Flat lead. I use a sheet lead with an adhesive back. This can be purchased from a golf shop. Commence from the rear of the hook and take it forward in close wraps, then double back and trim off before the place where you commenced. Then add a third layer at the thorax area. Take a pair of pliers and compress it flat. You should have a thin wedge-shaped underbody.

Back (head): This is two parts. The first is to tie in a piece of dark brown raffia at the front of the hook. I generally split the raffia into two and use one portion, which I wet with saliva before tying it in. Now take a piece of monofilament (15kg) and tie a short piece across the shank, in front of the lead, at right angles to the shank. Cut the length to about 2mm each side of the shank. Pull both the raffia and tying thread out of the way and heat the ends with a lighter to produce a ball at each end. A bit like an eye.

Tail: Three moose mane hairs dyed olive. Take the tying silk over the lead down to the tail position and tie in the moose mane hairs. Splay them by wrapping through them so that they are fixed with one in the centre and another each side. I use super glue to keep them there as an added precaution. This is a critical trigger in this fly, so take care to get it right.

Back (tail):   Clear nymph latex materials. You can use surgical gloves for this but it needs to be a strip about 2mm wide. Tie it in at the base just above the tails.

Rib: Clear monofilament. I use 1.5kg tippet material.

Body: Yellow/olive mix dubbing material. Use a mix that has Antron in it and is more yellow than olive. Dub this tightly onto the hook up to the thorax area. This colour is another critical trigger, as the bottom of most nymphs in streams is much lighter than the top. Your stream survey should inform you about what colours you need to achieve. Now pull the latex forward and loop the tying thread loosely over it a couple of times. This will allow the latex to move forward as you rib it. Bring the monofilament forward in turns and pull it hard into the latex to create segments. Tie off the latex and monofilament and clip the excess.

Thorax: Yellow/olive dubbing material. This is the same as the body and is dubbed onto the thorax, making sure that it covers both the area in front of the 'eyes' and the 'eye' materials. I try to cover all of the monofilament, including the ends. Try to end with the tying thread at the point where the body ends.

Legs: Olive partridge breast feather. This can be tricky. I pull the fibres backwards, leaving a small tip which I tie in on top of the thorax. Take some head cement and dab it along the top of the thorax and then bring the feather forward to a point immediately behind the eyes. Take the tying thread along the thorax and tie off the feather. Clip off the excess. You should have fibres sticking out at right angles from the hook. Take the thread back to the point between the thorax and body, bring the raffia back and tie it off. Trim off the excess raffia and trim the legs to about half the fibre length. These legs are another critical trigger.

| Colour: | Permanent brown/olive marker (Pantone marker pen). This finishes off the fly. Colour the back all the way down to the tail, making sure that the ribbing is highlighted. |

Don't forget to make it barbless.

Czech Nymph (Caddis)

Hook:	Size 16 to 10 grub hook. I don't expect anyone to have the Czech hooks, but Partridge and Mustad do produce them.
Thread:	Yellow 8/0, very strong.
Underbody:	Flat lead. I use the same method as for a mayfly, but I place the thorax in the middle and increase the turns. Don't flatten it: you want it round.
Back:	Clear latex nymph materials. Use the same material and size as for the mayfly. Take the tying thread all the way along the hook and a good way around the bend. Tie in the latex.
Rib:	Clear monofilament, the same as used for the mayfly. Tie it in at the same point as the latex.
Body:	Pale yellow dubbing materials. Again, your stream survey should indicate the right colours. I use a variety from olive through to yellow. Dub the materials right up to thorax area.
Thorax:	Hare's ear (natural). Dub the material onto the thorax, making sure that lots of guard hairs are sticking out; this is a critical trigger in this fly. Bring the latex forward to the eye and tie it off loosely to allow the latex to flex. Rib the body and thorax right up to the eye, making sure that each loop is tight, to accentuate the segments. Tie off and remove the excess materials.
Colour	Permanent marker (Pantone marking pen). I use a colour that matches the insect colour. This can range from olive through to dark brown. I use dark brown on the head irrespective of the colour used.

Don't forget to make it barbless.

Baetis Nymph

This pattern is one developed by Oliver Edwards. It is quite a difficult fly, but very deadly on its day, so a bit of effort is worth it. This pattern differs only slightly from Oliver's pattern.

Hook: Size 16 to 10, 3x long shank. This nymph is very long and cylindrical.

Thread: Light olive or yellow 8/0, very strong.

Underbody: Flat lead. Commence from the rear of the hook and take it forward in close wraps, then double back and trim off before the place where you commenced. Then add a third layer at the thorax area. You should have a cigar-shaped underbody.

Tail: Three moose mane hairs dyed olive. Take the tying silk over the lead down to the tail position and tie in the moose mane hairs. Splay them by wrapping through them so that they are fixed with one in the centre and another each side. I use super glue to keep them there as an added precaution. This is a critical trigger in this fly, so take care to get it right.

Body: Light olive green latex strip. Tying commences after you have tied in the thorax. Use a piece of latex and either colour it with a marker pen or colour the tying silk. When ready to tie the body, take the latex forward in close wraps so that segments are formed. The latex needs to be taken right forward to the head of the fly. When you reach the wing case, undo the tying thread; this will let the two wing case slips spring backwards. Once you have reached the eye of the hook, reverse the latex so that it sits flat on the top of the thorax, and take the tying silk back to the start of the thorax and tie down the latex. Let the latex remain for the present.

Wing case: This is a tricky part of the fly. Take the tying thread back up to the point where the thorax commences. Keep it in close wraps to cover off any lead that may be exposed. Take two pieces of crow feather. They should each be about 5–6 fibres wide. Tie one each side of the thorax and then bring them forward and loosely loop the tying thread over them at the head of the fly.

Legs: Olive partridge breast feather. This can be tricky. Pull the fibres backwards so that they splay out. Tie the tip in and remove the excess fibres.

Thorax: Olive green dubbing. At this point you should have the wing cases sticking out each side and the latex pointing backwards, away from the eye. Now dub a thorax up to the point where you can form a head.

Finishing the fly: Put some head cement along the top of the dubbing. Bring the feather forward and tie it off. Remove the excess. Now bring each of the wing cases forward over the top of the feather fibres and across to the opposite side of the eye. Leave the excess for the moment. You should now have the feather fibres at right angles and sloping slightly downwards. Bring the latex forward and tie it off, removing the excess. Trim the wing case about 1mm from the eye. These give the impression of eyes on the nymph. Tie off.

Don't forget to make it barbless.

Rhyacophila Larva (Caddis)

This pattern is another one of Oliver Edwards'. He maintains that this is his best pattern using Czech nymphing techniques.

Hook: Size 16 to 10 grub hook. I use Czech hooks.

Thread: Yellow 8/0, very strong.

Underbody: Flat lead. I use the same method as for a mayfly, but I place the thorax in the middle and increase the turns. Don't flatten it: you want it round.

Rib: Clear monofilament, the same as used for the mayfly. Tie it in at the same point as the body.

Body: Oliver uses 4 ply wool that has Antron in it. The colour he uses is similar to a green apple. This can vary depending on the colour of the species in your streams. Tie the wool in at the bend of the hook. You will need to use only 1–2 of the plys. Thin down the end which you tie in by pulling excess fibres out. Now twist the wool tightly and wind it forward to the eye, making sure that the wool is twisted each time you make a wrap. Keep the turns slightly apart to emphasise segments. Bring the ribbing forward between each segment.

Legs: Olive green partridge. Take 3 feathers and remove most of the fibre, leaving a small 'tag' at the top. Bring the tying silk back 3 segments. Turn the fly upside down. Now tie the tip of one feather in and pull on the feather so that the tips start to point downwards. Trim off the stem. Take the tying silk back to the second segment from the eye and repeat. Again repeat at the first segment. Tie off.

Colour   Permanent marker (Pantone marking pen). I use a colour that matches the insect colour. This can range from olive through to dark brown. I use dark brown on the head irrespective of the colour used.

Don't forget to make it barbless.

Now that I had a good idea of the patterns required, I really needed to study the techniques, or more importantly how the flies were rigged. Yes, 'flies'. In Czech nymphing 3 flies are normally used. Sometimes this is reduced to 2, but multiple flies are always used. This is because the 'rig' is so important to getting the flies to the correct depth. The two patterns given here are not the only ones I use, but they definitely are the most important patterns.

For this technique you need to use a leader with two droppers about 50cm apart (or 18 inches for us old guys). Each dropper should be less than 12cm (6 inches). I use a simple 4 turn water knot for these, as it allows each hook to be pulled against the monofilament immediately above the knot. You don't have to worry about casting problems with this technique, as I will explain later. Three flies are attached to the droppers, with the heaviest fly on the middle dropper.

This rig allows the flies to sink very rapidly, with the middle dropper below the other two flies. It also allows for the lighter flies to be slightly higher than the middle dropper, thus ensuring that they are in the feeding slot immediately above the bottom.

To make this outfit I use a single piece of tapered leader down to 4lb. I remove a third of it, then attach the two additions. One at 6lb and the other at 4lb. This rig works well for me. It is important that the leader is not longer than the rod you are using. I use nothing less than 9ft and the Polish fly fishers use anything up to 10ft.

Degrease the leader before you use it. You want the rig to sink as quickly as possible.

While Czech nymphing requires specific flies and leader set-up, it really is your ability to read a river and be brave enough to put yourself in situations where you might get wet. The Polish and Czech fly fishers wade right out into the water, some of it very fast and strong. So you have to be brave (or foolish). I use chest waders, strong wading boots and at times have had the water come right over the top. I have even tip-toed down the stream as the strong current unsettled my balance. And I caught fish doing it. So get out into the middle.

All fishing is done upstream, never to the side or downstream. The trick is to get the flies to the bottom as quickly as possible and let them 'free fall' along the bottom. Just like an insect that has been dislodged.

You will only need about 50cm of fly line out the end of the rod. This is a lesson in constraint, as most fly fishers want to cast the whole line. 'Far off' is definitely not the way to go here. Control yourself and cast the flies immediately upstream or slightly off to the side where you think fish may be holding. Keep the rod tip up and watch the leader like a hawk. I don't need strike indicators as I am only 2–3m away from the point where the leader enters the water. You could use fluorescent line if it helps.

At the slightest pause – lift. I cannot emphasise this enough. You will see a slight straightening of the leader, and it is at that moment that you lift. You won't always have a fish on, as the middle fly 'ticks' itself along the bottom and can catch up a little. Make sure you check the flies now and again to remove any rubbish.

When the flies have come level with you, lift and recast. This is really rapid-fire stuff. Cover the water quickly and make sure that your flies cover all possible lies. You don't need to thrash the air. One false cast and back into it.

You will be surprised how many fish you catch right at your feet – as long as you move deliberately and don't crunch the bottom too much.

Does it work? Well the first time I did it I was really learning. For the better part of the day I struggled to get out in the deep water, let alone keep my balance and restrain myself from letting out line.

In fact you basically only use one arm. The other could be used to hold a stick if you feel uncomfortable wading in deep and fast water. But once I gained confidence I began to hook onto fish.

Now an average day for me would be 20–30 fish. The best I have had was in excess of 50 fish and that was in the 'Strid' on the Wharfe. The stream that is similar to the Kiewa.

I must admit I love this new adventure. I am tying flies that challenge the representation element of fly-tying. I just love the challenge of getting into the water and using this deadly technique.

Yes I still fish dries, but I keep that for the special occasion when the insects are hatching and the fish are up on top.

I can't wait to get back on those Australian streams that I had long ago discarded in deference to lakes.